The Winemasters

In memory of Fred Hirsch

THE WINEMASTERS

NICHOLAS FAITH

HAMISH HAMILTON · LONDON

By the same author

THE INFILTRATORS
MONEY MATTERS
WANKEL: THE STORY OF THE ROTARY ENGINE

First published in Great Britain 1978
by Hamish Hamilton Limited
90 Great Russell Street London WC1B 3PT

British Library Cataloguing in Publication Data

Faith, Nicholas
    The winemasters.
    1. Wine and wine making—France—Bordeaux
    —History
    I. Title
    380.1'45'66322094471   HD9382.8.B/
    ISBN 0-241-89867-6

Printed in Great Britain by
Ebenezer Baylis & Son Ltd, The Trinity Press, Worcester, and London

Contents

List of Illustrations

I

Hollywood-sur-Gironde

Location: the lobby of the Waldorf Astoria on a June day in 1973. Occasion: the visit to New York of a delegation from Bordeaux aiming to persuade the American public to buy more of their wines despite their spiralling prices, for these had trebled in the previous couple of years. Characters: Hugues Lawton, wine merchant, the sixth generation of a family of wine brokers and shippers settled in Bordeaux since the middle of the eighteenth century, and Henri Martin, president of Bordeaux's leading wine trade association, but himself of peasant origins, a man who had built up the reputation of the wine from his Château Gloria through fifty years of unremitting toil.

Martin is triumphant: the wine-growers of Bordeaux are finally getting their due reward, expressed in prices which enable them to live in comfort after nearly a century of suffering, in many cases real poverty. Earlier in the year he had proclaimed that "at last Bordeaux was seeing the end of its misery".

Lawton, closer to the customers and aware of the swings to which the trade—and his family—had been subjected over past centuries, counselled caution. There had been other booms in Bordeaux's history and they had all ended unhappily, because of the growers' greed, a fall in the quality of Bordeaux's clarets, or a sudden worsening in the world's economic situation.

Their argument was, inevitably, inconclusive: where Lawton's inherited instincts warned him of the dangers, Martin's bones told him that a grower could never trust a merchant, however friendly. The conflict between the two was too ingrained for real co-operation to be possible.

The boom so joyously celebrated by Martin was real enough; In 1972–3 the civilized world was imploring growers like him to sell their precious red wine at any price. Wine had become the talking point of the financial and fashionable world, whose representatives, bankers, speculators, middle-men, had descended on Bordeaux like a well-heeled plague. Each week, it seemed, record prices were being set in the London sale rooms, each week brought news of record prices charged for wines most of which would not be drinkable for a decade or more.

Yet Lawton was right: as so often happens, no sooner was a trend being publicly described as irreversible, as a permanent turning point, than there was a sharp swerve, followed by a slump, and one as sharp as the boom which led up to it.

Happily both Lawton and Martin survived the traumatic years that followed their conversation. But, just as heating a piece of metal too swiftly and quenching it too suddenly can make it snap, so many apparently permanent features of the Bordeaux scene broke apart under the strain: and none more notably than the most famous shipping house in Bordeaux, Cruse et Fils Frères. Before the end of June, before prices had started to crack, their fate was sealed, by the same arrogance and greed which had made generations of growers like Martin distrust them so profoundly.

It was 9 a.m. on 28 June when a team of a dozen inspectors from the French Ministry of Finance's tax squad arrived at the Cruses' shabby warehouse on the Quai des Chartrons, the stretch of riverside in Bordeaux where for generations the Lawtons, the Cruses and their like had conducted their business. The inspectors demanded to test and verify every drop of wine in the cellars. The Cruses were dumbfounded: for sixty years there had been a gentleman's agreement under which merchants' cellars could be inspected only after due warning had been given. The tensions, the telephone calls to lawyers and to their colleagues lasted all day, ending only when Lionel Cruse lost his temper and refused to allow the inspection to continue, which brought an immediate accusation of obstruction of justice.

Behind the bluster lay a guilty secret, given away by the fact that the first person they telephoned that morning was a shady wine-broker, Pierre Bert, asking him to rush round to their offices. For the Cruses had been working with Bert in an ingenious and elaborate fraud, devised by Bert to cheat the rigid French wine laws. The fraud was so ingenious that the 'wine' apparently 'sold' by Bert, which formed the main reason for the inspectors' interest, was not in their cellars, indeed did not exist, had only ever existed in the form of official certificates attesting to the existence of wine of that quality.

But beneath the guilt lay something even more fundamental: generations of aristocratic disdain. For the Cruses, among the noblest of the 'aristocracy of the cork', were not inclined to take orders from men they regarded as a bunch of petty officials, normally received by their employees rather than a member of the family. The Cruses, like the rest of Bordeaux, had been tested to breaking point by the heat of the boom. In it their proud ethical standards had melted.

It took six weeks for the news of the abortive police raid on the Cruse cellars to reach the press. Yet within three months the investigation had escalated into 'the affair', 'the Bordeaux scandal' or, as was inevitable in 1973, 'Winegate'; and when, eighteen months later, Pierre Bert, Lionel and Yvan Cruse and their associates went on trial, the world's press was in attendance *en masse* to gloat over the fate of some of Bordeaux's proudest citizens.

This intensity of interest in the trial in a French provincial town of a couple of executives in a medium-sized wine merchants on purely technical fraud charges was a tribute—although a profoundly unwelcome one—to the magic of the name of Bordeaux where wine was concerned. Indeed Bordeaux, like Hollywood or Detroit, is one of those industrial centres whose name is synonymous with a product, and one, moreover, with which the world is endlessly fascinated. The smallest scandal among the film-makers of Hollywood or the car-makers of Detroit causes far more ripples of interest than more portentous events affecting other cities which are synonymous with a particular product. The idea of 'filmgate' or 'cargate' is by no means absurd; the notion that the world's press would flock to Sheffield to report on 'steelgate' patently is.

Bordeaux has, of course, natural advantages for making good wine greater than those enjoyed in their respective spheres by Hollywood or Detroit. Yet Bordeaux was a great wine-growing and wine-trading centre for many centuries before it was discovered that a handful of gravel slopes scattered round the city were capable of producing some of the finest red wines on earth. And it is less than a century and a half since the secret of making Bordeaux's other great pride and joy, the sweet wines of Sauternes and Barsac, was discovered.

It is not primarily the potential capacity for making fine wines which has made Bordeaux famous: it is mainly the sheer quantity and variety of good wine the area can produce. Bordeaux can simply swamp its only real rival in quality, the slopes of the Côte d'Or in Burgundy. Bordeaux not only produces twice as much fine wine as Burgundy; unlike its rival, bound to narrow well-defined hillsides, its production potential is virtually limitless for wines of all but the finest quality.

With the size of Bordeaux's wine-growing area goes a variety of product inflated by the dogged individuality of French landowners, large and small, each determined that his (or her) product shall have its individual name, be called 'château' this or that. The saying goes that "there are more castles in Bordeaux than in Spain", over two thousand at the last count.

This combination of quality, quantity and variety has ensured that virtually every previous writer on the subject of Bordeaux's wines has found enough to occupy his attention in merely analysing and describing the wines, and the châteaux and cellars where they are produced.

By contrast, this book is an attempt to explore Bordeaux's other dimensions—political, economic, social—and to explain the tensions between the men growing the grapes and making the wines and the small band of merchants who provided the wines with their world-wide renown.

The tension, and the system it produced, have deep roots. Indeed one of the fascinations of Bordeaux is to trace the very clear links between past and present, and to see how many 'unprecedented' developments—like the periodic surges in prices due to speculation and accompanied by the influx of outside capital—have in fact been regular features of the Bordeaux scene for centuries past. Nevertheless the turmoil of the early 1970s, when an unparalleled boom and bust in wine prices was accompanied by the thunder from 'Winegate', did mark the end of the old system. It is being replaced not only by the impersonal forces of large-scale international capitalism (whose intrusions did so much to upset Bordeaux's previous delicate ecological balance), but also by a new and heady mixture of relationships and personalities among individual growers and wine-makers, co-operatives, merchants and customers, French and foreign. The new entrants to the field are discovering an old truth, that the production of fine wines demands above all an appreciative clientèle, one able and willing to pay for the care and attention required; and it also requires a very special style of salesmanship to ensure that potential customers can be persuaded that fine Bordeaux is a luxury necessary to their existence, and not one to be discarded in favour of other beverages, or indeed any other fashionable product.

In the past the wine-makers recognized only grudgingly, if at all, the need for such salesmanship and the costs it involved. In similar vein, the writers and directors who actually made the films in Hollywood were always slow to recognize as legitimate their dependence on the handful of tycoons who bulldozed their films on to the mass markets of the world.

The parallel with Hollywood can be carried further. When four famous stars founded United Artists in 1919 to establish their independence against the pressures from the studios which financed and marketed their talents, the lament went out that "the lunatics are taking over the asylum". A similar outcry used to go up in Bordeaux when anyone suggested any alternative to the time-honoured ways of selling wine. Yet, in Bordeaux, as in Hollywood, a formerly rigid system, with lunatics firmly confined by their keepers, has been replaced by a far more complex, enjoyable and less inhibiting series of relationships. This work is both a tribute to the keepers and a welcome to the former inmates discovering the joys and sorrows of a new-found freedom.

2

Not by quality alone

"There is the eternal hope that 'the next fortnight will be warm and sunny', the hope that has persisted throughout this disappointing season. A hot July would be enough to make up for a late and slow flowering; July was neither hot nor dry. A hot August could still give a vintage by the end of September; August was wet. Fine weather in September could still produce an acceptable wine and September is still with us. So is the rain . . . the dismal procession of wet weeks that followed the earlier bright days of June brought on the mouldy diseases of mildew, black and brown rot which became difficult to control with sprays that were continually washed off by the rain. Too much discouraging wet and too little encouraging sunshine have produced acres of half-starved, depressed damp little grapes hanging desperately on to dripping vines hoping that by some miracle they will eventually produce enough alcohol to enable them to forget their misery."

ALLAN SICHEL, September 1963

"The climate of Bordeaux is as near perfection as a temperate maritime climate can be . . . it is Southern England removed to the furthest point south at which it could remain both green and industrious."

CYRIL CONNOLLY

The Bordelais—the French name for Bordeaux's inhabitants—prefer to believe that it is the combination of their soil, their climate, and their own wine-making abilities, rather than their commercial or political acumen, which has given their home its unrivalled name in the world of wine. Even today the name of Ausonius—Roman poet, local Imperial official and wine-grower—is often invoked to symbolize the immemorial qualities of Bordeaux's wines (his name is more than worthily recorded in Château Ausone, whose vines grow over the supposed remains of his villa in St. Emilion).

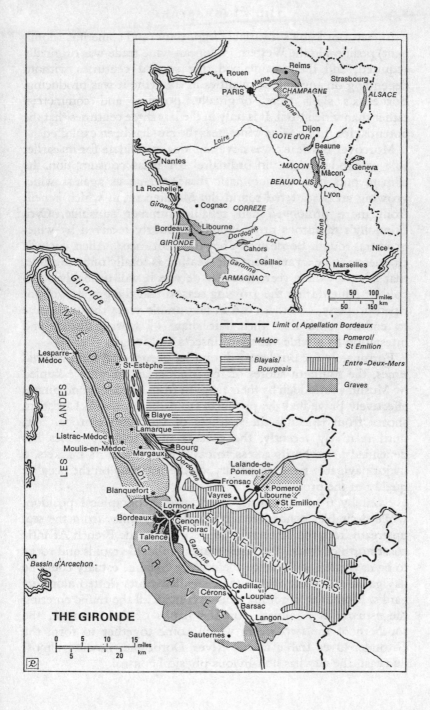

Rouen
Reims
PARIS
Marne
CHAMPAGNE
Strasbourg
ALSACE
Seine
Loire
Dijon
CÔTE d'OR
Beaune
Nantes
MACON
Mâcon
Geneva
BEAUJOLAIS
La Rochelle
Lyon
Gironde
Cognac
CORREZE
Bordeaux
Libourne
Dordogne
GIRONDE
Lot
Cahors
Nice
Garonne
Gaillac
Marseilles
ARMAGNAC
Rhône
Saône

0   50   100 miles
0   50   150 km

Limit of Appellation Bordeaux

Médoc

Blayais/
Bourgeais

Graves

Pomerol/
St Emilion

Entre-Deux-Mers

Gironde
MÉDOC
Lesparre-
Médoc
St-Estèphe
LANDES
LES
Blaye
Lamarque
Listrac-Médoc
Moulis-en-Médoc
Bourg
Margaux
Dordogne
Lalande-de-
Pomerol
Fronsac
Pomerol
Blanquefort
Vayres
Libourne
Lormont
St Emilion
Bordeaux
Cenon
Floirac
ENTRE-DEUX-MERS
Talence
Bassin d'Arcachon
GRAVES
Garonne
Cadillac
Cérons
Loupiac
Barsac
THE GIRONDE
Langon
Sauternes

0   5   10   15 miles
0   5   20 km

In fact, Bordeaux's invariably important (and sometimes dominant) position in the Western European wine trade was originally
acquired, and then maintained, for several centuries without
depending on any unique qualities in the wine it was producing.
Bordeaux's skills were, originally, political and commercial
rather than viticultural. It is only in the last three centuries that the
potential for making fine wines near the city has been exploited.

Moreover Bordeaux was never an ideal candidate for its earlier
role as producer of 'vin ordinaire' for mass consumption. Its
climate puts it at an automatic disadvantage as against wine-
growing areas scattered round the Mediterranean which benefit
from more prolonged and reliable summer sunshine. Cyril
Connolly's rapturous prose would be poorly received by wine-
growers round Bordeaux. They do not need Allen Sichel's
eloquence to be aware that their weather is totally unpredictable,
that in up to three years in every decade it will probably be so
cold or rainy during the growing season that the grapes will not
ripen properly, and that even in favourable years they will have
to endure more than their fair share of worry, disease and
infestation by a wide variety of insects and fungi.

Fortunately for Bordeaux, during its greatest days in medieval
times, the southern shores of the Mediterranean were occupied
by Muslims forbidden by their religion from drinking; and pirates
effectively prevented the products from the northern, Christian,
shores from reaching the markets of Northern Europe. For,
until relatively recently, the success of a region's wines has
depended more on its access to easy transport to its markets, a
major navigable river, an estuary, or the sea, than on the peculiar
quality of the product.

Even by these standards, Bordeaux's geographical position,
while desirable, is not ideal. It stands sixty miles from the sea,
upstream from the first navigable estuary on the French Atlantic
coast north of Spain. But there were formidable rapids and rocks
to be navigated at Cordouan before the Gironde estuary could be
navigated and there were other, smaller, ports dotted along its
banks. Moreover Bordeaux cannot control all the traffic entering
the estuary; it is situated on the banks of the Garonne, the
southern of the two rivers which come together to form the
Gironde. Over traffic in the River Dordogne, flowing almost
due east, the city has no obvious physical control.

But Bordeaux's merchants could, and did, ruthlessly exploit the possibility of monopoly power provided by their position on the Garonne. Their chance came in the early thirteenth century. By then, the whole of South-west France had been ruled by the Kings of England for half a century. Gascony and Aquitaine were not colonies; they were an integral part of an early Euro-centred British empire, and glad to be within it. For integration brought prosperity. Nearly a third of Britain's imports consisted of wine; and the wine growing areas clustered round the estuaries of Western France were uniquely well-placed to provide accessible supplies of wine far more reliably than English vineyards (by no coincidence, these declined with the rise of the Bordeaux trade).

But Bordeaux faced severe competition: in the twelfth century wines from the Charente area, shipped through La Rochelle, were infinitely more important that the product shipped by the Bordelais, who were not even mentioned as major suppliers at the time. Bordeaux, however, had two strokes of luck. First was when King John took a fancy to Bordeaux's wines at around the turn of the century—a taste which may well have been affected by the credit terms made available by the merchants to a king who was notoriously short of cash. But the second stroke of luck was even more political. In 1230 La Rochelle surrendered without a struggle to the King of France. At a stroke Bordeaux became virtually a monopoly supplier of wines to England; and for two more centuries, until the British were finally driven out of the city—significantly their last stronghold in France—in 1453, control of the Gironde estuary was a major commercial prize.

For the British appetite for wine was greater then than it is today, or at any period between then and now. At the height of their prosperity in the early fourteenth century, the Bordelais were exporting the equivalent of over 110 million bottles of wine a year. And of these nearly half were going to England, a country which then had only four million inhabitants, in other words virtually thirteen bottles per head per year. Consumption was not, of course, evenly spread; at the festivities surrounding one royal wedding over a million bottles were allegedly consumed, and celebrations like this helped the averages along very nicely.

Moreover the wine itself was by modern standards pretty thin stuff, and invariably drunk in the course of the year after it was

made. The English preferred their red wine light, so much so
that the French called it 'claret', a word derived from an old
French adjective meaning a wine which was clear, light and
bright enough to be distinguished from other red wines. But,
perversely, the British then wanted their claret strengthened—
one of the first references to claret in English literature, in
Chaucer's *Canterbury Tales*, mentions fortifying it with stronger
wines from Spain.

The Bordelais used the political clout they had acquired as a
result of their continuing loyalty to the English crown to prevent
the uncontrolled intrusion of stronger wines from up-country—
'the Haut-Pays', the hinterland. They so organized their rights
that the wine from their own 'Sénéchaussée'—the county
governed from Bordeaux—got automatic preference over outside
products. The preference was clearly political in origin, since
the preferred area—which corresponds to the modern French
département of the Gironde—had no particular geographical
significance. It extends east from the Bay of Biscay, north to a
low range of pleasant hills looking down on the Gironde, and
stretches fifty miles east of Bordeaux. It thus covers the wine-
growing areas of Bourg and Blaye between the hills and the
Gironde estuary, the vineyards round Bordeaux, and those
between the Dordogne and the Garonne—the Entre-Deux-Mers
(literally between two seas).

But the favoured vineyards did not include those in a number
of districts which were geologically as favoured as Bordeaux and
which enjoyed the advantage of a greater freedom from frost.
The wines from these areas tended to be better prepared for
travelling than Bordeaux's own wines, and were, in any case,
vital for the Bordelais—who could supply under a half of the
wine they sold from their own vineyards—but they were permanently inhibited from developing their own trade with the
outside world, and thus their own distinctive brand names, by
the commercial implacability of the Bordelais. To the east, the
Haut-Pays included Gaillac and Cahors, where strong 'black
wines' are still made, requiring as much ageing as Bordeaux's
best, and to the south, embraced the area round Auch which
eventually turned in despair to distilling its wines into the brandy
now renowned as Armagnac. The only areas the Bordelais found
difficult to control completely were the plateau of Pomerol and

the slopes round the hill-town of St. Emilion, both conveniently near the little port of Libourne on the Dordogne, and both within the 'Sénéchaussée'.

But for the rest, the citizens of Bordeaux cleverly used the normal pattern of wine-buying by the English for monopoly purposes. English ships would descend in their thousands in October in time to buy the latest vintage and depart six weeks later to reach England before Christmas. To use this seasonal rhythm to the best advantage they obtained the rights to forbid the sale of wines from outside the 'Sénéchaussée' before 11 November (St. Martin's Day). Indeed wines from outside simply could not be brought into the city from the Haut-Pays as from 8 September, well before the vintage, until either St. Martin's Day or, if the Bordelais preferred, Christmas.

The arrangement was supervised by a special 'police des vins', and to guard against possible infringements the burghers were even allowed their own special design of cask, the 'barrique Bordelaise'. Its size, shape, binding and contents (225 litres, about 24 dozen modern bottles) were strictly controlled, and its use sternly confined to the Bordelais. The barrique became so famous that the English imitated it in their 'hogshead'; and even today the wine trade measures shipments by 'tonneaux'—tuns— of four 'barriques' (a purely notional quantity, since there are no containers that size). And one final threat, from the small ports along the Gironde, was removed by simply forbidding the loading of wines destined for the export trade at any point between Bordeaux and the open sea.

The only internal commercial force the merchants of Bordeaux were forced to recognize was the wine-broking fraternity—the courtiers. These were middle-men between the English merchants and the wine-growers, operating on a commission of around four per cent. They were vital to both sides: the foreigners had no time to scour the countryside for wine and needed honest middle-men to assure supplies; and the growers needed protection against the less reputable English buyers who were in the habit of taking the wine, and then either trying to change the agreed terms of payment or, worse, of claiming that they had never bought it in the first place. Even at this early date, the courtier was also useful as a one-man quality control system.

So a pattern was established which did not change greatly for over four centuries. Even the much-bemoaned end of English rule in the middle of the fifteenth century did not make much permanent impact. At first, naturally, the French were inclined to trample on the rights of the Bordelais, who had been such staunch supporters of the enemy. But it only took a few years to convince the French kings that there was so much revenue to be derived from the wine business that Bordeaux's rights were restored, to be swept away only in the flood of the French revolution, at the end of the eighteenth century.

But before then the historic pattern had been badly disturbed. Even in the fifteenth century foreign merchants had been forced outside the walls of Bordeaux if they were to trade freely in wines from the 'Haut-Pays' and to ensure that these were not mixed illicitly with 'real' claret. So they established themselves on the Quai des Chartrons. This lay outside the city's walls and separated from Bordeaux by an unbridged rivulet, on the other side of which stood the formidable bulk of the 'Château Trompette', a fortress built after the French re-occupation of the city to overawe the potentially rebellious citizens. The name 'Chartrons' arose quite naturally because the spot had first been colonized by a group of Carthusian* monks driven from their previous home inland by the fighting during the Hundred Years War which ended in the British evacuation.

But it was not until the seventeenth century that the grip of the Bordelais first slackened, and the outlines of the modern wine trade based on the Quai des Chartrons became apparent. The pioneer iconoclasts were the Dutch, who dominated the seas of Northern Europe for much of the century.

They found Bordeaux convenient for many purposes: first, simply as a port of transhipment. They were, intermittently, at war with their former masters, the Spanish, still a people rich from their American colonies, so that the Dutch wished to continue to trade with them. They found they could use for this purpose Bordeaux's small colony of Jews and 'New Christians', former Spanish Jews who had been forced to convert to Christianity a hundred and fifty years before. But the Dutch were also looking for the agricultural products shipped from Bordeaux to sell throughout northern Europe: not just wine but also nuts of all kinds from the forests of the Haut-Pays, prunes and other

* 'Chartreuse' is the French word for a Carthusian monastery.

dried fruits, paper, resin and other forest products, and other more exotic commodities like goose feathers and woad.

But the Dutch were also famous as traders in beverages. They had been largely responsible for introducing tea and coffee from the Far East into Europe and they spread the habit of using hops to improve the quality of beer—a commodity sternly forbidden by the Bordelais with the same instinctual reaction towards alien beverages which has induced them to lead more recent French campaigns to restrict the advertising or sale of Scotch and Coca Cola.

To make matters worse, the Dutch were interested in wine from the Gironde not for its own sake but, primarily, as the basis for fabricated products. They were relatively uninterested in claret but were large-scale purchasers of cheap, sour white wine for distillation into 'brandywijn'—as it was called even in France until the rise of the products of the town of Cognac a hundred years later.

They needed brandy for their sailors: wine was for their customers, at home and all through Germany and Scandinavia—so it had to be capable of surviving a long sea voyage. The Dutch had also learned to appreciate the sweet 'muscaty' wines of Greece. So they dosed the wines they bought with sugar and spices, and strengthened them with brandy before selling them.

They disrupted the traditional pattern of Bordeaux's wine trade—and not only by treating the wines as merely the basis for an industrial product which would be acceptable to their customers. They also encouraged the peasants of the Entre-Deux-Mers to replant their plots with vines suitable for making white wine and paid them promptly, or even in advance. To this day, the districts from which the Dutch bought their requirements still mostly produce white wines—and these account for over two-fifths of the wine produced round Bordeaux, though only a quarter of the better vintages.

The Dutch also explored far up the Dordogne; and to add insult to injury, some of them settled in Bordeaux and became naturalized citizens, thus avoiding the export taxes paid by foreigners—indeed one firm of Bordeaux merchants, Henri Beyermann, can trace its origins as far back as 1620.

So complaints were inevitable; the first, grumbling about 'the commercial practices of the foreigners', appears in the 1646 records of the 'Parlement', the law-court which brought together a powerful legal aristocracy, the Parlementaires, whose rights and titles were passed down from generation to generation.

But the French authorities were in a difficult position: they were fully aware that the complaints of the citizens of Bordeaux were founded not on any desire to maintain the reputation of their wines, but simply to preserve their monopoly. At the behest of the indignant Bordelais, Colbert, the great French statesman, tried to forbid the blending ('coupage') of wines, but then realized that the Dutch would simply do the work anyway and sensibly concluded that 'the merchants could have more right on their side than the lawyers'. The foreigners could not, he concluded, be beaten: so why not join them? "If it is necessary to work on these wines during the winter, and to adulterate them, as the Dutch are wont to do, that could just as well be done at Bordeaux." He even suggested that the greatest experts in these mysterious practices be summoned to Bordeaux in case the whole art of mixing wine was a dark Dutch secret.

But the argument was swiftly submerged in politics. Colbert opened a tariff war with the Dutch in 1667, and five years later his master Louis XIV started a more deadly conflict with them. For the next forty years the two countries were, intermittently but regularly, at war. This state of affairs did not entirely stop trade—although Bordeaux suffered badly when the Gironde was blockaded in the 1690s—but it did prevent a complete take-over of the city's wine trade by the Dutch.

Bordeaux's privileges lasted, in one form or another, for a further ninety years, and in doing so achieved a major object. The wines from the area did not suffer the fate of, say, 'Eau de Cologne' in being entirely separated from its original source.

The Dutch left a double legacy. On the positive side they had demonstrated the commercial advantages of flexibility in a hitherto rigidly formalized business. A free-trade bridgehead had been established—an invasion commemorated in physical fact by the existence of the Quai des Chartrons. Negatively they had muddled two ideas: that of wines shipped through Bordeaux, and the narrower and more valuable description applying only to wines produced round the city. Fortunately, within a few years, Bordeaux was to find a product worthy of the second description, and thus ensure that the name of Bordeaux would henceforth be associated with vinous quality rather than quantity.

3

The birth of the crus

Although the Dutch used to complain of the poor quality of some of the wines offered to them, they were primarily interested in cheap beverages. "The Dutch live very frugally," explained one wine-grower early in the eighteenth century, "they are accustomed to the most severe economies, and are less attentive to the quality of their purchases than to the lowness of the price."

But the English were different. The writer's pen seems to glow with appreciation when he contrasts them with the Dutch: "no nation in the world trades in more noble a fashion. It is a generally recognized truth that, everywhere the English land, they spend a great deal, force up the price of the commodities they purchase, and seek out the dearest and best."

Fortunately for the Bordelais, the second half of the seventeenth century witnessed the blossoming of a society in London tailored to conspicuous consumption. The restoration of the casual, sociably amoral Charles II to the British throne in 1660, after eleven years of Puritanical republican government, was the signal for the creation of a social scene modelled on the king's character, sceptical, enquiring, scientific, witty, and deeply hedonistic. The king was famous for his saying that he wished never to go on his travels again. Fortunately for Bordeaux, he and many of his courtiers had been exiled in France, and brought the habit of wine drinking back with them. And, by a happy coincidence, an important minority of the Bordelais were waiting to cater to London's needs. By 1663, only three years after the Restoration, Samuel Pepys noted that he had drunk "a sort of French wine called Ho Bryan that had a good and most particular taste that I ever met with."

Pepys had sampled this delicious novelty at the Royal Oak Tavern in Lombard Street in the heart of the City of London, and the proliferation of smart taverns, coffee houses and clubs played a useful role in spreading the fame of the better clarets and persuading the English upper classes that it was worth paying much more for certain names which should provide some guarantee of superior quality. Previously, while the Bordelais themselves had drawn up properly graded price lists (one, dated 1647, divides the area's wines into no fewer than seventeen price brackets), the English had been less choosey.

Until the eighteenth century, social habits did not encourage the spread of fine wines as an item of conspicuous consumption. Louis XIV had dined alone: and it was only in the second decade of the eighteenth century, when the dissolute Duke of Orleans ruled as Regent of France in place of the infant Louis XV, that the consumption of fine wine became a major social factor in France. Even then, the fashionable world in Paris and the court at Versailles rarely if ever drank claret. They slaked their thirst on the wines from the more conveniently placed vineyards in Burgundy and in the Champagne area round Rheims.

The development of fine wines can indeed usually be traced to the requirements of a hedonistic court or society. The habits formed at the end of the seventeenth and in the eighteenth century proved permanent. The court of the Emperor of Austria in Vienna spread abroad the fame of the Hungarian 'Imperial' Tokay. The English made the name not only of claret, but also of port—the wines of Oporto, duly fortified with brandy; and sherry—the blended and sweetened white wines of Jerez in Spain. At the same period a handful of merchants, mostly from the Channel Islands, established themselves in Cognac and spread the fame of the brandies they distilled from the wines of the Charente.

In Rheims, in Oporto and in Jerez, the nature of the final product ensured that it would be the merchants who would dominate its production, and whose names would be associated with it. Cognac, port, sherry and champagne have in common the need for capital-intensive production processes; they were and are always deliberately manufactured products, requiring elaborate and well-financed commercial organizations to market them.

Even when the product was a natural one—like the rich dessert wines of the Atlantic island of Madeira, or those of Marsala in Sicily—the merchants quickly established their supremacy over largely peasant wine-growers. So the names that occur to every connoisseur, Krug, Hennessy, Osborne, Harvey, Sandeman, and countless others, commemorate not growers but long-dead merchants—and, in some cases, their still-active descendants.

But Bordeaux has always been different from the other suppliers of luxury beverages; the balance of power between the growers supplying the basic product and the merchants selling it has been, from the beginning, a disputed affair. This was partly because of the nature of the product. Great claret requires only the skills—though elevated to the highest level—normally associated with agricultural production. The vines—themselves selected only from those varieties likely to produce the best rather than the greatest number of grapes—need to be carefully tended, the wine-making meticulously supervised. But all the qualities required are those of the skilled husbandman, not of the industrialist.

To be sure, the producer has to be patient and allow the wine to age. But simply nursing the wine produces a uniquely fine product: by contrast champagne requires elaborate blending and second fermentation, port is manufactured, sherry blended, all fabricating, quasi-factory processes.

But there were other distinctions: first, because of the vagaries of nature, the quality of the product could not be entirely standardized, could never be guaranteed to remain the same from year to year—a crucial drawback when thinking of 'châteaux' as brand names. Furthermore, the innovators who originally made fine claret famous were not merchants, they were the local 'parlementaires', the rich local upper middle class. These lawyers inherited their titles as 'president' of the Parlement (there were uncounted dozens of officials entitled to the name); and, like many worthy citizens before and since, they sought to establish themselves as landed gentry by building up country estates, by marriage to the daughters of local aristocrats, or by purchase from peasants or impoverished gentry.

In Bordeaux the pace-setters were the Pontacs, the owners, among other estates, of Haut-Brion, the vineyard Pepys called Ho Bryan. By Pepys' time the Pontacs had been flourishing for over a century. Armand, the founder of the line, was a merchant who became Mayor of Bordeaux in the middle of the sixteenth century. But it was his son, Jean, the richest man in Bordeaux (who, allegedly, lived to the ripe old age of 101) who built up the family's land-holdings. He inherited Haut-Brion, at Pessac, in the Graves district just south of Bordeaux (the vineyard and a few others round it are now islands of green, trapped in the dreary wastes of suburban Bordeaux). But he also built up his holdings to the north of Bordeaux at Blanquefort—where he produced wine known simply by the family name.

For he, and indeed the other Parlementaires, concentrated primarily not on the Graves—historically one of the most important vine-growing areas near Bordeaux—but on the Médoc, an area which, until the late seventeenth century, was largely waste land with a few peasants struggling to gain some sort of a living.

The Médoc is the sixty-mile-long peninsula north of Bordeaux between the sea and the Gironde. Previously the citizens of Bordeaux had, effectively, blocked all attempts to develop the area by refusing to allow any road to be built north from Bordeaux which might have diverted traffic to the ports of Pauillac and Lamarque, and might have encouraged foreign merchants to go direct to growers in the area. (They already had enough competition from Bourg and Blaye, ports on the eastern shore of the Gironde; before the development of the Médoc the claret from the gentle hills behind Bourg had attracted the best prices from foreign buyers.)

Again it had been the Dutch who had shown the way—though not as wine-buyers, but in another role. As leading civil engineers they helped to drain Médocain marshes. The newly-drained land, the 'palus'—the marshes—proved fertile and easy to cultivate. And the parlementaires quickly appreciated what a few local landowners had long known, that some of the gravel banks which sloped down to the river were capable of producing rather better wine than that from the 'palus'.

Ever since that time a passionate—and still inconclusive—argument has raged over the exact ingredients, climatic, geological, and geographic, which result in the particular qualities of claret; and indeed it is because the final product is the result of so many factors, many still mysterious, that 'claret' covers such a wide variety of tastes, such a uniquely varied gamut of taste and smell.

Nevertheless the elements of the mixture have long been known. They begin with Bordeaux's weather, still the subject of the most passionate local interest, since on it depends the quality of a particular vintage. (Bordeaux is such an enclosed society that particular years have associations completely different from any they may possess in the outside world. Elsewhere 1945 may mark the end of World War II; in Bordeaux 'another 1945' means another vintage comparable with the superb wines produced that year. Elsewhere, 1956 is generally associated either with the Russian invasion of Hungary, or the Anglo-French incursion into Suez. In Bordeaux 1956 is unhappily memorable for a disastrous frost, which wreaked havoc on thousands of vines.)

Meticulous records exist of the weather every day in the growing season for the past century and a half. Nevertheless, although there is general agreement about the broad outlines of the best (and worst) weather for the grapes, the relative importance of sun and wind, rain and cold, are by no means precisely established. The weather of the Médoc is so fickle that it is simply impossible to establish more than the most general relationships, and to say, broadly, that in any decade, three years will produce great or very good wines, four will be good-to-humdrum, and three poor-to-terrible (though modern methods of vinification are reducing the number of years when truly awful wines are produced).

Right through the growing season the crop is constantly threatened by the vagaries of Médocain nature. In 1977 a late frost wiped out up to a third of the buds before Easter. In many other years an unseasonably cold spring can delay the 'flowering' when the first tiny green grapelets appear, normally in early June, only to turn into flowers. If the weather is wet at the time rot can set in, as it can during any summer when there is too much rain in July or August—'June', the saying goes, 'makes the wine, August makes the taste.' Too cold a summer prevents the grape from ripening, too hot a summer can burn the skins so badly that the burnt taste comes through to the wine itself— as happened in 1949. The vintage can be made or ruined by the weather in early September as the vintage approaches, while the weather at the time of the vintage is so vital that an owner can fail through harvesting too early (thus picking still-unripe fruit) or too late (thus running risks from late rains). This difference can be dramatic. In 1964 the weather was perfect until 8 October. So, growers who had completed their harvest by then (or who confined themselves to producing wine from early-gathered grapes) produced superb wine.

But 8 October saw the start of a week of drenching rain which virtually ruined the chances of any grower who, anxious to harvest at the last possible moment, delayed just a couple of days too long, only to see his grapes rot away on the vines.

Even more fatally, a local hailstorm can completely ruin one estate's work for the year, while sparing a neighbour completely. In 1880 a hailstorm 'with stones as large as pigeon eggs' but lasting a mere 4½ minutes, completely destroyed the crop at Château Loudenne. And in 1975, just before a vintage which promised to be of superb quality, 'the worst hailstorm in living memory swept across' three villages in the Médoc, then, by a sudden quirk, changed direction, and instead of sweeping further north and destroying the finest grapes in the Médoc, turned to the east, crossing the river just by the ferry route from Lamarque. "In some of the vineyards of Blaye," said one report, "the stricken vines, stripped of all their leaves, display for all to see the bare bones of their battered branches."

Yet, ironically, the very fickleness of Bordeaux's weather is a major factor in establishing its ability to produce great wine. For all the great vineyards of the world, whether in California, the Andes, Burgundy, or Bordeaux, are situated at the extreme edge of the areas where vines flourish. Either (as in the great vineyards of France) the vines are grown at or near the climatic limit, or on relatively cool mountainsides above a torrid plain. The Médoc, on a suitably narrow edge between success and disaster, but sheltered from frost—and from the over-moist Atlantic air—by a belt of pine forest, was far better placed to produce limited quantities of fine vines than for the mass production of the ordinary wines in which Bordeaux had previously specialized.

But the Médoc differs from other areas where great wine is made in several ways. It was largely uncultivated—indeed it is probably the only area in the world producing wine of any distinction which is not renowned for its natural beauty. But the scrub and pine-forest which constitute the Médoc's natural covering did not provide much of a temptation for agriculturalists. So the land was not intrinsically expensive, and the peasantry were easier to buy out than in a more favoured countryside.

Moreover, the area of potential wine-growing land was, relatively, limitless. Prolonged wine booms have simply meant that vines have been planted further away from the river and into the forest. The wine from these clearings never reaches the quality of the most precious vineyards, but much of it is good enough to figure in the various classifications that have been made of Médoc wines.

It would be a mistake to believe that good or great wine can be produced only where it actually is made. The potential for making good wine exists in a lot of other places—Fronton north of Toulouse and in the Minervois district, for instance—less famous than the Médoc. But only near Bordeaux could be found the particular combination of men and geography required to turn potential capacity into actual wine.

For good wine is in every sense a Puritanical product, flourishing only through a barrier of suffering. If the weather must not be too uniformly warm, the soil must be poor. It must also be very well-drained—the old Médocain wives' saying that "the best wines can see the river" has met with modern scientific approval, since the finest vintages invariably come from slopes which drain the majority of the rainfall they receive into a stream or, best of all, the Gironde—which also helps to keep the temperature even. Yet grapes are even more finicky: to be ideal the slopes must face east. Only grapes with an eastern aspect have the opportunity to warm up gradually with the rising sun, and cool gently of an evening (the sun would set too abruptly on a western-facing slope to allow the grapes to ripen to perfection).

Because of the importance of drainage, the wines of the Médoc can easily be divided by experts into those produced by different 'communes' or parishes. Geographically each of these—St. Estèphe, Pauillac, St. Julien, Margaux—is divided from its apparently similar neighbour by a stream—or 'jalle'. Each parish sits on a slightly different gravelly hillock (or, in the case of Pauillac, two gently-sloping mounds separated by a 'jalle'). A fanatical drain-theorist could even point to the softer profile of the central Médoc—where the 'jalles' tend to form water-meadows to give an even flatter valley floor—as a major reason why wines from these parishes, Cussac, Lamarque and the like, are less appreciated. A more balanced judgment might be that the same geological processes which produced this gentler profile deposited less of the valuable pebbles and gravel at this point.

Far more crucial even than the physical position—according to most authorities—is the soil, or rather the lack of nourishment near the surface, and the contrast between the composition of the soil and the sub-soil. For the ideal vine needs to draw its nourishment from barren soil on which nothing else will grow (as witness the stunted and scrubby wilderness which marks former vineyards which have been allowed to revert to their natural state). Rich soil produces grapes too easily: great wines come from relatively undernourished fruit. Only, it seems, by painfully extracting water and traces of mineral elements from roots which go down fifty feet or more can a vine produce grapes worthy of good, let alone great, wine.

So there is a fairly standard pattern if the soil is to be suitable. The top soil must be gravelly or pebbly—the name Beaucaillou (beautiful pebble) attached to one leading growth could apply to many others—for the pebbles reflect the heat of the summer sun and prevent the soil from drying up. The sub-soil should be different—probably stony or sandy—with the water level well buried in earth strata which contain minute traces of minerals to enhance the subtlety of the wine. Thus the soil of Pauillac, the parish which grows three of the four finest wines of the area, is "fairly heavy gravelly soil with stony sub-soil and iron underneath".

The unpredictability of the weather, combined with the stringent requirements of the vine, necessitate the large-scale production fortunately possible in the relatively underdeveloped Médoc. Only a big estate can support a fifty-year growing cycle in which the ground will lie fallow for at least a couple of years before being planted with vines which will yield good wine only after ten years or more.

A century later, Thomas Jefferson, himself an agricultural expert, noted that "the vines begin to yield an indifferent wine at three years old, but not a good one till twenty-five years, nor after eighty . . . they dung a little in Médoc and Graves, because of the poverty of the soil, but very little, as more would affect the wine".

But the pattern was set in the late seventeenth century, as we can see from a letter written by the English philosopher, John

Locke, who in 1677 visited the estate of the Président de Pontac at Haut-Brion. His report contains most of the elements which were to recur in the history of Bordeaux over the succeeding three hundred years (including the difficulty which any English visitor finds with the local dialect).

"It is a little rise of ground . . . white sand mixed with a little gravel; scarce fitting to bear anything. The vines are trained, some to stakes, and some to lathes; not understanding Gascoin, I could not learn the cause of the difference from the workmen. This yield may be estimated to yield about 25 tun of wine, however the owner makes a shift to make every vintage 50 which sells for 105 écus per tun; it was sold some years since for 60, but the English have raised the price for themselves. This, however, they say, that the wine in the next vineyard to it, though seeming equal to me, is not so good. A tun of wine of the best quality at Bordeaux, which is that of Médoc or Pontac, is worth 80 or 100 crowns; for this the English may thank their own folly; for whereas some years since the same wine was sold for 50 or 60 crowns per tun, the fashionable, sending over orders to have the best wine sent them at any rate, they have, by striving who should get it, brought it up to that price, but very good wines may be had here for 35, 40 and 50 crowns."

Note the element of fashion built into the price; the premium over apparently similar wine from a neighbouring vineyard (probably that of La Mission Haut-Brion, donated to the Church by the Pontacs earlier in the century); the attempt to maximize the yield of a fashionable wine. But there is one element missing from the equation, ageing, the crucial quality involved in the making of claret as we know it. For the wines so appreciated by the fops of Restoration London were young wines, drunk within the year after their fermentation, light in colour and in alcoholic content. It was only gradually, during the succeeding half-century, that the new breed of wine-makers began to explore the possibility for improving the quality of the wine by allowing it to age for several years in barrels, and then bottling it in the glass bottles with proper corks which were slowly evolving at the same time.

The literature of seventeenth-century Bordeaux is full of accounts of wine forgotten in cellars, dredged out of wells in the course of cleansing, or simply left for several years, and which was found to have greatly improved with age and not turned into vinegar, the fate normally expected of wines more than a year old. Such old wines were often supposed to have miraculous curative properties and were venerated as veritable elixirs to be given, in carefully regulated doses, to the sick.

Slowly, the Parlementaires started to capitalize on these old wives' bottles, and to cherish their wines for several years. This again was an expensive business. If the wine were left for long the normal process of evaporation meant that it had to be topped up repeatedly—in modern cellars this 'ouillage' is carried out three time a week for the wine's first year of life. Three times in the first year the wine had to be 'racked on its lees'—carefully transferred from one cask to another, leaving behind in the old container a deposit of vinous sludge. And to clear the wine dozens of egg-whites had to be poured into the casks to take with them the impurities and solid detritus suspended in the liquid.

Cherishing wine in this way involved a great deal of labour. It also reduced the yield, since up to a fifth of the cask was lost in the course of the two or three years it was left in wood to mature. According to one estimate, it cost nearly twice as much to produce a bottle of mature Graves compared with more ordinary wine. Nevertheless it gradually became the done thing in Bordeaux society to offer your older wines to your guests, and in the first decades of the eighteenth century the better wines began to be appreciated in London.

Ironically the first full records we possess of the value of superior claret date from the first decade of the eighteenth century during the War of the Spanish Succession which temporarily reduced imports of claret to a trickle—although smuggling, and shipping via Spain, ensured some continuity of supplies.

More permanently, the fact that the Portuguese fought at Britain's side resulted in a preference for the wines they produced. By the terms of the Methuen Treaty of 1704 French wines were obliged to pay a third more duty than Portuguese, regardless of the general level. The result was that even when peace returned the English had to pay the equivalent of 1s. a bottle in duty on French wine, an enormous burden at the time. But the duty was at a flat rate, the same for all qualities of wine. So while the provisions of the Treaty removed for a hundred and fifty years the possibility that claret could regain its medieval rôle as the staple beverage of the British people, the duty bore progressively less heavily on the more expensive wines.

The war, seemingly, had merely whetted the thirst of English snobs. A number of advertisements in the official *London Gazette* at the height of the war between 1707 and 1711 record forthcoming sales of "New French Prize clarets, lately landed, being of the growths of Lafitt, Margouze and La Tour . . . new Obrian and Pontack Prize wine . . . new Pontac and Margose wine . . . remarkable fine high flavour'd claret . . . New French Bourdeaux Prize Claret, of the best growths, deep, bright, fresh, neat". Moreover the buyers were prepared to pay up to four times the price of ordinary claret. It is an extraordinary tribute to the tenacity of fashion that these, the very first records that have been traced of a group of named clarets fetching far more than ordinary wines, should single out the four major names which have dominated Bordeaux in the two and a half centuries since then—Margaux, Lafite, Haut-Brion, and Latour. Only one name, Mouton-Rothschild, has been added, and that, officially, only in 1973.

For the fashion survived the Methuen duties. Indeed the preference given to the Portuguese wines made the consumption of French wine more distinctive, and therefore more desirable in a fashion-conscious capital. English country squires turned almost unanimously to port. As if by a reflex action to distinguish themselves from a class they despised as country bumpkins, the fashionable of London would prefer claret, a drink which, because of the additional duty, it was inevitably conspicuous to consume.

Although the wine was usually shipped in cask, yet even at this early date there are records of "the excellent wine of Margaux, old, black and velvety" being shipped to London in wicker-covered bottles, stoppered with corks sealed with wax, a shipment which brought together all the technical advantages—bottles, corks, ageing, fining, racking, bottling—which had emerged together at the turn of the century. This was an exceptional case. But, according to the merchant involved, it could not fail to be profitable, for the wine would be saleable in London at "5s. sterling the bottle, which will give us a considerable profit, since duties only amout to 1s. a bottle", and the fall in the value of French currency meant that an écu was worth only 3s. (In other words the wine cost only 3¼d a bottle, leaving a margin of 300 per cent to cover transport, the retail margin in London—and the merchants' 'considerable' profit.)

We know that the buyers included Brooks's, the smartest club of the time, and also Sir Robert Walpole, one of the first Britons to be truly a Prime Minister, responsible to Parliament, rather than to the king. Walpole was himself a notoriously hard drinker, and judging from his account books, he concentrated on claret, and on two châteaux at that. According to his biographer J. H. Plumb, Walpole "in the main stuck to Lafite and Margaux with the obstinate loyalty which was so much part of his nature". In practical terms his loyalty resulted in the purchase of four hogsheads of Margaux at a time and one of Lafite every three months—and each hogshead represented 24 dozen bottles.

Walpole and his guests were epic claret-drinkers. One guest, John Hervey, Earl of Bristol, the original of Alexander Pope's hated 'Sporus', is recorded as being "up to the chin in venison, geese, etc., over the chin in claret, strong beer and punch". But then eighteenth-century drinkers in general downed quantities to make modern topers blink. Thackeray's *Four Georges* records a conversation which supposedly took place in the 1780s between a bishop and a wine merchant who asks him how much claret his Lordship possesses that "you wish me to remove". "Six dozen," says the bishop. "Why then," replies the merchant, "you have but to ask me six times to dinner and I will carry it all away myself."

The tradition—of a select few drinkers each putting away vast quantities—persisted for two centuries. In the early 1930s, an elderly client of a distinguished London wine merchant reckoned that "in fifty years I have drunk more than my share of finest red Bordeaux, certainly over 10,000 bottles", not a ludicrous claim when considering that at the age of seventy-two he could "still get into the second bottle if it be old and of fine vintage". Such customers ran up similarly awesome bills—Walpole spent £1,118 (over £25,000 in modern money) on wine during a single year. They also expected their wine merchants, like their tailors, to provide credit over an unlimited period—Walpole paid his bills two years late. He and his friends, however, did not drink old claret—there are records of him buying 'old' Burgundy but the term is never applied to any of his claret purchases, frequent though these were.

But even though the English may not have understood the crucial part ageing played in enhancing the essential qualities of claret they were good clients. They bought little wine, but the best: once trade resumed officially in 1713 they were prepared to pay two or three times the price of the lesser wines sold to the Dutch—and, in money terms, accounted for between a third and two fifths of all Bordeaux's wine exports.

4

The first winemasters

A "former proprietor" of Rausan-Ségla who, "dissatisfied with the price which the merchants of Bordeaux gave him for his wines, freighted a ship with them and set sail for the Thames, determined to try his luck with the Londoners themselves. Arrived in port, the wines were tasted, criticised, and generally approved of; still he was unable to obtain the prices he demanded. Remembering the story of the Sybilline books, he gave orders, in the presence of the merchants with whom he was negotiating, for one cask after another to be breached and the contents discharged into the river, demanding, as each cask was emptied, the same price for what remained as he had originally asked for his entire cargo which, as the somewhat doubtful story goes, he is said to have eventually obtained".
HENRY VIZETELLY, *Glances Back Through Seventy Years.*

The Bordelais needed every market they could find for their wines. For they, even more than other French wine-growers, had been seized by a 'fureur de planter'—a craze for planting vines. In Bordeaux's case the impetus was vastly increased by the unexpected results of the dreadful frosts of the winter of 1708–9.

The knowledge early in the year that the next vintage would be small or virtually non-existent led the more sophisticated Bordelais to hold back their 1708 vintage, aware that keeping their wines another year in the cask would, if anything, improve their quality. (Since then, the same phenomenon has recurred repeatedly, most recently in 1957 and 1977.) This, the earliest demonstration that conserving your wines was not merely a fad but a potential source of profit must have vastly increased the Bordelais' interest in ageing their wines.

But the craze was directly opposed to the policy of a government which had seen thousands starve during 1709 for lack of bread, and was naturally haunted by the fear that a similar shortage could recur because land suitable for grain had been planted with vines. For much of the new planting in the Médoc

was on the fertile palus and not on the pebbly slopes above.
Throughout the century, therefore, the central government
acting through the provincial 'intendants' (governors) tried in
vain to forbid new vineyards; as an indication of their seriousness
they even tore up a few acres of vines here and there. But, as
always in France, an autocratic, if frequently logical state faced
implacable and ingenious opposition from those likely to be hurt.
For there was a loophole even in the original stern decree of 1725:
new vineyards could be established if proper permission were
obtained, not too difficult a matter for influential local nobilities
like the Parlementaires. The ineffectiveness of the decree is shown
by the frequency with which it was repeated in the course of the
century.

The opposition was expressed in loftier form by Montesquieu
the philosopher, a keen wine-grower who had a beautiful estate
in the woods at Labrède, south of Bordeaux. He promptly
denounced it as an infringement of personal liberties and free
trade; individuals, he declared, were infinitely better judges than
governments of market requirements. He did not, however,
mention that he had just purchased some land strategically placed
next to Haut-Brion. Nevertheless he did make a couple of valid
points—that neighbouring provinces were free to plant as many
vines as they chose, and that foreigners were eager to buy Bordeaux wine. More typical was the cynic who wrote that Bordeaux
could offload even its poorer wines on the less choosey markets
of Northern Europe.

Dozens of Parlementaires caught the fever, concentrating on
the finer wines. By the middle of the century they owned a full
quarter of the land in the Médoc, as against under a fifth of the
traditional Graves wine-growing district south of Bordeaux, and
only one acre in thirteen of the county's total wine-growing land.
These Parlementaires were a rather special breed. In other parts of
France, municipal officials ('noblesse de cloche'), traditional landowning aristocracy, or the 'noblesse de l'épée'—landowners who
owed their fortune to the military exploits of someone in the family
—were often of greater importance. But not in Bordeaux. Moreover the Parlementaires came to depend overwhelmingly on their
vineyards. In 1755, according to one calculation, they derived
three-quarters of their income from wine, as against only five
per cent from their seigneurial dues.

In their time the Pontacs were dominant, owning not only Haut-Brion and their estate at Blanquefort, but another major holding at Margaux in the Southern Médoc, which also figured early and permanently as one of the top four. The tradition still persists; five-sixths of the wine-growing land in Margaux still belongs to large owners. For these estates were of considerable size, sometimes including over a hundred acres of vines. But the deaths of Locke's friend Armand de Pontac ('much learning made him mad', was the baffling comment of John Evelyn) and then of his son in 1694 ensured that, although Haut-Brion was for much of the eighteenth century still reckoned the finest of wines, historical fame as the 'prince des vignes' came somewhat later to another owner, Nicolas-Alexandre de Ségur (his name is, of course, commemorated in two well-known vineyards in the Médoc, Calon– and Phélan–Ségur). Indeed most of the names of major landowners from the end of the seventeenth century on are well-known to wine lovers because of the habit of adding one's name to any estate which produced better-than-average wine. This was obviously a pointless practice when wines were simply anonymous beverages, but during the eighteenth century it became a matter of pride for the Lalandes, the Pichons, the Branes, the Léovilles and the d'Estournels to immortalize their names in this way. The habit—like so many others established at that time—has continued to the present day. The Rothschilds now have three estates which include their names. The American wine merchant Alexis Lichine has one, as does the French aircraft manufacturer Marcel Dassault.

But Nicolas-Alexandre de Ségur was something else. Even a big landowner like Montesquieu might count himself fortunate to produce 200 tonneaux (nearly a quarter of a million bottles) annually from over 150 acres of vines. But Ségur owned a thousand acres of which up to a third was planted with vines. His estates included Lafite and Latour—the latter brought into his family through his mother. To these estates in Pauillac, in the Médoc thirty miles from Bordeaux, he also added Mouton and Calon in St. Estèphe, the next village north from Pauillac.

Almost as rich was the Marquis d'Aulède, with over 300 acres of vines within estates three times as large. As one of the heirs of the Pontacs, his proudest possessions were Margaux and Haut-Brion, but he also owned the major and productive estate of Pez, also in St. Estèphe.

Although Ségur and d'Aulède monopolized—albeit for only one generation—Bordeaux's most expensive wines, other lesser-known Parlementaires were also major producers. M. de Brassier, 'Councillor' to Bordeaux's overstaffed Parlement, owned at least three estates, producing in all nearly 200,000 bottles a year, as much as his classier contemporaries. Two of his estates produced relatively unremarkable wine. But another, Beychevelle, at St. Julien between Margaux and Pauillac, has been famous ever since, not only for the elegance of its wines, but also for the same quality in the long, low, pavilion-like mansion de Brassier built there (neither of the two major 'princes' left behind any comparable monument). It is a mark of the under-developed state of the Médoc before the 'fureur de planter' that there are relatively few noble buildings in the district dating back to before the eighteenth century, apart from the Château d'Issan.

As the century progressed, so the Parlementaires were able to establish a bigger premium for their better wines—and for an increasing number of them. A price list dating from 1714 shows Pontac top of the list, its wines costing four times as much as ordinary wines from the Médoc. Latour and Lafite were priced about a quarter below Haut-Brion, but Margaux had not fully emerged from the ranks. Another list, drawn up forty years later as part of an enquiry into the capital owned by the Parlementaires, shows a much more dramatic contrast: four growths, including Lafite, Latour, and another 'bordering Haut-Brion' fetched nine times the price of the humblest wines produced on the Parlementaires' estates. And other names, like Beychevelle and Malescot (now Malescot-St. Exupéry), were also emerging from the ruck.

The Parlementaires needed the higher prices, for wine-growing was a capital-intensive business. Ségur's tax returns for 1745 show that he made only an annual five per cent on the capital value of Lafite and Latour—and the tax authorities promptly deprived him of a fifth of his profits. On a revenue basis he was doing better: expenses accounted for only 40 per cent of the proceeds from his wine. And his wife's attempts to minimize her income by merely copying out an old tax declaration made

by her father a generation earlier, an hilarious enough episode in
itself, leads one to suspect that, as usual, reliance on French
taxation returns will tend to underestimate the wealth of those
involved.

All these major figures also owned town houses in Bordeaux,
and Ségur at least also had a house in Paris and land near the
capital, to a total value of 2.4 million livres (well over £10
million in modern currency). But, for all their grandeur, these
estates were bound to crumble, thanks to French inheritance
laws, which ensured that every child had the right to a share of
a parent's estate. Inevitably, the estate of Ségur, who died in
1755 without male offspring, provides the most spectacular
example because his Médocain estates formed two-thirds of his
fortune. Lafite remained an integral part of the family; but
Latour had to be split. The man responsible, his eldest son-in-law,
Alexandre de Ségur-Calon, had to provide for his three sisters-
in-law's dowries, mainly from Latour. And Ségur, typically, was
an absentee landlord—indeed was the official Prefect of Paris.
The legal problems were considerable and the result—a dispersal
of shares in the estate, combined with a steady loosening of
direct family supervision—provided a spectacular foretaste of
future trends. The present Marquis de Beaumont is the direct
descendant of the 'prince des vignes" second daughter, the
Comtesse of Mirosmesnil and still owns a small share of Château
Latour. But, when control passed to English interests in 1963,
it was found that the 155 shares were in the hands of sixty-eight
members of three families, the Beaumonts, the Courtivrons and
the Flurs, all descendants of the 'prince des vignes'. And the six
biggest shareholders controlled under a third of the estate.

Latour was an extreme case because of the size of the estate,
and the length of time during which the shares passed through
successive generations. But even an apparently solid family like
the Achille-Foulds, descendants of the banker who bought
Beychevelle a century and a quarter ago, numbers a wide scattering
of small, distantly related shareholders, uninterested in anything
except an annual dividend in cash, or failing that, some of the
property's wine—lucky owners of one of the very few shares in
Lafite are entitled to two barriques, equivalent to 48 dozen,
of the wine a year, equivalent in 1977 to an annual dividend of
up to £5,000. But few properties could boast single ownership for

any length of time, and inevitably control of most of the estates soon passed from the hands of the Parlementaires' families.

This dispersal was the sadder because the Parlementaires often showed a very close interest—intellectual as well as agricultural —in their wine. The records of the Academy of Bordeaux throughout the century contain numerous useful (if rather turgid and pretentious) notes on such questions as the best vines to plant, the need to root out over-productive varieties, and whether you could satisfactorily clarify wine without using expensive egg-whites (this last was the subject of a competition in 1756; it remains unresolved to this day). For while the peasants tended to treat their vines in the most casual fashion, considering them as merely one element in a mixed holding, the parlementaires grew vines only on the most suitable parts of their estates, rigidly separating them from other plants. This specialization, and the care which, at their best, they lavished on vine and wine alike, provided the base on which Bordeaux's fame as a producer of fine wine has rested ever since.

For, well before they ceased to dominate the Médoc, the Parlementaires had demonstrated the particular qualities which combine in the notion of a 'grand cru' (not to mention the profit that could be derived from such wine). They had first established the names as recognizable 'brands' in the modern sense. But behind these brand names was a whole complex of qualities. The first were the soils on which they were produced; and, although the particular qualities for which a 'cru' is famous are based on one patch of ground, yet there is still an astonishing licence in the area from which wine bearing a famous name can be produced. For the name is not, as in Burgundy, attached to a narrow strip of hillside, strictly delimited for generations. It allows for much greater flexibility—even in the last couple of decades the Rothschilds of Lafite and Mouton have gradually exchanged small parcels of land to straighten out the boundaries of their estates, a process which is constantly being carried on throughout the Médoc. And an ambitious owner, like Jean-Eugène Borie of Ducru-Beaucaillou, can even buy land in other communes to add to his production (while, at the same time, enhancing his reputation as one of the most reliable of winemakers).

This flexibility extends to the varieties of vines which can be planted. Even now that these are relatively strictly controlled, it is possible, indeed desirable, to plant very different varieties to distil the potential subtleties inherent in the land—the neighbouring vineyards of Mouton and Lafite produce wines which are as distinct as any made in Bordeaux, partly because the balance in the varieties used is different.

Yet there were further elements in the making of a 'cru' which tended to rule out its production by any but the most exceptional landowner. Ageing, topping up, racking and fining, are costly enough processes. 'Assemblage' is an even more delicate operation. At vintage time wines from different plots in the vineyard are fermented in different vats, and during the wine's first winter these are blended together to produce a wine worthy of the château's name. Now there is a clear temptation to label too much of the production with the name that will bring in the most money, so it requires a continuing—and very expensive —discipline to reject some of the wine; in a bad year this should be the majority.

But even when the wine is 'assembled', matured and ready for the consumer, it has to be marketed, and here the owner stands at a major disadvantage. He can never increase production sufficiently to finance a proper sales operation to establish or maintain his product's reputation; and since, from the start, the best clarets were appreciated virtually exclusively outside his native France he could not rely on direct sales to the final customer.

These complications are inevitable—the creation of a 'cru' involves landownership, the making of the wine and its marketing, and these are three activities which it has never been easy to integrate. The more numerous the 'crus' and the markets in which they were sold, the more difficult it became to combine all three elements.

Inevitably, the majority of owners have always had to rely on the merchants: and it is significant that the majority of châteaux whose ownership has stayed in the hands of one family through a number of generations have been those owned by merchants' families. For it is a mark of the relative power of the men who made the wine and those who sold it that there are virtually no recorded cases of a landowner buying a wine merchant's business. There are, however, plenty of instances, dating back to the middle of the eighteenth century, of the reverse process.

The absence of continuing unitary ownership helped the merchants by preventing the owners from building up one essential for the making of good claret—a solid financial base. For the process requires enough capital to finance the holding of the wine in cask for several years—nowadays it is almost invariably bottled during the second year after it is made but, in the days when bottles were scarcer, and the bottling was almost invariably carried out nearer the consumer than the producer, the period could be twice as long. And the wine had to be stored, if not in an actual cellar, then at least in a building substantial and well enough insulated to ensure that the maturation process would not be adversely affected by sudden changes or extremes of temperature. The Bordelais greatly envied other wine-growing districts their natural caves, often tunnelled into chalky mountainsides. But the Médoc's rocky soil meant that digging was difficult, if not impossible (dynamite had to be used on a large scale when new cellars were blasted recently at Mouton-Rothschild). Hence the basic Médoc compromise, the 'chai', the semi-cellar, half-underground, topped by a substantial (and often very handsome) stone building.

Here the Chartronnais—as the merchants on the Quai des Chartrons came to be known—enjoyed a major advantage. The banks of the Garonne were far more suitable for the digging of cellars and the storage of wines than the Médoc: the temperature was more stable, and the loss from evaporation significantly less than at any but the most lavishly-appointed vineyard. And the Chartronnais increased their advantage by binding their casks with iron rings, whereas the owners used looser wooden staves which allowed more wine to escape.

Even so, the combined effort of ageing the wine and housing it in suitable cellars would not have imposed impossible burdens on a unitary estate. Indeed some estates, for varying lengths of time, have managed to assert their independence in a fashion inconceivable for individual landowners supplying wine for champagne, port or sherry. But most châteaux, most of the time, needed the regular annual injections of cash—as well as the marketing skills—which only the merchants could supply.

Moreover, even a grower with adequate sources of finance and a suitable cellar was in no position to provide the British market with the exact product it required. For the British had never lost their taste for wines rather stronger than the Médoc could produce unaided: indeed the wide spread of gin and rough strong port wines in the eighteenth century hardened the British palate. So any wine—even the most expensive—destined for the British market needed mixing with stronger ones, generally those of Benicarlo from Spain. The fabrication of the wine—generally known as 'Travail à l'Anglaise'—was not a haphazard process. About ten per cent of stronger liquor, and a little 'stum'—semi-fermented must—were mixed in to each hogshead, to encourage further fermentation to produce an acceptable final blend. To be truly satisfactory the 'travail' involved further fermentation (for otherwise the mixture would have been more obvious, the final result too raw even for English tastes). So it had, logically, to be undertaken before the various rackings and finings carried out from the first spring after the wine was made. Thus both financial pressure and manufacturing convenience dictated that the wine should be removed as soon as possible to the merchant's own cellars. Yet, even in the late eighteenth century, the battle for direct contact with the client was by no means entirely lost. For then as now customer snobbery was strong: and a know-ledgeable wine-buyer like the future American President Thomas Jefferson was quite sure, as he wrote to a friend, that it was from the grower alone "that genuine wine is to be got and not from any wine merchant whatever". As Minister of the newly-founded impoverished United States to the French court in the 1780s he may have been, as one biographer puts it, "the lowest and most obscure of the whole diplomatic tribe", but none the less he was a valued client. The letter he received from the Marquis de Lur-Saluces, just after the latter had taken over management of the estate of his father-in-law, the Marquis d'Yquem, is a treasure.

The noble lord was evidently overjoyed to treat with Jefferson, and the fulsome sentiments with which he concludes his letter are worthy of the most grovelling old-style tradesman dealing with the gentry—even though it was Lur-Saluces who came from a noble family whose origins dated back to the Middle Ages. One almost expects the noble lord to offer Jefferson special wholesale terms. For his wine proved very popular, "a most excellent wine and seems to have hit the palate of the Americans more than any wine I have ever seen in France". It has remained popular. It was a favourite of President Eisenhower; another, less welcome, tribute, lies in the number of 'Sauternes' on sale, which do not come from the village of that name.

Jefferson was not alone among Americans in buying large quantities of wine—John Adams found that at one point he had ordered more than the diplomatic duty-free allowance. And, later in the decade, the French gourmet Brillat-Savarin, noted that the price of good claret in New York was lower than in France "because so many cargoes had arrived that the market was too fully stocked". But—partly because the financial problems of the American Consul in Bordeaux gave him a good excuse to visit the city—Jefferson was in a uniquely good position to observe the scene. He even used gifts of wines as means of flattery. "I cannot deny myself the pleasure," he wrote to Francis Eppes, "of asking you to participate of a parcel of wine I have been choosing for myself. I do it rather as it will furnish you a specimen of what is the very best Bordeaux wine. It is of the vintage of Obrian, one of the four established as the very best, and it is of the vintage of 1784, the only very fine one since the year 1779." Not surprisingly, there was money to be made from keeping your wine: the Sauternes of 'M. Diquiem' doubled in price within a couple of years (though even at its peak it was worth only a third of the first-growth clarets). And 'de Corbonius' in Graves (home of the modern Château Carbonnieux) then belonged to "the Benedictine monks who make 50 tonneaux and, never selling till three or four years old, get 800 the tonneau".

For at that point the wines were ready: "the wines of the first three are not in perfection till four years old. Those of la Fite, being somewhat lighter, are good at three years." Nevertheless "all red wines decline after a certain age, losing colour, flavour and body. Those of Bordeaux begin to decline at about seven years old".

The hierarchy of 'crus' was already elaborate. If the big four sold at 1500 to 1800, then the second-quality wines like 'Rozan', 'La Rose' and 'Durfort' fetched around 1000 louis—two-thirds of the firsts. The third-quality wines (like 'Calon', 'Mouton', 'de Terme') fetched ten per cent below the seconds, and "after these they are reckoned common wines and sell down from 500 to 120 the tun"—less than a tenth of the top prices.

But even in Jefferson's time the power of the merchants was growing. He was fully aware of the merchants' tricks. Although a wine broker assured him that the merchants "never mix the wines of the first quality, but that they mix the inferior wines", he wrote to the then owner of Lafite (Président Pichard) asking him to bottle and despatch the wine himself as a "guarantee that the wine will be natural and the racking properly carried out". But he also reported how even the owner of Margaux, the Marquis d'Agicourt, "has engaged to Jernon, a merchant", as had the Comte de Funelle, the owner of two-thirds of Haut-Brion. In other words the merchants already had a grip on the business, for 'engagement' involved the selling of the whole, or a guaranteed percentage of the crop, either from year to year, or on an 'abonne-ment' (subscription) basis for a period of years, usually to a group of merchants, since none was big enough to gamble regularly on such a scale.

But the names were emerging which were to dominate the trade for nearly two centuries: Jefferson's list of leading English merchants, "Jernon, Barton, Johnston, Foster, Skinner, Copinger and McCarthy", is complemented by another of those who were regular buyers of Yquem, "Toebarts et Fils, Schroder and Schyler, Wustenbery, Weltener, Geissler, Brack and Batie, Cock and Muller, Bart and Cie, Brown, MacCarthy brothers, Barton, Johnston and Bauer, Cabarrus et fils, Duboscq Pere".

5

The Chartronnais muscle in

The prevalence of Irish names in both lists is not surprising. A few were Catholics—like the MacCarthys who had followed King James II into exile in 1688 rather than submit to a Protestant king. But the majority were Protestant from Ulster—like the Bartons and the Johnstons. Partly this was through sheer need: the English ruined the Irish wool trade in the early eighteenth century, and Ulster was full of young men, from respectable but suddenly impoverished farming and merchant families, anxious for any outlet for their talents—and if the opportunity involved a spot of smuggling, why, no real sin was being committed in Irish eyes.

Inevitably then Bordeaux, as a major market for Irish salt beef, would have attracted the attention of these likely lads. But added to this motive was the remarkable Irish thirst for Bordeaux's second-rank claret. For during the eighteenth century a hierarchy of markets grew up, matching the rough classification of 'crus' noted by Jefferson. At the top, the four great growths sold mainly to the English. At the bottom, the poor, sour stuff sold to the thrifty Dutch and Germans. The pecking order was clear enough —Vizetelley tells of the owner of Château Larose, who "was in the habit of hoisting the flag of the particular nation which he considered his wine most likely to suit. Thus, when it was thin and low in price the German colours were run up; when full in body and correspondingly dear, the British standard was unfurled; while, when the wine proved to be of an intermediate character, the Dutch flag was seen flying from the square tower of the château."

His sentiments were echoed by the régisseur (estate manager) at Latour, who achieved his major objective when he was able to sell his whole harvest immediately after fermentation ('en primeur'), to a single firm of 'British' merchants—thus getting the best price for his wine without the cost of storage, racking or evaporation. In the first half of the century the firms of Kater and of Jacob Albert—one of the first recorded as buying property in the Médoc—were frequent buyers. Later on the Bartons and the Johnstons were often prepared to take up the majority of Latour's wine in a good year, the remainder being divided among a small handful of other mainly Anglo-Saxon names— Keystone, Eady, West, French, Bonfield, MacCarthy, Boissière and Morgan. As so often, the prices depended almost entirely on the quality of the wine, so that large-scale and profitable exports were recorded even at the height of the Seven Years War in the late 1750s, simply because it coincided with a run of excellent harvests.

But the lesser vintages—and the second wines of good years— were associated with merchants trading with Holland, Germany and the Baltic and Scandinavia—often lumped together in the eighteenth century as the 'gens du Nord' who were prepared to pay only half the price of those supplying the English market.

Despite a number of wars and several increases in duty, the English continued faithfully to buy relatively small quantities of the very finest wines—barely more than one cask in twenty sold abroad, around half a million bottles. By contrast the Scots and the Irish fitted in lower down the scale: the Scots bought over twice as much wine as the English, the Irish probably four times as much (the figures are unreliable and, especially where Ireland was concerned, were inflated to an unmeasurable extent by smuggling). But they paid less per cask than the English— the Scots just over half, the Irish under half as much. In the scale adopted by the owner of Larose they would still have fitted above the Dutch, but resembled the other non-English markets in that claret was still a comparatively wide-spread beverage.

The reasons—apart from price—were many and various: until later in the century duty was lower in Scotland and Ireland than in England; there was also a strong emotional attachment to France, as the home of the 'lost' Jacobite cause for the Scots, as a Catholic country for the Irish. But there were other, more purely social reasons why terrifying quantities of second-grade claret were consumed in both countries. The mighty thirst of the Scots and Irish is symbolized by the glasses and decanters which were widely used. They had no flat bottom so they could never rest on the table but had to be passed continually from hand to—

increasingly unsteady—hand as interminable rounds of toasts were drunk the long night through. According to Lord Chesterfield "one gentleman in ten in Ireland are impoverished by the great quantity of claret which, from mistaken notions of hospitality and dignity, they think it necessary should be drunk in their houses". No wonder, according to Lecky's *History of Ireland in the Eighteenth Century*, the "immense consumption of French wine was deplored as a national calamity". Berkeley noticed that, while "in England many gentlemen with £1,000 a year never drank wine in their houses, in Ireland this could hardly be said of any who had £100 a year".

Chesterfield's disdainful remark of the Irish that "the affectation of drinking wine has even got into the middle and lower ranks of the people" would have been greeted with a hoarse laugh in Scotland, where claret remained a relatively classless drink throughout most of the century. According to Henry Cockburn, when a cargo of French wine arrived at Leith, the port for Edinburgh, "the common way of proclaiming its arrival was by sending a hogshead of it through the town on a cart with a horn, and that anybody who wanted a sample or a drink under pretence of a sample, had only to go to the cart with a jug, which, without much nicety about its size, was filled for a 6d. The tax ended this mode of advertising; and, aided by the horror of everything French, drove clarets from all tables below the finest."

So it is not surprising to find that Leith and Dublin were probably more important centres for wine imports than London, or, indeed, that the North of England, down as far as Manchester, was supplied with 'Leith-bottled' claret (at first the wines had been shipped via Boulogne often simply because of the ease with which goods could be smuggled across the Channel, but this habit died out during the latter half of the century).

In all this hierarchy the domestic French market scarcely seems to have figured at all. This is surprising, given the fuss made about the alleged discovery by the court of Louis XV of the virtues of claret, and, in particular, of Lafite. This, supposedly, dates from the late 1750s, when a famous rake, the Duc de Richelieu, was exiled from Paris to be governor at Bordeaux.

During his few months' residence he galvanized and shocked the city with his all-night orgies, in the course of which he acquired a taste for claret—a wine previously virtually unknown in Paris or at the court at Versailles. On his return he attributed his good health to his new discovery and supposedly converted the King, his mistress Madame de Pompadour, and thus, inevitably, the whole of fashionable Paris, to the Bordelais cause.

Nevertheless, the Anglo-Irish merchants continued to monopolize the purchase of the finer clarets. But the Irish merchants, in particular, created as much trouble as the Dutch had a century before. Because they preferred to buy their claret pure in Bordeaux and then work on it in Cork or Dublin, they were, paradoxically —if hypocritically—against allowing such mixing anywhere near Bordeaux. So, in a famous row in 1764, they posed as the sternest defenders of the old rules which forbad the mixing of 'foreign' wines with claret in Bordeaux itself. Their problem was that the Bordeaux-based merchants had imitated their methods so successfully as to gain most of the business.

The Irish complainants were touching on a sore nerve. For the foreign merchants in Bordeaux—the Chartronnais—were already under attack, like many other groups of hard-working immigrants before or since. One ground for dislike was that they were "cold, calculating, disciplined and rich". An anonymous enemy in the 1740s had summed up all the complaints made against them: that they went directly to the wine-growers, avoiding the brokers—and their commissions; that they monopolized foreign sales, and dictated prices in all the wine-growing districts.

One typical defence (made twenty years later when requesting permission to build a Lutheran church) claimed that it was they who had developed Bordeaux's wine exports in the first place, and that they had used their foreign contacts to good purpose when they had provided Bordeaux with grain after the frightful winters of 1709 and 1747 (they were to render a similar service in 1770).

They could have added that they were already famous for their charitable ways—("it is," said one appreciative inhabitant, "among the foreigners at Bordeaux that you find most of the treasurers of St. Andrew's Hospital").

In 1746 the Irish had tried a different line of approach. They declared that they were being condemned without being heard, that they only mixed wine to save the growers from having an unsaleable crop (a fundamental fact of Bordeaux life to this day), and that the growers themselves did the same thing—quoting the case of the white wines of Bergerac, which were specially mixed with 'sirop' for the Dutch trade.

Nevertheless the Parlement issued one last thunderous decree on the subject. Its futility is demonstrated by the sonorous roll-call of its predecessors "notably that of the 16th March, 1683, which recalled those of 1602, 1616, 1619 and dates back to earlier centuries; more recently still those of the 10th May and 2nd July 1741, the latter preceded by Letters Patent; that of 17th July, 1744 and 16th December, 1755".

The 1764 declaration was doomed to be the last on the subject. The French minister, Turgot, tried to break up Bordeaux's monopoly in 1776; and, although local pressure forced him to restore the *status quo*, Bordeaux's privileges—as well as everyone else's—were finally swept away in the first onslaught of the French Revolution, thirteen years later. Yet they had served their purpose: for Bordeaux had kept a good deal of protection during a crucial century when it was establishing the name of its wines for quality, as well as quantity. It was nearly a century before the challenge to the Médoc gathered strength.

But, for all their mixed feelings about the wine merchants who made so free with their products, growers could not deny their success, although this was of less importance to Bordeaux as a whole than at any other period in its history. For during the eighteenth century France was busily building up a colonial empire in the West Indies, and Bordeaux enjoyed enormous prosperity as the country's major colonial port. (It also helped the look of the city, which was remodelled, largely under the inspiration of an Intendant, Tourny, in a handsome, dignified but not overpowering style that has set it apart ever since from the usual run of French provincial towns.)

The colonies were enormous customers for Bordeaux, and thus for the wines shipped through the port. They bought up to a third of Bordeaux's steadily growing wine exports—and these rose steadily through the century. Prices, too, rose at a rate steady enough not to frighten the customers, but fast enough to ensure that the actual value of the wines shipped nearly tripled in the sixty years.

Yet wine accounted for only a twelfth of the goods shipped to the colonies, and in the course of the century, wine, and indeed

Bordeaux's own produce as a whole, gradually withdrew into the background. Wine, which had accounted for half the city's exports around the turn of the century, was responsible for less than a third by 1789. This was part of the general trend: as Bordeaux's official history puts it, "Bordeaux detached itself from its hinterland"—an important development in separating the inward-looking wine-makers from the outward-looking merchants. These were selling forty per cent of their wines abroad, whereas the average for French wine was only one-tenth.

The general increase in trade—which made Bordeaux France's biggest port—was, in general, helpful to the wine business. The Irish, for instance, could not have afforded so much claret if they had not been supplying French sailors and French colonists with so much of their wool and salt beef. The Germans from the Hanseatic ports were primarily interested in reselling French colonial products, sugar and the like, at home. They also reduced the Dutch share of the wine trade very sharply, for at the beginning of the century the Dutch had acted as middlemen, re-exporting a great deal of wine they bought to Germany and Scandinavia.

For if one set of foreigners ever lost out it was only to other aliens not to the Bordelais themselves. The natives' Gascon temperament and lack of foreign contacts has kept them from participating in Bordeaux's wine business over the past three hundred years. Their place was taken by other Frenchmen, by the English and Irish, by the Dutch and by the relatively large number of Germans who arrived early in the century.*

Of course shipping throughout the eighteenth century and into the nineteenth was a business for gamblers, speculating on the chance—often well-founded—of a fabulous fortune from one shipment. Nor did an aspiring merchant require much capital. Stendhal, who visited Bordeaux in 1828, describes how a young man from up-country "would get a job as a clerk in a business house. After two or three years in which, by good conduct, he proved his worth (for things move fast in Bordeaux) he would obtain permission to place a small cargo of sundry articles on

---

* There were eighteen such families recorded in 1743, of whom eleven had arrived in the previous dozen years, and thirty years later it was estimated that fifty out of the city's four hundred and fifty merchants were of German origin.

board one of the firm's vessels. He would then call on one of
the merchants who furnished those articles and make his request."
The merchant then made his enquiries, and, if these were satisfactory, would extend six months' credit till the ship's return.
The would-be merchant had only to furnish a small deposit.
Stendhal reckoned that a clerk could hope to do well enough
after ten years or so to be able to join with three or four of his
contemporaries while still in his mid-thirties and start up by
themselves. Even then they needed only enough capital to hire,
rather than buy, a ship.

The risks were of course tremendous, for the chances of a
ship returning in six, or indeed any number of, months were not
good, but the route described by Stendhal is the one trod by
future wine-merchants, as well as by the more general traders.
Typically, the founder of the still-thriving Johnston business,
William Johnston, first came to Bordeaux in 1716 as an adolescent
to learn French. He went back to Ireland to marry, then returned
to work in the firm of Pierre Germe. After Germe's death the
estate was divided and Johnston went it alone.

Despite the risks, a real fortune could be made very quickly.
Thomas Barton (described though not, one suspects, to his
face, as 'French Tom') worked in Marseilles and Montpellier as
a factor, before finally settling in Bordeaux. According to Cyril
Ray, "he was twenty-seven when he first went to France, thirty
by the time he set up his own business in Bordeaux in 1715". Yet
"many years before 1742", according to a legal document of the
time, he "was engaged in a great and extensive trade, by which
he had acquired a very considerable fortune". By mid-century
he was rich enough to buy property: Château le Boscq in St.
Estèphe, and, even further north, his "country house in the
Médoc" at the very tip of the peninsula. But his roots remained
in Ireland, and at the same time he bought an estate in Tipperary
for £30,000, then an immense sum.

His riches endowed his children more than adequately: "Of
the six sons, one became a member of Parliament, two became
generals, two lived on their spacious Irish estates. Of the three
daughters, one married a peer, and another a baronet. The
Bartons, from being a modestly well-to-do family, with merchant
in-laws, had become immensely wealthy landed gentry, with
lordly connections—and all thanks to 'French Tom'," who, not

surprisingly, was reckoned to be one of the biggest, if not the biggest, single purchaser of fine claret during the second half of the century.

But other merchants, German, Dutch, English, did almost as well. For virtually all the foreign inhabitants of Bordeaux in the late eighteenth century were rich. Indeed the only exceptions, the Swiss, testified to the wealth of their fellow-aliens, for they included five patissiers, a watch-maker and at least one jeweller. The strangers had by that time turned the Quai des Chartrons into what was described as "the finest suburb in France, because of the beauty of its houses, the importance of its trade, and its advantageous position". The foreigners had spread further down river, to what was called the Quai de Bacalan and had built behind the Chartrons itself.

Today the whole quarter, especially the Quai itself, has that sad, run-down, dusty appearance which characterizes many handsome decaying streets in unfashionable areas near city centres the world over. Some of the shippers still defiantly retain their offices on the Quai and, even more defiantly, refuse to modernize their premises. In the late 1950s an unsympathetic foreign competitor declared briskly that "Charles Dickens would have considered their offices old-fashioned. The shippers stand at high desks, doing their calculations on the backs of old envelopes. The clocks on the walls are out of order. In some cases the name of the firm doesn't appear on the door; the owners claim there's no need for a nameplate because their company is so well known that anyone can find it."

The Quai and the triangle behind it still house the majority of firms which provide the essential services for the wine trade— the printers who supply the labels, the makers of corks and boxes, the coopers, the insurance and shipping companies, the consulates of maritime nations. But the gaps have been filled by 'clubs', by seedy newsagents with their displays of pornography and by shabby bars. Their sleazy signs contrast with the wrought-iron balconies above and the solid strength of a stretch of uniform stone buildings which closely resemble the four-storey eighteenth-century terraces which are still the pride of many English towns. The only stretch which still looks as immaculate as ever is the former Pavé des Chartrons (renamed in the 1920s the Cours Xavier Arnouzan after a famous local doctor). This runs at right

angles to the Quai at its city end and the flats into which its
dignified houses have been divided are still much sought after
residences—and not only by the Chartronnais.

Yet a hundred and fifty years ago the Quai itself was as exciting
and handsome a commercial centre as any in the world. Thomas
Jefferson admired its elm trees, a later visitor "the magnificent
crescent of houses in the Italian style". And, at the end of the
nineteenth century, the excitement of the whole quarter was
indelibly recorded by those two stalwart Anglo-Irish ladies,
E. Œ. Somerville and her cousin who wrote under the name of
Martin Ross. *

It was only when they reached the Chartrons that "we began
to realize what the wine country could do when it put its mind
to it. The great quays were packed close with barrels as far as the
eye could follow—barrels on whose ends were hieroglyphs that
told of aristocratic birth as plainly as the armorial bearings on a
carriage; the streets were full of long narrow carts like ladders on
wheels, laden also with barrels, one behind the other, and about
every five minutes, as it seemed to us, some big ship moved out
from the wharf, filled to the brim with claret, and slipped down
the yellow current to other climes."

Somerville and Ross were seeing the Quai after a century of
triumph. For it had been the upheavals of the French Revolution
and the Napoleonic period which had provided its inhabitants
with their real opportunity.

* Their book on Bordeaux and the Médoc *In the Vine Country* was not
their first travel book, though rather more adventurous than their
previous *Through Connemara in a Governess-cart*.

6

The triumph of the Chartronnais

1789 was not a good year for Bordeaux, not because of mere external events: for the Revolution had, at first, little effect. But, because the vintage was poor, the Bordelais could not continue to take full advantage of the opportunities which had opened three years before with the signature of an Anglo-French Treaty of Commerce, which effectively halved the English duties on French wines. Although the Portuguese quickly clawed back the general preference they had enjoyed during the previous eighty years, exports of claret to England jumped five-fold in as many years.

By 1789 Britain accounted for a fifth of Bordeaux's wine exports by volume, and nearly a third by value. In the long term, this jump confirmed the Bordelais in their free-trade beliefs, very different, then as now, from the basic protectionism felt by most Frenchmen; more immediately, it reinforced the importance of the English trade—and thus of the merchants of the Chartrons— and enabled the upper end of the wine trade to float unharmed over the general economic crisis afflicting France, and the specific crisis of over-production and competition which hurt Bordeaux's traffic in ordinary wines and many other goods.

The first effects of the Revolution actually helped the Chartronnais. In 1790 the route to naturalization was made infinitely easier, indeed it became automatic after a relatively short stay, provided that the alien affirmed that he or she would remain permanently in France—until then the process had been so complicated that many foreigners did not bother (no one is quite clear, for instance, whether two of the leading merchants of Dutch origin, Messrs. Schröder and Schÿler, who arrived from Hamburg in 1739 and whose descendants are still active, were naturalized or not).

But eventually the Revolution began to make itself felt in earnest. A number of owners, including Président Pichard of

Lafite, and the then owner of Margaux, were guillotined, their heirs—and many others—fled the country after the King's execution in 1792, and their estates were confiscated. At the same time, the revolutionary monetary system broke down. The results helped the British merchants, who emerged in far more dominant a position in 1815 after the Revolution and the Napoleonic Wars. This was, at first sight, a startling development, given that many of them were still citizens of a country which had been at war with France intermittently for nearly a quarter of a century.

But the owners, whoever they were, still depended on a flow of cash which only the English could provide: they had always acted as bankers for the growers—Guestier let the Comte de Lascases, owner of Léoville-Lascases, have an open account in the 1820s. They bought the previous year's crop on terms which assured the owner that his costs for the next year would be covered. In general they kept their word—when in 1795 payment in coin was forbidden they arranged for the money to be paid through the Hamburg market. The period imposed a terrible strain on the merchants, and probably the biggest of them all, Forster, Chalmer and Forster, went into liquidation in 1808, leaving a trail of debts to other merchants and to many estates. But the survivors emerged as completely dominant. They had proved conclusively that they, and they alone, could market Bordeaux's best wines.

The most astonishing rise during the period was that of Daniel Guestier, one of the very few merchants of French origin to make any permanent mark on the wine business before the 1870s. Not that the Guestiers were locals, or even Catholics. They were Huguenots from Brittany; indeed Daniel's grandfather had been forced to give up his career as a naval officer when, in 1685, Louis XIV revoked the Edict of Nantes, which had provided for the toleration of Protestants, and he eventually settled in Bordeaux. His son François was a lawyer, a legal secretary to Alexandre de Ségur, indeed helped the 'prince des Vignes' to sell Lafite's wines (there is a famous advertisement, dating from 1736, proclaiming that "the great wines of Lafite and Latour could be bought at the town house of the Président de Ségur in the Rue Porte Dijeaux, and at the house of Mr. François Guestier in the Rue du Cerf Volant").

François conformed sufficiently to have his children baptized Catholics, although neither of the parents attended the christenings. Daniel, born in 1755, was his second son, and even before the Revolution had demonstrated remarkable entrepreneurial talents. He had gone to sea at the tender age of fourteen taking with him a job lot of trade goods. He had done so well that he eventually owned an enormous coffee plantation on the then French West Indian island of Santo Domingo, settled a younger brother there to manage it, and travelled all round Northern Europe exchanging its produce for the goods required by the colonials. He was enterprising enough to dodge the British blockade of the Gironde during the American War of Independence by building two schooners specially designed to operate out of the Basin of Arcachon, fifty miles west of Bordeaux on the Atlantic coast, for the shoals and tides of the Bay were too tricky to allow the English to close the Basin entirely.

The Revolution immediately ruined his plantation: the slaves who worked it were freed and took it over. So he had to look elsewhere. His first step was to join the radical 'Jacobin Club', a political master-stroke, since this membership seems to have provided him with an immunity unique among wine-merchants from persecution by the revolutionary leaders. These, fairly naturally, reflected the general Bordelais suspicion that the foreigners were parasites and speculators.

His elder brother, Pierre-François, was arrested with his business colleague Nathaniel Johnston in 1793. So was the young Hugh Barton, the grandson of 'French Tom'. Hugh Barton had been taken into partnership by his father William in 1786. William had never been on good terms with *his* father (indeed conducted a law-suit against him which provides us with a glimpse of the size of his fortune); but by the Revolution was a relatively old man, and was left in peace by the revolutionary authorities.

Hugh Barton had married Johnston's sister Anna (known by him as Nancy) in one of the earliest of the dynastic marriages which were, for two hundred years, to provide the socio-economic cement which held the Chartronnais together so effectively (as Edmund Penning-Rowsell puts it, "all the wine families are so connected with each other by marriage that a Jewish family gathering has nothing in the way of kinship on a large dinner party of the Bordeaux wine trade").

The Bartons and Johnstons were well enough treated. In Cyril Ray's words, "the conditions of internment seem not to have been too severe; Anna Barton, perhaps because she was a nursing mother, perhaps because she had been born in France and could claim French citizenship, was soon released and permitted to visit her husband daily. He, for his part, was granted a parole to visit his dying father, but too late: William died on 29th October, 1793".

Hugh himself was released later that year and cleared of any suspicion of criminal activity early in 1794—he was treated as 'Citizen Hugues Barton', because his father had had him naturalized some years previously. Nevertheless the Bartons and the Johnstons had to leave the country. The legend has it that Johnston escaped from prison in a female disguise smuggled in by his wife. Allegedly he took with him on his flight to Dublin the keys of the guillotine, thus effectively stopping any further executions in the city. He soon returned to France, though Barton spent most of the next fifteen years either on his Barton Hill estate in Ireland or in Portman Square in London busy with French & Barton, the family-owned business which dominated the import of wines into Ireland. Before he left Bordeaux, however, he arranged for his business to be handled by Daniel Guestier.

Originally the Barton–Guestier arrangement was a temporary one. Indeed Barton wrote to Nathaniel Johnston that he "had no intention of continuing the partnership longer than the war". But Daniel took full advantage of the revolutionary situation, ideal for an entrepreneur with privileged access to markets, for he enjoyed a unique advantage as the agent in charge of both the Johnston and Barton businesses—buying wine, as he told Hugh Barton, "as if it were my own".

Once the revolutionary fervour died down, a new stability emerged in 1795. But by that time many of the estates were being sold up as 'biens publics'—confiscated property in public hands. Because of their continuing insecurity about their political position, the merchants—even Guestier—hesitated over trying to buy up any of the properties, but there were two other ways of getting their hands on the wines, leasing the properties or contracting with the owners to take the wine on long-term contracts or 'abonnements'. The most spectacular instance was Margaux, one of the first growths on the market in the 1790s—the other, Lafite, was sold at public auction in 1797 to a Dutch syndicate. Five years later they sold the domaine to a Dutch businessman, Vanlerberghe, who had made a fortune supplying Napoleon's armies, in probably the first instance of outside capital being invested in Bordeaux's vineyards—previously only local merchants and ship-owners had bothered. In 1802 Château Margaux was sold—cheaply—at auction to a Spanish banker, the Marquis de la Colonilla, and since then the Médoc has, periodically, received massive injections of outside capital in the course of several subsequent booms.

Before that it had been leased to one Mathieu Migneau, who neglected the vineyard most grievously—even now it can take several years of hard pruning, of continual ploughing and expensive chemical treatment to restore a neglected plot. Guestier was probably the only man in Bordeaux able to restore the position. So, in the late 1790s, he took a lease of Margaux and cut the Forsters, Johnston and the absent Barton in on the deal. His only possible rival, Johnston, was probably in no financial state to take on so big a burden—he had, for instance, defaulted "because of persecution" on the payments he owed for his share of the 1792 Latour. In other words, Guestier made himself indispensable to Barton and, within a few years, was offered a partnership, which lasted for a hundred and sixty years until the death of the last Daniel Guestier.

The date of the partnership, 1802, was significant, for it marked a short interlude of peace during which the wine business sprang back to life. The shippers were helped by neutrals, who enabled Bordeaux to receive the supplies of Spanish wine necessary for making up the claret for the English market—they even managed to sell the inferior 1799 vintage, duly 'worked on'. But the relief was only temporary—just as Bordeaux's reliance on the English market had helped it in the 1780s, so it suffered from this same dependence twenty years later when, for the first time, trade with Britain virtually dried up as a result of Napoleon's 'Continental System' and Britain's consequent blockades. The Chartronnais tried for alternative markets—in 1807 one of the Johnstons sailed for New York, armed with an introduction from

Lafayette himself, and, within a couple of years, had, allegedly, acquired a thousand customers. But, by and large, the English market was irreplaceable. 1808 was the blackest year. The bankruptcy of the Forsters was by no means the only one that year, nor unique in Bordeaux's history—the substantial Dutch firm of Sellschop had gone under as recently as 1788. But the Forsters' historic importance ensured that the debts they left behind were enormous and widely spread: and the bankruptcy was so unexpected that even Daniel Guestier was owed 44,000 francs. (Lamothe, then estate manager of Latour, which escaped virtually scot-free, commented smugly that Guestier "was a terribly difficult man to deceive; but this was an instance when, you could say, that even the most famous got it wrong".)

Yet, as so often in Bordeaux, recovery was remarkably swift. Lamothe may have lamented that the vintage of 1808 was lovely but unsaleable, but within four years—while the war still raged—the cellars of growers and merchants alike started to clear. Indeed the first decade of the century seems to have established the pattern for a century and a half to come. Lamothe's battles with the buyers at the time show the ingrained hostility between the two sides, and the emergence—or rather the re-emergence—of the power of those medieval specialists, the 'courtiers', the wine-brokers.

They had survived by throwing themselves on the King's mercy in the seventeenth century, thus ensuring the continuation of their monopoly. But the cost of their royal charter was that they were lumbered with a number of taxes and became the victim of every sort of royal hanger-on. Although they managed to salvage some sort of official monopoly power after the Bourbon restoration, this petered out, and since then they have relied on their wits and qualities defined by Philippe Roudié as "speed of decision, and extraordinary knowledge of wines, and a scrupulous honesty as wine-tasters". Despite the breakdown of their official status, the role they play as honest middle-men is governed by some fairly rigid conventions (their commission could be up to two per cent, though for large transactions it was—and is—usually set at between $1\frac{1}{4}$ and $1\frac{1}{2}$ per cent. They were expected to set an order in motion within two days, one for dealing with the owner-grower, the next for agreeing a price with the merchant). In time a whole host of legends have accumulated round the

fabled palates of the better brokers, and this sensitivity remains
even today their most important asset in advising on the particular
qualities of wines, especially of new wine, and deciding whether
it is likely to develop well. There was, for instance, the dying
broker whose parched lips were moistened with a little wine.
"Lafite '70" are recorded as his dying words.*

The majority of brokers have always been the poor relations
of the system. Today it is reckoned that only twenty out of the
hundred in Bordeaux earn a decent living. Most of them are still
treated by the merchants with some disdain, as mere 'carriers of
samples'. Indeed a group of them, weatherbeaten and indistinguishable from peasant wine-growers in their workmen's
ragged blue denims, can be seen every day before lunch hanging
round the reception desks of merchants' offices, carrying with
them their little bottles of wines white and red, waiting for the
honour of a tasting.

Some of these will be 'country brokers' based on Bordeaux's
small satellite towns—Pauillac, Bourg, Blaye, Cadillac, Cernon,
Langon—lesser fry, only too glad to act as half-commission men
for the all-powerful handful of brokers who have the ear of the
biggest buyers. These were, and are, a much more vital element
in the Bordeaux system. During his visit to Bordeaux Stendhal
dined with one of them. His description—at least of the top few
brokers—is still accurate. In the intervening century and a half
only the means of transport has changed: until towards the end
of the century brokers had to travel by boat or on horseback, and
they were often away for up to three weeks at a time. But the
opening of a railway from Bordeaux up the Médoc enabled
brokers to cover a much wider area than before. Stendhal's
broker "was teased about the good life he led. The only capital
these gentlemen put into their business is a horse and a Tilbury
in which they run all over the Médoc. They taste the wines of the
various proprietors and, with a piece of chalk, mark the quality
of the casks. You can imagine how the proprietors pay court to

* Many of these stories are of considerable antiquity. One, which
dates back to Cervantes' *Don Quixote*, but still circulated in Bordeaux
earlier this century, concerns the broker who detected a faintly metallic
taste in a particular cask, together with a suspicion of cardboard.
When the cask was drained, why, in the bottom was found a metal
key, with a cardboard label.

them! And woe betide the owner who would dare to rub out the broker's chalk mark! No broker would take it upon himself to sell that man's wine.

"After he has received his mail, a merchant will say to a broker: 'I need 200 casks of wine, of such and such a quality, at such and such a price.'

"The winebroker replies: 'There are some in this place and that place.' He then goes to the proprietors and charges two per cent above the price paid by the merchant, in addition to gifts from the proprietors who are always eager to sell. These brokers are like ministers: they always call on people who need them. Many of them make 8–10,000 francs a year from their travels around the Médoc and by allowing themselves to be urged to accept good dinners. Besides they can never lose."

A broker like this was M. Baguenard, the only one used by the English wine merchants, Walter and Alfred Gilbey, when they were major buyers of claret in the last quarter of the nineteenth century. They mourned him when he died, for "he had made himself one of us". Cannily his firm had established an office at Lesparre, forty miles from Bordeaux but conveniently close to the Gilbeys' cellars at Château Loudenne, one of the most northerly of major Médocain estates.

Baguenard was a partner in Mermans, one of the two broking firms who were the most powerful influences on the history of the Bordeaux wine trade. But pride of place belongs to the Lawtons, the only brokers to have been accepted into the Chartronnais' clan system, and the only ones to have survived and flourished continuously for the last two hundred years. The Mermans, a Dutch Protestant family, were established well before Abraham Lawton arrived from Cork in 1739, and had become much involved (as were so many other brokers) in shipping and commodities other than wine. But only the Lawtons survived. The offices of 'Tastet and Lawton' (Tastet was a Frenchman taken into partnership early in the nineteenth century) are still at 60 Quai des Chartrons, and Daniel-Georges Lawton is still the most important broker in Bordeaux. Not that the offices give any indication of past glories or present significance. They consist merely of a small tiled tasting room on the ground floor, and a secretary's office and partners' room on the first floor. There is no conclusive visual evidence that the building has been painted since Abraham Lawton's arrival. Obviously the Lawtons, like Stendhal's dining companion, have never believed in excessive capital expenditure—indeed this compulsive shabbiness, a characteristic of many of the offices of the Chartronnais, is typically English, a mark of inner security, demonstrating a superiority so self-evident that it would be diminished by any outward and visible display of riches or power. Yet, within these few offices are records giving Bordeaux's weather, day by unpredictable day, over the past hundred and fifty years, the prices paid over the same period for its wines, and volumes of comments on the Bordeaux scene.

It was Abraham Lawton's son William who, together with the contemporary member of the Merman family, emerged as one of the most powerful figures in Bordeaux during the Napoleonic period—"they are all-powerful", was one contemporary view.

In general the brokers were accepted by the growers as necessary evils: one proof of the horrors of 1808 was that "no broker is moving around the Médoc any longer". But this did not stop the flow of Lamothe's eloquence on the subject of "the inexorable Lawton . . . the bird of prey, who hovers from time to time over the Médoc, more especially over the head of the needy, whom he menaces with his cruel talons". Already, it seemed, the brokers and merchants had adopted the habit, which they have still not completely abandoned, of touring the Médoc together, visiting numerous châteaux, tasting carefully, but then subjecting the wretched proprietors to a silent war of nerves. Lamothe exploded about one such visit that although "these big-wigs had ample funds with which to buy the whole crop and although they tasted amply, they said nothing about any transaction in the near future".

But growers—or managers like Lamothe—enjoyed their moments of revenge, especially when demand was rising. One such came in 1814 when a new English firm, Messrs. Blackenbury from Liverpool, broke up what was otherwise a relatively cosy ring and bought the whole crop of all three Médoc first-growth châteaux. Blackenbury's arrival was, according to Lamothe, "just in time to free us from the despotism of Lawton and Merman . . . who have recently started to work together to acquire the 'grands crus' at 16 or 1800 francs . . . The reefs of Cordouan are not

3

more dangerous for ships than are these two gentlemen for proprietors."

Although the coming of peace and of a few new buyers like Blackenbury helped the growers temporarily, yet they and the final buyers both admitted that direct dealing was virtually impossible, that the merchants were an indispensable link in the commercial chain. For they emerged from the wars not just as dealers, but as 'négociants éléveurs', wholesalers whose role include the storage and treatment of the wines in their cellars, playing two distinct roles. From their point of view the actual purchase was crucial: "the intelligent members of the family do the buying" is the hoariest of Chartronnais truisms. And, for all the growers' grumbles, the process was something of a gamble, even for the merchants. Charles Cocks, the English journalist who played a major role in publicizing the wines of the Gironde, tells of the "high prices followed by serious losses" on the 1820 vintage, which obviously deceived the brokers and merchants into imagining that they would mature more satisfactorily than they actually did. "The red wines," he wrote, "had body, a fine colour, and good maturity, but, in developing, they remained hard, and were destitute of suavity and bouquet." The merchants clearly made up for their losses by their profits on the 1823 vintage, which started so badly that "several proprietors, in despair, left the grapes on the vine . . . however, in developing, they were found to have much bouquet and to be light and delicate. In consequence of their low prices these wines were found profitable for the trade".

But what "the trade" wanted varied from country to country. The 1840s, for instance, were found "particularly smooth, but rather deficient in body". The vintage "met with much approbation in the German market; but its want of body precluded the possibility of its being used for England". By contrast, the 1841s, with their "fine colour, body and flavour" were "certainly better qualified to suit English taste than any years for several years past". Even the prices were "moderate . . . until the quality became known, and then very high."

For speculation remained endemic in Bordeaux, especially in the 'good' years—which tended also to be those producing wines likely to be appreciated by the English. Then the difference in price between first and second growths was accentuated, and the price of the new vintage was greatly affected by what was happening to the older ones. The process Jefferson had noted in the 1780s was repeated—the prices of the 1844s were boosted because those same 1841s had been bid up so high.

Once the gamble had been taken, the merchants' second rôle emerged, as the 'éléveurs' responsible for their ageing and, if they were for the English market, their treatment. This, again, changed during the Revolution. For much of the time it proved impossible to import wine from Spain. This led to a marked increase in the use of the Hermitage wines produced in the Rhône Valley. For half a century, indeed, the area's whole production was destined merely to strengthen Bordeaux's wines (though, ironically, they have emerged in recent years as serious rivals in their own right to claret). But in the early nineteenth century the connection was colonial: Nathaniel Johnston took leases on a number of vineyards by the Rhône to secure his supplies of Hermitage; and in 1819 Jean-Marie Calvet, a young wine merchant from the area, came to Bordeaux to sell his wines for blending—only to stay and found what is still one of Bordeaux's biggest firms.

To age— and prepare—the wine, the merchants required enormous cellars. In the eighteenth century much of the ageing and blending was still done nearer the customer. But by the beginning of the nineteenth the business was concentrated on the Quai des Chartrons, and the merchants' cellars, some of which stretched back half a mile behind the offices, became major tourist attractions. Three, in particular, became famous: those of Fred Cutler, the English Vice-Consul; those of Barton and Guestier's—over 50,000 square feet in all—which were called "the Lions of Bordeaux" in Murray's guidebook, and the 'caves anglaises' of the Johnstons, which held the equivalent of nearly six million bottles. Cocks recalled their appearance when they were illuminated: "Nothing could equal the magical effects of the innumerable wax candles, revealing interminable rows of casks, and reflected in many hundred thousand bottles in this subterraneous fairyland, or rather Kingdom of Ganymede."

Despite this magnificence, the Chartronnais were interested in many other goods besides wines. A price list of Nathaniel Johnston's of the 1820s gives a list over a page long of imports, from aloes to snake root and including forty varieties of sugar. By contrast the list of exports is much shorter and includes mostly local agricultural produce (almonds, aniseed, prunes), with only six varieties of wine—the best of which was simply 'Good Médoc'. Obviously Johnston did not list his better wines, but as late as 1914 the house of Barton and Guestier made more money from handling olive oil than from its wine business.

It is not surprising that after 1815 the wine merchants emerged as major powers within Bordeaux, especially as the strictly colonial trade had diminished with the evaporation of France's first colonial empire. They played a very active part in any new commercial or financial development. Daniel Guestier was especially active. He had survived the return of the Bourbons so well that he had become President of the Chamber of Commerce and been made a baron by Louis XVIII (though he never used the title, preferring to sport the insignia of the Légion d'Honneur). But, in later life, he left the wine business to the next generation, to his son Pierre-François and to Nathaniel Barton (the Christian name chosen, presumably, in honour of his mother's brother, Nathaniel Johnston). Daniel returned to his first love, shipping, he bought shares in the Sandeman port business and devoted much of his time and capital to new ventures. With Nathaniel Johnston he was active in promoting such novelties as the first steamships on the Gironde, the Bank of Bordeaux and the first railway in the area, across the marshy Landes to the Atlantic at La Teste and Arcachon.

Not all these ventures went well: the Bank of Bordeaux got into terrible trouble in 1830 when the Bourbons were finally ousted, was propped up by the Rothschilds, and finally succumbed in the even more revolutionary year of 1848, when it was absorbed by the Bank of France; and the railway was rescued only when it became an extension of the main line from Paris.

One of the sufferers from the railway's financial problems was a wine merchant of Swiss origins, Domeine Guillaume Mestrezat, who had to be rescued by his banker father in Geneva. Mestrezat had arrived in Bordeaux in 1814, the first of a number of new-comers in the first decade after the war, men bearing names still well known in Bordeaux. Mestrezat (now known as Mestrezat-Preller) is still in the hands of the family—and of a member of the Lawton clan. So is Hanappier–Peyrelongue, founded in 1818 by a merchant from Orleans (the centre of a major pre-Revolutionary wine-growing area). When the family needed financial protection in 1968 it looked to the Calvets, the other family business of French origin dating from that time.

But most of the newcomers came from further east—Switzerland or 'Northern parts'—probably because the Johnstons and Barton and Guestier had the British market so well sewn up. Among the founders of firms still active—if no longer independent—Louis-Frederick Eschenauer arrived from Strasbourg in 1821 and specialized in the German market. Almost the same year a young Swiss, Alfred de Luze, arrived from New York, where he and his brother Louis-Philippe had emigrated a couple of years before from Neuchâtel (this small Swiss county had been a possession of the King of Prussia, who bestowed the baronial title still sported by Alfred's descendants). The brothers had originally emigrated to New York to sell European luxuries, like olive oil, and settled on Bordeaux as a European base on the advice of a banker uncle in Frankfurt. But Alfred quickly specialized in wines and in Cognac.

But the most significant newcomer proved to be Hermann Cruse, who arrived in Bordeaux at the age of twenty-nine in 1819. He was the son of a Lutheran pastor in Schleswig-Holstein—a buffer state between Denmark and Prussia which became entangled in some of the most obscure diplomatic convolutions of the whole century (the problems of the family ancestral home have had their compensations, providing the Cruses with a sort of dual nationality, useful when selling to both markets—or in times of war against the Germans).

But the family fortunes owed more to speculation than to nationality. The most famous coup in Bordeaux's history was accomplished by the founding father with the 1847 vintage. For 1848 was the most troubled year Europe was to see during the whole century. In February—just as the 1847s came up for sale— the French King, Louis Philippe, fled to England and a Republic was proclaimed. By the end of the year Louis Napoleon, nephew of the great Napoleon Bonaparte, and himself later crowned as Napoleon III, was firmly in control, but only after a year which had seen revolutions in much of Europe, as well as considerable further disturbances in France.

These were ideal circumstances for an entrepreneur like Hermann Cruse with stout nerves. Right through the year he kept buying enormous quantities of the very best clarets, at prices as low as a third of those paid for the popular 1844 vintage. He virtually monopolized the crop, buying in all the amazing quantity of 13,650 tonneaux from over 130 growths—enough to fill nearly 16 million bottles. Once the dust had settled and Napoleon was firmly in power, prices rose again and Cruse graciously allowed competitors like Barton and Guestier and Johnston to purchase some of his hoard—at prices which have not been disclosed.

Since then, many merchants have dreamed of repeating Cruse's coup—probably Edouard Kressman, founder of another firm, came nearest with the fine vintage harvested during the height of the Franco-Prussian war in 1870, and other merchants have given their fortunes similar boosts (the most spectacular newcomer of the last generation, Jean-Pierre Moueix, a gambler on the grand scale, hoisted himself into the big league in Bordeaux with his massive purchases of the 1959 vintage, without an external calamity to assist him).

To sober observers, Cruse's example is precisely the one which Bordeaux should *not* follow, since it encourages the trade to think in speculative, rather than marketing terms. But speculation is so much more fun than marketing that the trade is still addicted to it.

Cruse employed some of his gains to buy châteaux in the Médoc; and the supremacy of the merchants at the time is shown by the numbers they bought, and the many long-term 'abonnements', which often provided for a growth to be pledged to one house or, more usually, a small group of merchants for up to ten years at a time. And with the coming of peace, in 1815, there was no longer any reason why the merchants should not buy estates. In 1818 Daniel Guestier bought the estate of Beychevelle, and four years later his partner, Hugh Barton, bought Langoa, another estate surrounding a delightful eighteenth-century house. Over the next ten years Barton also acquired a quarter of the great Léoville estate which, before its break-up at the Revolution, had comprised over three hundred acres. He also bought numerous little plots from the local peasantry to round off his purchases. (The two are neighbours, but it is typical of the Médoc that Langoa is in the 'commune' or parish of Beychevelle, while Léoville is in St. Julien). Hugh Barton bought the properties personally and they have remained in the hands of the family ever since. Indeed Ronald Barton, a direct descendant, universally known as 'Ronnie' and one of the best-loved characters in the Médoc, still lives at Langoa, still, in his seventies, actively supervising the wine-making and still proud of being of Irish, rather than of English origin.

But the amiably squirearchical position of Ronnie Barton was not the most obvious role of the Chartronnais. To the owners they were still predators: to the estate managers a painful contrast to the absentee descendants of the original families. The wretched Lamothe who had guided Latour's fortunes so ably through the disturbances of the years before Waterloo suffered badly from the business-like habits of the Bartons and the Guestiers. They bought just under a tenth share in the estate in 1833 and went through the books with a fine toothcomb—comparing the costs with those on their own estates (by contrast the Comte de La Pallu, another shareholder, had visited Latour only twice in twenty-six years and the then Marquis de Beaumont only once).

Lamothe's sins—including allocating a large percentage of the crop to cover his private expenses—led to his dismissal years later at the age of nearly eighty-three. In 1840 the merchants gained a tighter grip by converting some of their loans to the other owners into shares to give them a fifth of the total. The other proprietors were so alarmed that they set in motion a legal device called 'licitation', which ended in a compulsory auction in 1841. After spirited bidding the other owners finally secured the whole estate, but the cost of acquisition of the merchants' shares, combined with the redemption of the outstanding loans, was so great that they were forced to grant a ten-year 'abonnement' to Barton and Guestier. Even this caused trouble: costs rose more than predicted, the crop was smaller on average than expected—and the two sides got into an argument over the exact amount of wine being delivered in each cask. The cost of defying the merchants was high, even for the best-placed of vineyards.

7
The search for quality

"A certain fraternity of chymical operators who work underground in holes, caverns and dark retirements, to conceal their mysteries from the eye and observation of mankind. These subterraneous philosophers are daily occupied in the transmigration of liquors, and by the power of magical drugs and incantations, raise under the streets of London the choicest products of the hills and valleys of France. They can squeeze Bordeaux out of a sloe and draw champagne from an apple."

JOSEPH ADDISON, The *Spectator*,
quoted in André Simon, *Bottlescrew Days*.

The triumph of the merchants inevitably meant that the quality of wine would be judged on their names. For a long time, even the first-growth clarets fetched better prices if they had been through the hands of a house as reputable as Barton and Guestier. In the English market, the merchant's name was especially important because the claret was so heavily 'treated' and because so many English merchants were not very good judges of quality.

According to T. G. Shaw, one of the select band of British merchant-writers who propagandized for better wines—and lower duties on them—"some English wine merchants have pure refined tastes; but as port, sherry and other kinds with between 30 and 40 per cent proof spirit still constitute upward of 70 per cent of total consumption, it cannot be fairly supposed that men who have little else in their mouths all day, can have palates capable of appreciating the delicacy and bouquet of great growths."

There were immense numbers of these merchants—over two hundred crammed into under three hundred houses in four narrow streets in the City of London alone. And they could do untold harm to wine. They could simply neglect it: only their employees were allowed into the bonded warehouses in the London docks; inevitably, according to Shaw, many of these

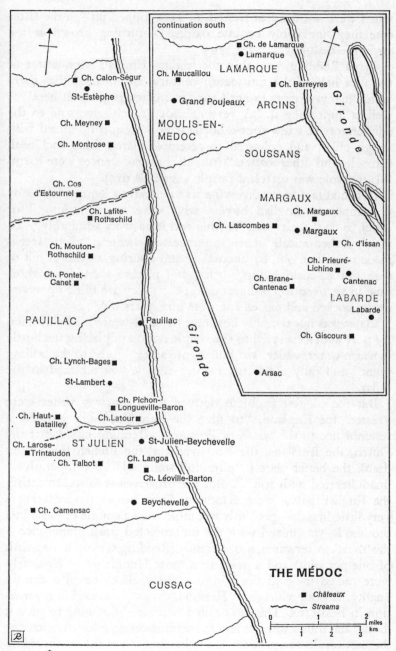

continuation south

Ch. de Lamarque
● Lamarque

Ch. Maucaillou ■   LAMARQUE

Ch. Calon-Ségur ■   ■ Ch. Barreyres
● St-Estèphe   ARCINS   G
                ● Grand Poujeaux   i
Ch. Meyney ■   MOULIS-EN-   r
                 MEDOC   o
Ch. Montrose ■   n
                     SOUSSANS   d
                                           e
Ch. Cos
d'Estournel ■   MARGAUX
     Ch. Lafite-   ■ Ch. Margaux
     ■ Rothschild   Ch. Lascombes ■ ● Margaux
                                        ■ Ch. d'Issan
Ch. Mouton-
Rothschild ■   Ch. Prieuré-
                                   Lichine ●
Ch. Pontet-   Ch. Brane-   ● Cantenac
Canet ■   Cantenac ■
                                        LABARDE
PAUILLAC   ● Pauillac   ● Labarde

                    G   Ch. Giscours ■
                    i
Ch. Lynch-Bages ■   r
                    o
● St-Lambert   n   ● Arsac
                    d
      Ch. Pichon-   e
      Longueville-Baron
. Ch. Haut- ■
Batailley   Ch. Latour ■
Ch. Larose-
■ Trintaudon   ST JULIEN   ● St-Julien-Beychevelle
    Ch. Talbot ■   Ch. Langoa
                    ■
                    Ch. Léoville-Barton
                ● Beychevelle
■ Ch. Camensac

                            THE MÉDOC

        CUSSAC   ■ Châteaux
                            ⌇⌇⌇ Streams

                    0   1   2
                    └────┴────┴────┴────┘ miles
                    1   2   3
                                        km

3*

wines were not fined or racked, or kept topped up—in the latter case they 'inevitably became oxidised'—turning brown as the air in the cask attacked the wine.

Cyrus Redding, probably the leading English wine-writer of the first half of the nineteenth century, commented that there were "many receipts extant" for "manufacturing claret here" as well as improving it. "A very inferior French wine sold to the adulterators at a few sous a bottle is now frequently mixed with rough cider, and coloured to resemble claret, with cochineal, turnsole, and other matters" (not all these substances were harmful: turnsole was merely a purple vegetable dye).

In brutal fact, even this wine was perfectly adequate for many contemporary English buyers who were simply asking "for claret to cool their port. To this end it answers admirably". To satisfy a theoretically more sophisticated clientele "new claret is made to imitate old, by uncorking and pouring a glassful out of each bottle, corking the bottles, and placing them for a short time in an oven to cool gradually; then they are filled up again, finally corked and passed for wine nine years old."

Claret was not the only beverage to be ill-treated. The demand for port with a crust led to the simple notion of placing the bottle in warm water, which was boiled, or rather "urged to the boiling point" and duly threw up a crust once it was replaced in the cellar.

But the biggest problem derived from the way wines were 'treated' for England, "to give the pure Bordeaux growths a resemblance to the wines of Portugal". Redding noted that the Dutch, the Russians, the Prussians and the French themselves drank the better clarets "pure and unmixed . . . comparatively unadulterated with spirit". But the processes required to satisfy the English palate were elaborate. Even before fermentation a very little brandy—probably not more than a couple of parts in a thousand—was mixed with the unfermented fresh grape juice—the 'must'. Afterwards, more brandy (Redding says up to one-fifth of one per cent) and a great deal more Hermitage or Benicarlo were mixed in—and the additive had itself to be of a certain quality. A poor vintage in Hermitage in 1810 caused consternation in Bordeaux. This was called 'working' the wine to give it 'body' and thus a warmer and more intoxicating effect. To achieve the best results the process had to be carried out before the wines had been racked and fined. Larger proportions could be added to older clarets which were 'nearly worn out'—had become thin and undrinkable, often because they had been left too long in the cask.

Redding admits that "much of the delicate flavour was destroyed . . . by these additives". In time, he said, they "give it a brick dust flavour and cause it to deposit. It is often too artificially flavoured. Wines so treated never recover their natural bouquet . . . Orris root is employed to give the perfume destroyed by mixing, and sometimes a small quantity of raspberry brandy is used, two ounces to a cask, in order to flavour it factitiously and replace the natural flavour it has lost." The only advantage of the resultant beverage was its strength: Shaw notes that the average strength of the 1858 vintage was nearly 18 per cent, half as much again as modern claret.

Nevertheless, out of this morass of chicanery a few merchants were emerging whose name became synonymous with quality. Judging by Christie's auction catalogues of the early nineteenth century, the merchants—Barnes Plaskett, Randolph Payne, Carbonnel, Maxwell and Keys—whose names provided some form of guarantee of quality were not, generally, among the three hundred in the City, but clustered in St. James's, near the clubs and the London houses of their private customers. These were immense buyers—a number of executors' sales of wines at Christies in the second half of the century each totalled between 500 and 1200 dozen bottles, and the blending skills of their suppliers were correspondingly impressive. (Two of the world's leading brands of Scotch whisky, Cutty Sark and J and B, were first blended by two such firms, Berry Bros. and Rudd and Justerini and Brooks respectively, to satisfy their customers' desire for a natural-coloured blend.)

The Bordeaux merchants were well aware of the varied requirements of their customers. As early as the turn of the century Nathaniel Johnston was writing that Barnes Plaskett "have got such a reputation for their claret, in a great measure, I believe, from their greater care and management than others that their demand is daily increasing . . . therefore for them the wines should be neat and very lightly made up."

For gradually the quality improved as purer wines were shipped. Merchants like Johnston wanted to minimize the impurities.

He wrote to his English importer about the 1801 vintage that "if the wines have the body and flavour which others represent more favourably than you do, I think they ought to be made up very lightly this year—the first and even second growths with not more than three or four gallons of Spanish wine and about three gallons of Hermitage and the other wines not to have more than five gallons of Spanish wine"—so that even lesser wines had under two per cent of 'foreign' wines in them. Moreover he was anxious not to use wine from Roussillon, in the shadow of the Pyrenees, instead of the Spanish Benicarlo as the "harshness" of the Roussillon "never wears off".

By mid-century the censorious Shaw noted that "shipments are now much purer" than formerly when the "large quantities of Hermitage . . . gave the appearance of body but deadened the flavour and, after a few years in bottle, the wine became of a brownish hue, hard and flavourless."

Even so, the best "guarantee for fair dealing" lay "in the position and respectability of the merchants" under whose names the vast bulk of the wines were sold, and who verified the quality even of the 'grands crus'.

For the owners of the major châteaux were not averse to cheating—especially if they had contracted to sell their production for some years ahead by contracts which generally guaranteed them a price similar to that obtained by comparable wines. Charles Tovey, another writer-merchant, pointed out that "treaties for several years are inclined to encourage the lessees to get as much produce out of the vineyards as possible . . . gossip says of Lafite and Margaux that their wines of late years are much depreciated in quality, through former proprietors having worn out the land by heavy manuring to get the largest possible yield".

By contrast the merchants who took on such contracts were aware that their outlets were limited and were therefore inclined to be more concerned with quality than mere quantity. In the late nineteenth century Latour's owners were pinned down by merchants who would pay the full price for only a hundred and twenty tonneaux a year, paying only half-price for any surplus wine. Earlier a ten-year 'abonnement' for Margaux obliged the proprietor "not to manure more than a seventh of the estate's area every year".

This precision is not surprising: an early nineteenth-century owner of the château, the Marquis de la Colonilla, was in the habit of mixing his wine in off-years with that from the 'palus'.

But many owners were becoming more conscientious: the years after Waterloo saw the implantation on a wide scale of the Cabernet Sauvignon vine which provides Médoc wines with their tannin—their 'backbone' so to speak—and which to this day occupies at least half of any Médoc estate (up to ninety per cent in the case of estates like Latour and Mouton, famous for the solidity of their wines).

The local merchants felt no compunction about doctoring their lesser wines, enhancing the alcoholic content by adding sugar to the must before it was fermented ('chaptalisation') or even afterwards. And, of course, they mixed the wine with wines from the 'palus' and then, as the railways spread throughout South-western France, with wines from Narbonne in the Midi and with those from Roussillon so disapproved of earlier by Nathaniel Johnston. A contemporary English visitor noted that "Bordeaux is by no means a place for good ordinary wines; on the contrary the stuff they give you for every day tipple is particularly poor and flavourless". Many other apparently undesirable practices were accepted as normal. Bernard Ginestet, himself a wine merchant, discovered a 'spiritual guide' to this effect furnished in 1847 by the Bishop of Toulouse to a village priest, one of whose parishioners was a wine merchant with a troubled conscience. The reverend gentleman managed to use to quite extraordinary effect the orthodox Catholic doctrine that there is a 'just price' for any product, and that mixtures (including water in wine) can be tolerated provided that the price is adjusted accordingly—and also that no harmful or noxious substances are employed.

New wine, affirmed the Bishop, could be treated so that it resembled old and could be sold as if it were of the same quality —though pretending that the wine was older than it was clearly constituted a sin. Wine that had aged badly could be restored to its pristine quality and value and alcohol could be added to a vintage which lacked sufficient strength, possibly because the grapes were picked while still unripe. It was also legitimate to make up for nature's deficiencies by mixing the wines of two vintages—as Latour had done when the 1814s were used to 'restore' the 1807s. The only provision was that the final product should be sold bearing a description which applied to a majority of its contents, a loose enough condition which still applies to California's better wines. The only exception—apart from the reiterated injunction not to use substances which could be 'injurious' to the drinker's health—was that wine destined for the Holy Sacraments should not be doctored, even though missionaries in heathen parts often asked for wines sufficiently fortified to survive the journey.

These missionaries could have found many supporters for whom it was an unquestioned article of vinous faith that life on the ocean wave was an incomparable method of improving the quality of a wine. A journey to the East Indies was one favoured method of treatment: in other cases, wines were loaded on to the fishing boats at Arcachon and buffeted by the waves. The habit left at least one physical mark on the Médoc, the extraordinary 'Chinese' cupolas tacked on to Cos d'Estournel. These were added by the grateful M. d'Estournel after one vintage was sent to the Indies, there rejected as of inadequate quality and found, on its return to Europe, to have greatly improved and to be immensely saleable. (Claret was not the only wine to be subjected to the same treatment: it was far more commonplace, for example, for Madeira.)

But in the long run by far the most important step forward in promoting quality was the increasing trend towards keeping wine in bottle, rather than in cask. This pinned the final responsibility for the quality of the wine on the bottler, and it overcame the problems associated with wine which had been kept—as was so often the case—five years or more in cask and was either 'tired' or so hard and tannic that no amount of ageing or treatment would enable it to develop further. At the end of the eighteenth century, when the modern shape of bottle was first developed, and storage became easier, its first use was, probably, to rescue 'tired' wines. It was used very early in the Channel Islands, Nathaniel Johnston's base during the early part of the Napoleonic period, and he took the practice with him on his return, first to England, and then to Bordeaux. The process of ageing was still mysterious. "The amelioration of wines in the cellar," noted Redding, "is not by any means clearly understood." Nevertheless bottling at the grower's, or at least in Bordeaux, offered a guarantee of authenticity, as sophisticated customers like Jefferson had already realized. The battle for authenticity lay between the grower and the merchant, not only in Bordeaux, but also the specialists in London, Bristol, Edinburgh and Dublin, and it was over a hundred years before even the first growths decided to bottle the whole of their production at the château, a further forty-five years before other classed growths followed suit, and even today a handful of English bottlers, most notably Berry Bros. and Rudd, can claim a far greater expertise in the delicate task than the great majority of growers in the Gironde.

But the tension was extremely healthy—bringing with it a similarly positive concentration on the vintage of a wine and an increasing confidence that it would be drinkable long after the seven- or ten-year limit generally accepted at the end of the eighteenth century. It is noticeable that the first wines to be treated as objects of veneration in their old age were produced at the very end of the eighteenth century. The earliest example in the famous *vinothèque*—wine library—at Lafite is the 1797; and 1798 was what might be described as the first modern vintage. The Lafite of the 'Comet' year of 1811 was drunk at a luncheon at the château in 1926 and found still to be in splendid shape.

The search for quality led, inevitably, to a steadily growing formalization of the various classes into which wines had been divided since the first years of the eighteenth century. There were two such divisions: between the wines of the different 'communes' —parishes—of the Médoc, and between wines made by individual proprietors. These were expressed on an increasingly elaborate price scale.

The big four—Lafite, Margaux, Latour and Haut-Brion—were usually quoted in that order. Cyril Ray noted that with one exception every list gave them in roughly the same order. "Lafite is always first—in Jullien's list based on that of 1782; in William Franck, writing in French in 1824, and in Henderson in English in the same year; in a French list of 1827 in the possession of Mr. Ronald Barton of Léoville and Langoa; and in Cocks in 1846." Already in September 1797—or as the revolutionary calendar had it, 'Fructidor in the year five'—when Lafite was put up for public auction after its owner had perished on the guillotine and his daughter fled abroad, it was described as a 'premier cru du Médoc' and producing the 'first wine of Bordeaux'.

It was obviously in the merchants' interests to try to categorize wines, to ensure that there was not too much upward mobility and that, especially in a good year, there was no general surge of prices.

By the second quarter of the century—according to Redding's very detailed table—the second crus like Rausan (now Rausan-Ségla), Durfort (Durfort-Vivens), Lascombe, the three parts of the Léoville estate, Mouton, and Branne (now Brane-Cantenac) were fetching prices within ten per cent of those obtained by the big four. Earlier, the accepted gap had been roughly 25 per cent, and strenuous efforts were made by the merchants not to en-encourage the owners of the second-growths (especially the women, who seem to have had an enhanced notion of the value of their produce) to expect too much. The first growths set the price pattern and tried to stick together to outwit the merchants. If the vintage were good they would sometimes claim that the second growths were of so high a quality that they did not need the firsts. But the ratio stuck, even if the merchants sometimes arranged the terms of payment so that the first growths got their money more quickly as compensation for not getting a bigger price; and, at least once, the owners of the second growths were promised a bonus—which, needless to say, never materialized—if the price of the first growths went above a certain level.

The growers were fully aware that the merchants were charging double the buying price—indeed the catechism answered by the Bishop of Toulouse specifically sets out the charges which were likely to be added to the purchase price: the final buyer would expect a discount reckoned at eight per cent; transport costs added another 20 per cent, interest and foreign exchange costs were three or four per cent; even so the profit margin was a handsome 30 per cent on the purchase price.

Inevitably the growers, aware that the framework was relatively fixed, tried to climb the class ladder. As Redding describes the process "the wines are classed by the brokers, who decide to which class the wine of each broker shall belong. The latter use all their efforts to place their wine in a higher class, and thus emulation is kindled and they are justified in their efforts by the profits. The price of the wines is less governed by particular merit than by the number they occupy in the scale of classification". In his table, Redding gives the names of five grades of châteaux (in the eighteenth century there had been only four, but the fourth division was gradually split into two, and the lower half became the fifth category). In a good year the fifth fetched only half the price of the firsts. In a bad year the differences, then as now, were much less marked. In a good year, even the best 'commune wine' —Pauillac, Margaux, etc.—fetched only two-thirds the price of the fifth crus, and 'common' Médoc only half that amount, a mere seventh of the price of the firsts. But in a bad year the differentials were so reduced that the firsts fetched only double the price of the most ordinary Médoc.

According to Redding, the keener growers were prepared to keep their wines for many years "to give it a superior title" instead of selling it the first year according to custom. "By this means an individual will get his wine changed from the fourth to the third class, which he had perhaps occupied before for many successive years." And there were other cases—like the creation of a major estate by one of Wellington's generals, Palmer, out of the remains of a much smaller one—where a virtually new growth was involved.

Unfortunately for aspirant social climbers, the classification was frozen in 1855 in one of the most-publicized and least-understood events in Bordeaux's history. The 1855 classification sprang from the innocent request to the Bordeaux Chamber of Commerce by Prince Napoleon, organizer of the Universal Exhibition to be held in Paris that year, for a comprehensive display of the wines of the Gironde, arranged by category. The Chamber, aware of the emotions engendered by the whole subject, sent back a list based on historic prices paid, with the wines in the different classes arranged in alphabetical order. But the Prince insisted on a 'new' classification; and he was the cousin of an emperor who took a keen interest in claret, and had actually stayed at Château Margaux, owned by the Marquis d'Aguado, a great friend of the Empress Eugénie. So the embarrassed Chamber handed the job over to the brokers' 'syndicat'—their federation. And the famous list was duly produced, giving information which, basically, was known to the whole of Bordeaux. The only difference was that the brokers did not rely entirely on price comparisons. They tasted the wines more or less carefully (though they were not helped in their job when Lafite provided only some immature wines, and Latour and Haut-Brion refused to submit any samples at all). Then they placed the wines in order of merit within the classes.

They carried out a similar procedure for the white wines of Sauternes and Barsac, a much simpler job, since everyone was agreed, then as now, that the Lur-Saluces produced the finest white wine in the world at Château d'Yquem. Moreover fewer châteaux were involved and the price differentials were smaller. Indeed there has never been much subsequent pressure to change the white wine classification.

But the classification of the Médoc (the only Graves included was Haut-Brion, which could not realistically be omitted) has bedevilled Bordeaux ever since. This was inevitable: even though the order was based on historic prices, vineyards are constantly changing hands, eternally getting bigger, improving or decaying. Much of the Médoc has changed in the hundred and twenty years since 1855. But the classification remains—with only one change. In practice, of course, the actual prices paid for wines have allowed for newcomers, and for those châteaux—notably Brane-Mouton and Palmer—which were being reorganized in 1855 and thus were undervalued. Some communes like Margaux seemed unduly favoured, compared with others just to the north. Some estates were really too small to have been included in the first place and the owner of Château Lanessan supposedly refused to allow the name of his château to go forward although it has often produced wine of classed growth quality since 1855.

Had it not been for the 1855 classification, these imperfections would have been ironed out by gradual changes over the years, but the classification that year froze the class structure: aspirants, whatever the price they received, could not receive any patent of nobility; and owners of classed growths felt themselves able to rest on their laurels, no longer constrained by the threat of demotion.

At the time, the classification was seen largely as a tactical move, helping the trade against the growers. A few years earlier, the latter had encouraged an English journalist, Charles Cocks, who had published a guide book on Bordeaux, the Médoc and its wines, an effort which had concentrated on publicizing the individual properties, thus by-passing the merchants.

In return, the merchants ensured that none of the bottles actually displayed at the 1855 exhibition in Paris were allowed to show the names of the owners of the estates, information which would have enabled the growers to sell their wines directly.

Only Lafite and Haut-Brion had the initiative to display their wines separately but the next year Mme d'Aguado of Margaux carried the war into the merchants' camp by demanding that she and the other proprietors should be able to see for themselves what happened to their wines during their stay in the merchants' cellars.

The classification was not, however, taken as an earth-shattering event. Lawton wrote the list down in his books, but without the comments which accompanied more significant events like a major frost or a change in purchasing patterns. And the estate manager of Latour did not think the event worth mentioning to his employers until 1856.

Yet the most extraordinary aspect of the classification is not its importance at the time or in subsequent Médocain mythology, but the overall accuracy of the historic price-levels-cum-folk-memory enshrined in it. Even today Ronald Barton, who makes both the wines, Langoa and Léoville, which bear his name, claims that he can never make as good a wine from the grapes from Langoa—a third growth—as from Léoville—a second. Yet the two vineyards are intermingled, the soil, subsoil and exposure virtually the same, the wines are made by the same people at the same time. No wonder, in every subsequent attempt to revise the classification, the vast majority of the wines listed are accorded exactly the same rank as they were awarded by the brokers in 1855.

8

The mushroom boom

In 1855 growers and merchants alike had much more to worry about than a classification which directly involved only sixty-two of their number in the Médoc, and a mere twenty-one in Sauternes and Barsac.

The overriding preoccupation was the oidium, a small mushroom growth which attacked young wood, young leaves, and young grapes, producing small, whitish spots which soon covered the whole branch, leaf or berry. The leaves curled up and dropped; the grapes darkened, split and dried. The disease was first noticed in England in the 1840s, and it arrived in the Gironde in 1852. The results were devastating. In the five years up to 1852 the average production of wine in the Gironde had been about 38 million gallons; in the four subsequent years it averaged less than a third of that amount. The better wines suffered even more badly, with production in some cases down to an eighth of the normal level, and even the wine that was produced had to be doctored to restore its colour.

It was quickly discovered that dusting sulphur on the vines cured the disease. But before the treatment became widespread prices had doubled because of the shortage. Already in 1854 Lawton was noting disgustedly that "the owners are making the most absurd demands . . . the sparks are flying everywhere . . . the growers are on top of the world". Indeed the course of the disease worked out to the great advantage of the growers.

The reduced quantities, coming at a time of general prosperity, led to doubled prices which were maintained, broadly, during the following couple of decades. More importantly, it provided the owners with a much-needed boost to their confidence. In the words of M. Clauzel, owner of Château Citran—a relatively unremarkable 'cru bourgeois'—"the alacrity with which our wines were pursued during these troubled times proved to the owners that the product of their land had an unquestionable worth abroad which they had never previously suspected".

The biggest jumps were recorded in the prices of the first growths which again fetched a quarter or a third more than their nearest rivals. The average price of Château Latour in the years from 1854 to 1858—not all outstanding wines, by any means—was two and a half times the level of the ten-year 'abonnement' which had ended the previous year. The price of its second wine was the same as that reached by a number of the most famous vintages earlier in the century, and the increase rubbed off on those below. In early 1857, after Clauzel's wine had sold at nearly the same price as Latour's second, Lawton exclaimed that "this excessive rise, coming on top of already inflated prices, has inflamed their owners' expectations and made it impossible to deal in run-of-the-mill wines for the moment". But in the end he had to deal, and moreover, at prices which were not to be exceeded for over a century: the prices paid for the 1856 Latour—were roughly the same in real money terms as the £2 being paid for a bottle of the new Latour in the mid-1960s.

The momentum provided by the oidium was accelerated by the provisions of the Anglo-French Commercial Treaty of 1860, and by treaties concluded by the French soon afterwards with a number of other major European markets, like Belgium and many of the German states. Through the centuries, French external economic policy has, basically, been protectionist: naturally, therefore, foreign countries had tended to respond in kind. Indeed British import duties on French wine actually rose during the first half of the nineteenth century.

Bordeaux had always been a free trade city, and it had not developed any sort of manufacturing base to harbour protectionist sentiments. So its representatives fought by the side of British free traders; even Queen Victoria's visit to the famous 1855 Exhibition played its part by helping to bring the two countries together.

As a result of the treaty, Gladstone, who was then Chancellor of the Exchequer, drastically reduced the duties on French wine. Within a year, for the first time since the Methuen Treaty a hundred and sixty years previously, claret came within the reach of the average Englishman's purse. Lawton's partner Tastet expressed the opportunity clearly: "ordinary wines will end up," he wrote, "by entering the everyday consumption of the English people."

Curiously, the rejoicing was less unanimous on the English side. Claret had been for so long the monopoly of the upper classes that the advent of what was speedily called 'Chancellor's Claret' or 'Gladstone Claret' did not endear itself to merchants snobbishly unprepared to cater for a mass market.

The opportunity was enlarged by the "Single Bottle Act" of 1861, which opened the way to the sale of drink through licensed grocers—'off-licences'—selling what was snobbishly termed 'grocer's claret'. In the very long run the opening spelt the end of a trade based on a small number of customers each spending relatively large sums. But at the time virtually the only English merchants to take up the challenge were the brothers Walter and Alfred Gilbey. Their father's carriage-making business had been ruined by the advent of the railways, and the same fate loomed for them with the 1860 reduction in duties. For previously they had specialized in selling sweet dessert wines from the Cape of Good Hope, whose major advantage was the lower duties they had enjoyed, but which could not face competition from French wines.

Within a few years the Gilbeys had an estimated 50 per cent of the wine business in England. Not for them a concentration on a few châteaux. The bulk of their business was in brands un-romantically labelled Castles A, B, C and D. The wines they sold were far from the artificially strengthened clarets of their pre-decessors. The English customer, according to them, wanted "clarets soft and velvety and of medium strength". It was the blends of the '65s and '66s "which produced most charming, soft, medium-bodied 'vins ordinaires', which were greatly appreciated in the Exhibition year of 1868 and did much to stimulate the consumption of light wines in England", qualities opposed to the "immense colour and body" required by the 'Bordeaux houses'.

Although the Gilbeys sold their wines through over two thousand outlets, all duly listed in their exceedingly business-like catalogues, Britain remained a relatively more important customer for the better wines of the Gironde. In 1863 the British Empire as a whole took a third of all the wine Bordeaux exported in bottles, as against only a sixth of the (cheaper) wines exported in casks.

For the euphoria of the twenty years which followed the oidium epidemic did not affect only the most expensive wines. The price of the most ordinary Bordeaux jumped nearly five times during the mid '50s, and never relapsed to its pre-oidium level. More important was the surge in production, not only in the Gironde, but in the rest of France as well. (Before the revolution, Bordeaux had accounted for over a tenth of French wine production. But the development of new mass-production vineyards in the South of France reduced that share to under six per cent. Even in 1875, when production in the Gironde had leapt to over 115 million gallons, three times the pre-oidium level, this still represented less than $6\frac{1}{2}$ per cent of total French output.)

Yet technical advances were such that this jump in production came from a production area—of about 360,000 acres—only a tenth bigger than before the oidium. Inevitably profitability leapt.

In the Médoc the opportunity was taken to cultivate many of the backwoods, particularly in the still little-known, still straggly stretch between Margaux and St. Julien, in Avensan, Arcins, Cussac, Listrac, Moulis and Lamarque, an area capable of producing perfectly adequate, if not top-rank wines. Inevitably the fortunes of these lesser-known communes mirror those of the trade in general more accurately than the more famous villages to north and south, for whose products there is always some sort of demand. At the same time the qualities of the white wines of Sauternes, and the clarets from the medieval hill-town of St. Emilion east of Bordeaux first showed themselves to great effect.

Previously the Bordeaux trade had largely scorned the wines made round St. Emilion and on the plateau of Pomerol which lies between it and the port of Libourne. In Redding's list, even the first wines of St. Emilion are priced below the best 'commune' wines of the Médoc, at about half the value of the fifth-growth crus. Cocks' guide did not mention any of St. Emilion's châteaux as outstanding, although he did list sixty of them. But the St. Emilionnais, stung by their exclusion from the 1855 list (which was supposed to represent the outstanding wines of the whole department of the Gironde), submitted their own triumphantly-received samples to the 1867 Exhibition in Paris.

In the long term, the growers of St. Emilion—like the mass-marketing efforts of the Gilbeys—represented a threat to the cosy world of the Chartronnais. For the owners in St. Emilion and Pomerol were not aristocrats, businessmen or bankers; like their brothers in the rest of France, they were peasant producers, selling their wine either directly to French customers, or through local merchants (usually in Libourne) who themselves were often of peasant origin. As in Burgundy, the relationship between grower and merchant was thus more equal, more relaxed, than in the Médoc.

The wines sold through Libourne had to wait nearly a century to fulfil the promise first shown in the 1860s. But for another class of grower—the largely rural gentry producing the sweet white wines of Sauternes—the period after the oidium (which hit them even worse than it did the Médoc) marked the start of half a century of relative prosperity.

This was largely because of another fungus—botrytis cinerea—which shrivelled the grapes and gave them 'pourriture noble', 'noble rot'. The effect of what the Germans called 'edelfaule' had long been known on the Rhine, and the Germans had used its effects to make natural wines of a quality and a unique natural depth of sweetness—for the act of shrivelling merely concentrates the sugar, does not alter the taste.

It was probably Foke, a German merchant who owned La Tour Blanche, who introduced the idea into Sauternes in the 1830s, but the habit spread slowly, if only because 'noble rot' was such an unreliable phenomenon. In some years, when the autumn weather is wet, it is entirely replaced by 'grey rot' which simply turns the grapes, and makes it impossible to produce any true Sauternes at all during a couple of years in every decade. Even when the weather is favourable, the need to pick only grapes which are adequately shrivelled means that the pickers have to go through a vineyard up to ten times over a period which can extend from early October to the end of November, against the ten days spent on a normal harvest. And, finally, the yield from these grapes is inevitably much smaller than that of more ordinary wines, white or red. At Yquem, indeed, the average yield is under 500 bottles for every acre of vines, only just over a third of the yield of

Sauternes permitted under French law, and under a quarter of the yield—of over 2000 bottles per acre—allowed in most of the red wine districts.

So Sauternes is, by definition, a luxury wine of intermittent profitability. This, combined with its relative inaccessibility from Bordeaux, is possibly why Bordeaux merchants showed much less enthusiasm for buying châteaux in Sauternes and Barsac than they did in the Médoc, even though the gently rolling countryside, with its toy castles perched on every hilltop, is infinitely more attractive.

Nevertheless the local landlords have been left largely in peace—the Lur-Saluces at Yquem are, indeed, the only proprietors of a major estate whose ownership dates back to before the French Revolution, and one of only three to have kept an estate in the same family since 1855 (the other two are the Bartons of Léoville and Langoa, and the Rothschilds at Mouton).

As the 'noble rot' spread, so did the fame of Sauternes. In a major publicity coup in the 1850s, the Russian Grand Duke Constantine paid the equivalent of over £8 a bottle for a cask of the 1847 Yquem, whose price rose to above even that of first-growths Médocs, though earlier in the century Redding had given the price of Yquem as barely that of a fifth-growth. A further boost was provided for Sauternes, as for St. Emilion, by the Universal Exposition of 1867. A jury of three 'neutrals'—a Dutchman, a Prussian and an Englishman—carried out a blind tasting, comparing the finest product of the Johannisberg estate on the Rhine with a wine from Bommes, just north of Sauternes— Vigneau (now Rayne-Vigneau, but then owned by, and called after, the Pontacs). Even though the German wine, unlike the French, was specially selected, yet the Vigneau emerged as the unanimous choice. The Cruses cashed in by buying the whole 1847 crop of Yquem, Filhot and Coutet, bottling it in Bordeaux, labelling it quite legitimately as 'Monopole of the Marquis de Lur-Saluces'—who owned all three estates—and selling it through their Russian agent.

But the Russians had not concluded a Free Trade Treaty with the French; and the great boom in sales in the 1860s was largely confined to those countries which had (as well as traditional markets like Sweden and Holland). The biggest jump was in the wines sold to Britain which, before 1860, was, in quantity terms anyway, a relatively small market.

But sales nearly doubled in 1860 compared with the previous year, and in 1861 they really took off—with sales in the first quarter three times those in 1860 and five times the 1859 level. By the end of the 1860s, sales at 2¾ million gallons were five times their pre-treaty levels.

The 1860s also saw a flowering of the Girondin trade with Latin America, partly because of an influx of wine-drinking European immigrants into countries like the Argentine, where sales, over five million gallons in 1869, had gone up six and a half times in a decade. Even Uruguay, which was buying 2½ million gallons in 1869, was drinking far more Bordeaux wine per inhabitant than England.

These new markets would, in the long run, provide the opportunity for newer merchants to break the grip of the Chartronnais—before 1860 it was estimated that a mere forty firms did the bulk of Bordeaux's wine trade. It was in 1865 that Alphonse Delor became the first native Bordelais—and one of the few Catholics—to found a firm of any consequence. (He was also a pioneer in escaping physically from the Quai des Chartrons by building his cellars over a mile away from the river, in the Rue de Macau.)

But, for the moment, the Chartronnais were well able to carve up the markets for themselves, with a handful of firms specializing in each market: the de Luzes and the Cruses had agents in St. Petersburg, the Johnstons and the Bartons were always important in England. This specialization extended to individual châteaux: even today there are names well known in one foreign country and virtually unknown elsewhere. La Lagune always went to Britain, Cantemerle to Holland, while Château Dillon at Blanque-fort—now a small training estate for apprentice wine-growers—was then owned by the Seignouret family who sent its production to the United States, where, as it happened, they had a branch in New Orleans.

But the United States provided an almost unique example of a market which collapsed during the post-oidium period. Before the Civil War it had been a major customer, buying over three million gallons annually. But by 1869 sales were down to a mere 500,000 gallons, the same quantity as went to Mexico, and sales never really recovered from the war and America's post-war economic difficulties.

The seeds of the trouble had been sown much earlier, based on a conflict between the habits of the American customs authorities and those of Bordeaux's less scrupulous merchants. US regulations were that each cargo had to have a certificate of origin for the purposes of 'ad valorem' duty related to the market price of the goods. Of course quality and name did not necessarily tie up. The muddle is well exemplified by a petition presented in the 1850s by the wine merchants of New Orleans to the Bordeaux Chamber of Commerce. They complained about the quality of the wines being shipped from Bordeaux bearing the names of the finest growths and the most distinguished houses. The Bordelais replied that the Americans were at fault for asking for wines bearing the most celebrated names yet at prices "well below those established in recent years". The merchants shipping their wines to San Francisco expressed themselves even more bluntly: "It is immemorial usage," they opined, "to send to the United States, under the generic names of St. Julien and Margaux, ordinary 'cargo wines'. The American customs men then assume that these come from St. Julien and Margaux and treat them the same as those that really do come from the Médoc, basing themselves on the name on the label"—and, inevitably, the Customs men, bewildered by the arrival of wines bearing the same description but at very different prices, would charge duty on the higher values charged for the real wines. None of this helped Bordeaux's reputation.

Furthermore, any possible recovery later was stymied by French protectionism in the 1880s. This started with attempts to ban the imports of salt beef from the United States because cases of trichinosis (a disease which affects the intestines) had been discovered near Paris. These, it was alleged, derived from parasites in the salt beef, an idea declared to be rubbish by the French medical academy ('protectionism that dares not use the name'). In revenge, the American federal authorities immediately started testing all imported wines and lifted duties by fifty per cent.

This combination of unreliable quality and retaliation against French protectionism was a foretaste of the disasters to come. But the good times left behind not only the seeds of future developments—new wines from outside the Médoc, new firms exploiting new markets—but also a major influx of new capital investment.

Much of the money was local. During the Second Empire the Bordelais were unwilling to follow the example set elsewhere in France and invest in industry, whose major yield seemed to be smelly factories and a troublesome proletariat, when they could make a steady return out of buying up the countryside. The value of an acre of the Landes trebled within thirty years provided that it were cleared and planted with vines, and the average yield on the land thus acquired was a steady and reputable $5\frac{3}{4}$ per cent. Because of the wine boom, Bordeaux largely escaped the worst consequences of the 1857 financial crisis (as it had enjoyed a similar immunity in the 1780s). And the many ship-owners and colonial merchants with estates could fall back on their vinous income. No wonder that over a quarter of the sixty-two classed growths changed hands in the twenty years before 1870. Many went to local merchants. Nathaniel Johnston bought two— Dauzac and Ducru-Beaucaillou. Hermann Cruse, who had bought the unclassified Laujac in 1852 on the proceeds of his coup with the 1847 vintage, later acquired one of the biggest of all the classed growths, Pontet-Canet, a neighbour of Mouton. Cruse's in-laws bought Rausan-Segla and Léoville-Poyferré. Lynch-Bages was bought by the Ceyrou family, while the de Luzes contented themselves with the unclassified Paveil—inevitably adding their own name to it.

The only merchants to sell during the period were the Guestiers, still coping with Pierre-François' legacy of six daughters and only one son—a classic example of the losses that could be caused by such genealogical accidents. The solitary male, François, had to sell Batailley and, finally, in 1874, Beychevelle, the pride of the family. Both, as it happens, went to Parisians (Beychevelle to a banker, Armand Heine, whose granddaughter married into another banking family, the Achille-Foulds, who own it today).

The better crus, it seemed, were so sought after that only bankers could afford them. They had always been expensive: in the 1830s Redding had estimated that every acre of a Médocain estate was worth between £60 and £70 (over £750 today). But the better estates fetched far more, £180 an acre for Lafite in 1803, twice that figure for Mouton in 1830. No wonder there had already been bankers (of Spanish origin) at Margaux for half a century. Then, in 1853, the Pereires, scions of a Portuguese Jewish family long resident in France, bought Château Palmer for 425,000 francs. The same year the Pereires' example was followed by their great rivals the Rothschilds, when Nathaniel, a member of the English branch of the family who had been crippled in a hunting accident and was looking to settle down in France, bought Mouton for 1.125 million francs (around £675,000 in today's money), or over 8000 francs an acre—several times its estimated value twenty-five years previously.

Traditionally, Mouton, under its old name of Branne or Brane-Mouton, had occupied a place between the first and second crus. Nathaniel's first step was to ask for the same price as a first growth: he succeeded only in pushing up the price of the big four and had to be content to resume its historic place.

But the most sensational purchase came fifteen years later, when Lafite came up for auction. The purchase of Mouton had stirred the latent spirit of rivalry which always lingered in the Rothschilds and which often expressed itself in evermore conspicuous consumption. In the 1850s, Nathaniel's brother Mayer had built and furnished a hideous palace at Mentmore, in the Chiltern Hills north of London. His French cousin Baron James promptly ordered the same architect to build him another Mentmore "only twice as big" on his estate at Ferrières.

He could not resist the urgings of his sons Alfonse and Gustave to bid for Lafite, for were not such estates then the most fashionable thing to purchase? In Cyril Ray's words, "as collectors, why not collect the greatest of all French vineyards?" But the Rothschilds had rivals, a syndicate of merchants prepared to bid high. And the final bid at the auction of 4,440,000 francs (over £2.5 million) was more than the combined prices paid by the Auguados for Margaux in 1836, by Pereire for Palmer, and by cousin Nathaniel for Mouton. Yet eleven years later another banking family, the Pillet-Wills, topped the Lafite deal when they paid five million francs (nearly £3 million in modern money) for Margaux.

But the Pillet-Wills got more than a mere vineyard. They also acquired one of the architectural glories of France, Château Margaux, built, together with its cellars, in the Palladian style much earlier in the century. Unfortunately the example of celebrating prosperity in a new house was widely followed during the Second Empire, a time when French architectural styles were at their most ornate, and bore least relationship to the gentle folds of the Médoc. The long, low, compatible lines of houses like Ducru-Beaucaillou were ruined by ostentatiously turreted additions, and dozens of new châteaux were built, all more or less grandiose, virtually all destined to appear on wine labels ever since, and thus to give claret as a whole the rather inappropriate feel of a pretentious and obvious beverage, whereas its actual qualities, its subtleties and delicacies are precisely the opposite of those symbolized by the labels.

Houses, owners, and their wines also required a permanent record to provide for the Médocain aristocracy the same status as European aristocracy and royalty then derived from the Almanac de Gotha, and the British gentry still does from Burke. The challenge was taken up by an enterprising local publisher, Edmond Féret, who took Cocks's guide book, removed the general description of Bordeaux and the Médoc, and turned it into a much more specific guide to individual estates. Since then his family have published twelve editions of the book still known simply as 'Cocks and Féret', still published in a charmingly old-fashioned format, still retaining many woodcuts among the pictures of the châteaux; the other illustrations, generally rather muddy photographs, do nothing to spoil the period feel of the volume.

Owners are still allowed to fill in their own entries, giving a short history of their château, its average production and some appreciation of their wine's qualities. The result is a prolonged ego trip. Even the most modest wines are invariably 'greatly appreciated' for qualities of elegance and delicacy which would shame Lafite, for an ability to live to an age which Latour and Mouton would envy, and are enjoyed by a 'faithful public' in many foreign countries. Inevitably, too, the arbitrary judgments of 1855 are challenged: in Pauillac alone, Duhart-Milon-Rothschild (4th class), Lynch-Bages, Batailley, Haut-Batailley, Pontet-Canet, and Mouton-Baron-Philippe (fifth growths) all claim to be selling wine today far "superior to the 1855 classification".

The only changes in this beloved volume over the past century and a quarter are in its size. While the 1868 edition could contain the glories of the Gironde in 470 spaciously laid-out pages, the latest edition, first published in 1969—which, however, contains a great deal of useful general information as well—weighs in at over four pounds, has over 1,750 pages, and contains details of nearly three thousand châteaux, 'crus', and more humble plots.

Outside interest was not expressed primarily in the purchase of the estates celebrated in 'Cocks and Féret'. It consisted largely of speculation in wine, a wave which reached absurd heights in the late 1860s: Vizetelly remembers in 1869 the "proprietor of the Hôtel de la Paix showing me in his cellars a score of bottles of the Château Lafite (the famous Comet year) which he had purchased at auction at the time the château was sold at a rate of nearly £5 a bottle. Some eight years later he parted with what remained of the wine—which was nearly the whole—to Bignon of the Paris Câfé Riche at the exorbitant price of about £13 a bottle". Like so many of the prices reached during the 1860s, these—the equivalent of over £100 a bottle in modern terms— were not again approached for over a century.

There was far more scope for speculation in newer wines. Within a couple of years the 1865s had nearly doubled their prices (as so often in the later stages of a boom the lower classes had risen proportionately even more than the first growths) and this rise in price set the stage for the hysteria over the 1868 vintage. This seemed at the time to offer everything, even to a critic as severe as Lawton. He wrote that the "wines were the outcome of a harvest gathered in exceptional circumstances. The temperature was uniformly favourable the whole time between the spring and harvest. Picking started early and our vines entirely are without blemish or disease". The circumstances were also ripe for a veritable price explosion. For the merchants were hoping to repeat the enormous profits they had made on the superb vintages of 1864 and 1865. Many had been unwilling to buy the disappointing wines made in the two following years and therefore had plenty of money to spend. They started buying the lesser growths 'sur souches', from July on, while the grapes were still on the vine; but it was the vintage month of October which triggered an unprecedented hysteria.

At the beginning of the month Lawton could not believe that the wines being made ("so firm that they sometimes tended towards sharpness"—inevitably, therefore, long-maturing) would be bought in any great quantity at the prices being asked. They were. At the end of October he was forced to admit that "the business done this month has been enormous. Almost the whole of the Médoc's production has been sold—only an eighth of the crop remains. In the Blaye district, the same thing: round Libourne two-thirds of the harvest has been sold". He reckoned that in one month the modern equivalent of £40 million was spent on a buying spree which—as so often with events in the 1860s—was not to be repeated for a century.

For after the boom came the inevitable anticlimax. As so often in Bordeaux's history this was not caused by the more obvious external events. The Franco-Prussian war of 1870, the siege of Paris, the bloody suppression of the Commune followed by the imposition of enormous reparations by the victorious Prussians had but a limited effect—indeed they are chiefly remembered locally because they enabled a relative newcomer, Edouard Kressman, to repeat on a smaller scale with the 1871s the coup which Hermann Cruse had managed with the 1847 vintage.

It was the 1875 vintage which acquired an almost symbolic reputation—far more so than the 1868s, which ultimately proved a disappointment and caused considerable losses among early and over-enthusiastic purchasers. For the 1875s were not only remarkable wines in their own right: the year remains famous in the Médoc as the last of the 'belle époque'. Later in the decade, a darkness descended which was to last, with only fitful gleams and delusory breaks in the clouds, for eighty years, during which the claret business remained seemingly petrified in the attitudes assumed in the sunlit years of Napoleon III.

1 *Top:* Pierre Bert: anti-hero of 'Winegate', in front of the Palais de Justice, Bordeaux, scene of his greatest performance. *Bottom:* Yvan (left) and Lionel Cruse in their tasting room.

6 *Top:* Barons Elie (left) and Philippe de Rothschild – smiles on
the faces of the tigers – a rare picture. *Bottom:* From two of
the labels commissioned by Baron Philippe: (above) by
Salvador Dali for the 1958 vintage; (below) by Georges
Braque for the 1955.

7 Château d'Yquem: Like many of its humbler fellows in Barsac and Sauternes, the château is smaller, prettier and set in more hilly country than comparable châteaux in the Médoc.

8 Ronald Barton: the much-loved squire of the Médoc, complete with Old Etonian tie.

9

Disaster: the slump, mildew—and phylloxera

Even in 1875, the growers were in no shape to withstand any prolonged misfortune. Despite twenty years of prosperity, little money had been invested in new 'chais' or cellars, so they were unable to take over from the merchants the role of 'élévage'. The Gilbeys were scathing on the subject: "Most of the chais in the Médoc are totally unfit for wines beyond a year old, neither do the proprietors appear to understand the care and attention that wines two and three years old require."

They found some of the famous 1875 vintage in stores so dry that the wine was thin and prematurely aged. Other châteaux possessed "underground cellars of the most objectionable construction, where the atmosphere had such a fungus (mushroom) odour about it that any cask wine, placed in such a store, must partake of the same bad flavour."

In this respect, as in so many others, the Gilbeys were a complete contrast. In 1875 they had spent £28,000 on buying Château Loudenne, an estate overlooking the Gironde on one of the most northerly gravel outcrops of the Médoc. The wine was good, if not remarkable, and the château elegant but then dilapidated—it is still used by Gilbey's as a guest-house, in an English country-house atmosphere rarely, if ever, found today in Britain itself. But the Gilbeys had bought Loudenne primarily as a warehouse for storing and blending the massive quantities of wines they needed. They spent nearly double the purchase price on the estate and were awarded a French government gold medal in 1887 for their improvements. Significantly, and notably unlike the majority of absentee Médocain landlords, they visited Loudenne twice a year, and the record of their visits provides an incomparably business-like view of the Bordeaux wine trade in the last quarter of the century.

4

The troubles which overwhelmed growers less provident (and less wealthy) than the Gilbeys in the decade and a half following their purchase of Loudenne are generally summed up in the one word 'phylloxera'. Indeed many people otherwise totally ignorant of the history of wine are vaguely aware that the French wine business was ruined by the ravages of that notorious aphid, a tiny stout 'vine-pest', barely a millimetre long. The phylloxera, an American import, multiplied frighteningly, producing twelve generations a year, attacking the roots of the vine so that it went into a lingering decline and eventually died. The image of the period, indeed, is of despairing growers demonstrating its ravages by pulling at a fifty-year-old vine, and showing how its shrivelled roots slid out of the earth. The phylloxera did indeed sweep through all the French vineyards during the twenty years after the Franco-Prussian war. It did indeed cost the French twelve billion francs, over twice as much as the supposedly crushing indemnity imposed by the victorious Prussians after the war of 1870.

All this is true: and the Gironde suffered as badly as the rest of France. By the mid-1880s, the harvest was down to barely a quarter of the record level of 1875, and never again reached that quantity during the last quarter of the century. During that time enormously expensive efforts were made to stem the tide: chemical treatments, fumigating and dosing the soil with carbon bisulphide and potassium carbonate, were liberally employed by the better-off. Owners on the 'palus', like their brothers on rivers elsewhere in France, flooded their vineyards to drown the pest.

But eventually the only solution proved to be complete re-planting, with French vines grafted on to roots from the United States, which were immune to the pest. This solution was resisted as a last desperate fling, partly because it was so costly, partly because the American vines had the reputation of producing wine with a disagreeable, 'foxy' taste.

The phylloxera also destroyed for ever France's position as the world's biggest exporter of cheap 'vin ordinaire'. For it struck other wine-growing areas, potential or actual, later than it did France. In the meantime, formerly good customers like the Argentine and the United States—often helped by European immigrants—found that they could grow perfectly satisfactory substitutes for the increasingly scarce French product. Other countries, Spain, Italy and Dalmatia, as far afield as Australia, discovered new outlets for their wines in export markets forcibly relinquished by the French. And French settlers in North Africa, primarily in Algeria, realized that they could produce wines which suited the French appetite for strong 'gros rouge' far better than the devastated vineyards of the South of France. No wonder that, even when the worst effects of the aphid had passed, French wine exports in the early years of the twentieth century were only two-thirds of the level of the 1870s.

But the effect of phylloxera was almost purely on the quantity of the wines, not on their quality: and Bordeaux's unique position depended ultimately on the quality of the wines it was producing, and the prices they were thus able to command abroad. Both the quality and the market were, in fact, afflicted by severe problems totally unrelated to phylloxera, but which struck the Gironde at the same time as the 'vine-pest' and their effects have been included within its fold, because elsewhere in France the phylloxera was so dominant a factor in the decline of the wine business. But in the special circumstances of Bordeaux the decline in world trade which gathered force throughout the late 1870s, and the mildew which afflicted the Gironde for five critical years during the early 1880s, were far more potent factors than the phylloxera. It is because Bordeaux shared this plague with the rest of France, and because—coincidentally—Bordeaux's fortunes then went into an eighty-year decline, that phylloxera had taken the blame for a far more complex set of troubles, in which it played only a minor part.

Foreign observers can be forgiven for failing to distinguish between the phylloxera and Bordeaux's other problems for 'well-informed' local opinion did the same. The basic myth was summed up as late as 1909 in an article in the newspaper *Gil Blas* on the occasion of the annual Ban des Vendanges (Harvest Festival): "It is as well to remember," wrote the paper's editor, "that the primary cause of this slump in the wine business is the phylloxera (1875) which destroyed the vineyards of the Gironde. For a number of years no one, so to speak, harvested a single bottle of claret, so that nowadays, many people still believe that this famous wine-growing area no longer exists."

Contrary to the opinion of *Gil Blas*'s editor, or indeed of his public, the phylloxera epidemic did not in itself affect the demand for Bordeaux's better wines: nor did it have a devastating effect on their quality. A great deal of nonsense is talked about the supposedly unique qualities of 'pre-phylloxera' wines. They did last longer than wines made from vines grafted on American stock. Nevertheless, in the words of Edmund Penning-Rowsell, modern methods of vinification, designed to produce wine ready to drink earlier than by more traditional methods "have had a more decisive effect on the life-span of claret than the adoption of American stocks". Indeed the pretensions of the antiquarians, mourning the glories that wine lovers have, supposedly, lost, cannot stand up to the fact that the supposedly 'post-phylloxera' vintages of the late 1890s and early 1900s were in fact made from a mixture of grapes, since the rate of replanting in the Médoc was slow and its incidence uneven. The first purely 'post-phylloxera' vintage in the Médoc was probably harvested as late as World War I.

So phylloxera alone would have produced a mere hiccup in the market for the better-class clarets and Sauternes, and might even have helped price levels, as oidium had done. But Bordeaux was facing grave commercial problems even before the phylloxera struck. It is typical of Bordeaux's narcissistic concentration on events within the Gironde, that the effects of the Great Slump which so devastated Europe in the twenty years after 1873 have been so largely ignored. The Gilbeys were infinitely more aware of the problems it caused: indeed their severe strictures on the inadequacies of the wine-growers' cellars had a practical basis. "The general depression of commerce throughout Europe", combined with "production of medium and fine wines far ahead of their consumption", meant that, by 1879, the proprietors had three vintages in hand. Demand had so slumped that even some of the fabled '75s were still in the chais.

Ward, the British consul, had already reported the previous year that prices in Bordeaux were down by a third. Even four years later, when production had slumped because of the phylloxera, the Gilbeys noted that "parcels of wines of two and in some instances three vintages were still on hand in the chais". And the next year it was "the depressed state throughout the world of trade generally and the consequent complete stagnation on the Bordeaux market" which "had compelled the proprietors to submit to prices that had not been known for very many years".

Within a couple of years, however, the trade was in no condition to supply, at any price, wines whose qualities could be guaranteed to remain stable—let alone improve—in bottle. Because the outbreak of mildew which swept through the Gironde after 1883 was so quickly checked—by a copper sulphate solution known as 'bouillie Bordelaise', 'Bordeaux mixture'—its importance has often been underestimated.

Mildew's 'parasitical mould' only attacked the leaves of the vine, leaving white spots underneath and yellowy-brown patches on top. Its effects were totally unpredictable, and well-described by W. Beatty Kingston, an English journalist who was a frequent visitor to Loudenne, and whose views obviously echoed those of his hosts. The ravages of the mildew, he wrote, "were soon found to be even more ruinous than those of the all but irrepressible bettle. Mildew told upon the grape juice after fermentation as well as upon the fruit before gathering. Wines that had apparently stood well for a couple of years in wood showing no symptoms of taint, suddenly became affected at the expiration of that period, went thin and bitter and were practically unmarketable."

Professor George Saintsbury, the great litterateur and oenophile, echoed Kingston's views. The 1878s were, he wrote, "the last 'fine' wines for many years . . . after 1878 there were catastrophes and catastrophes of mildew and the like till you come to the strong yet, like the 1870s, rather hard and dumb wines of 1887".

The classic problem year was 1884 when, according to the Gilbeys, "the '81s, with plenty of colour begin already to show signs of harshness and dryness and are really only suitable for imparting colour to their unfortunate thin and weak successors, the 1882s," a year when yet another disease, anthracnose, which stains the vines, was reckoned more serious even than phylloxera. And the '83s were no better, with "decided defects" due to the mildew and "neglect on the part of the proprietors", especially in the lower Médoc "to deal with the same".

The 1884 vintage showed the effects of the disease only too clearly. According to the Gilbeys, "important sales of the classified growths had taken place at high prices owing to Messrs. Lalande having led the way by giving 5,000 francs for Château Margaux, the best succeeded wine of the year". Nevertheless the extreme heat encouraged mildew and 'coulure'—the dropping of the flowers or newly-formed grapes, still a menace today in the Gironde—and this led to 'shanking' and the patter of tiny grapes on the ground.

Worse was to come. Lafite sold much of its wine in bottle, and the unpredictable effects of the mildew turned it so sour that the angry customers returned it to the Rothschilds, who had to reimburse them. In the words of the historians of Latour, "these 'mildewed' wines could not stand ageing; they turned acid when in bottle; they became sharp and disagreeable."

Although the mildew was checked by 1887 (reckoned by the Gilbeys to be the first 'normal' harvest for five years or more), the damage to Bordeaux's reputation for quality was infinitely longer-lasting. "Presently," wrote Beatty Kingston, "all confidence in clarets of a 'mildew year' collapsed. In the course of this gloomy period the esteem previously accorded to 'Bordeaux' in England gradually collapsed." And he noted that this "shortage of good, wholesome claret" left room for rival beverages from Burgundy, Australia, California and even Hungary.

Sixty years later, one of the most respected figures in the business, Ian Maxwell Campbell, summed up the disastrous decade succinctly: "1879, 1880 (with the exception of Mouton-Rothschild), 1881 (inky and dry), 1882, 1883, 1884, 1885, and 1886 were all thin, mawkish and more or less badly diseased. The taste for wine began to totter and some proprietors, and at least one firm of shippers, well-known in those days, took to pasteurizing their clarets to retain the sugar and check both growth and decay". Pasteurized wines were organically 'dead', but proved useful even for the Gilbeys, who found 'little difference' between the blends made with natural and pasteurized wines. Using treated wine enabled them, indeed, to reduce the price of their cheapest 'A' claret.

Other rivals were infinitely less scrupulous. Consul Ward noted that when the "old trade" could not find quality wines to export, "a larger share of the trade has fallen into the hands of less scrupulous houses who are less conscientious regarding the genuineness of the liquid which they supply to their customers, many of whom, it is true, often regard not so much the quality of the wine as a handsome and well-sounding label".

The emergence of these imposters merely reinforced Beatty

Kingston's sombre conclusions. The decline in claret's popularity as the favourite after-dinner drink of the English upper-classes coincided with a boom in champagne, a drink which seemed to accord well with the life-style of the Prince of Wales who was to become Edward VII—but this was only a part of the story. Some observers (including the Gilbeys, in public anyway) blamed the 'pernicious' after-dinner cigarette. But Beatty Kingston, quite rightly, pinned the greater part of the blame on "the mildewed specimens of the 1880s . . . the mishaps that befell the grands crus, year after year, throughout more than a decade". His analysis was especially convincing because it was written as late as 1895. This was two years after the 1893 vintage, which gave lasting promise of being of truly superb quality, and—rather more illusory—promise of marking a return to pre-1875 commercial reality.

The vintage has always been classed as the first of the 'post-phylloxera' era, a proof that the essential qualities of claret had not been destroyed by the change to vines grafted on to American roots. In fact its quality proved only that the years of the mildew were over, and that a *mixture* of vines, young and old, could carry on the tradition of fine claret.

The recovery in quality was real enough. The fillip given to the market proved delusory—though at first conditions indicated a return to the state of affairs last witnessed in 1868. Kingston remarked how "the merchants and speculators" who had bought "sparingly of the '91s and none at all of the '92s" were attracted by the quality and the low prices and bought "as if they meant never to stop . . . Bordeaux shippers found themselves in the unwonted position of being hardly able to buy fast enough". Many classed growths were bought without being tasted, and the proprietor of one first growth, "having announced that the wine could be tasted on such and such a day, found at 6 a.m. of that day no fewer than twenty-four carriages drawn up in front of his château" all containing courtiers and merchants or their agents.

What is more, the German market was booming. One Hamburg restaurant-owner boasted to Kingston that he had in his cellar at least one bottle from every single one of the sixty-two classed growths of the Médoc; and the Prussian habit of sipping wines en famille between meals proved a decided boon to the trade.

But the decline in the English market was unstoppable. Exports, even in 1894, were no more than two-thirds the level of 1875; the Gilbeys even shipped some of the 1893s to Saumur to be made into sparkling wine; the sale of better wines exported in bottles was only half the level of the boom years, and ebbed away even further after the turn of the century.

Typically, the terror of too large a harvest loomed in 1900, when, for the first time in a quarter of a century, the vintage was bigger than in the annus mirabilis of 1875. On 3 October Lawton wrote that he had just come back from the Médoc, and "I was frightened by the quantities we are harvesting . . . this enormous harvest, instead of being a cause for satisfaction, is merely asking for trouble in the market. One's got no idea whether to wish for good or bad wine; either way, and whatever the quality, prices will be so low that they will influence those of the '98s and '99s".

Lawton's fears were fully justified. The Gilbeys remarked how "the enormous production of this year" together with the large stocks of the 1898s and 1899s in the hands of the growers "has had the effect of reducing the value of Médoc wines beyond all precedent . . . Château La France, reckoned a first growth of Fronsac, sold at a price equal to £2 5s. a hogshead. In reckoning the cask as worth this year 15s., this will leave but 30s. for 48 gallons of wine, which is less than 9d per gallon"—then 1½d. a bottle, even today a mere 6p.

Trade in the 1890s and later was further crippled by the return of protectionism. In 1888 the British government had imposed an additional duty of 5s. a dozen on wines imported in bottle. "This," said the Gilbeys, "will give some trouble and will necessitate in future our bottling in England." And the new duty, combined with Lafite's troubles with the 1884 vintage, set back the cause of bottling near or at the grower's for a generation.

But the 1890s produced the worst troubles. The general rise in duties imposed in 1892 by the French led to retaliation, notably by the Americans. It also ruined Bordeaux's entrepôt trade by sharply increasing the duty on the strong wines still required in large quantities for mixing purposes—though these restrictions did not apply to Algerian wines, indeed provided them with their major opportunity. In the short-term, the government permitted the establishment of special free-trade warehouses to allow the blending to be carried on for the bulk wines destined for export. At the end of the decade even these were abolished—costing the trade, according to one expert, lost exports of over a million gallons a year.

Business was described as a "nullity . . . everything revolves round the stocks held abroad, hanging, like a Damoclean sword, as much in England as in Belgium and Germany, where all the buyers are waiting for forced liquidations of stocks to buy at low prices". Business failures were inevitable, not only in Bordeaux. A quarter of all the bankruptcies in France in the 1870s and 1880s were, supposedly, of wine merchants. Many of Christie's sales in the period came from the stocks of merchants who had gone out of business. In Bordeaux the merchants Markhausen folded up in 1898, the bankers Piganeau a year later.

The merchants' problems were complemented by the growers' financial headaches. Damagingly heavy capital investment had been necessary to attack the pests and diseases of the previous two decades—reaching the equivalent of over £10,000 a year at Loudenne alone for six or seven years at a stretch. This financial strain spelt trouble even at Latour where the proprietors had taken barely any money out since 1883, and the château had been in debt since 1887. Lesser estates simply could not afford the continuing strain—for the list of diseases seemed unending. Coulure remained a continuing threat; in 1896 the Gilbeys complained that "such diseases as mildew, oidium, etc. had been well kept under by the usual unceasing and costly treatment". The same year the 'noctuelle'—a grey caterpillar—was found eating the young shoots, and the next year (when, finally, the Gilbeys stopped any further treatment for phylloxera) "gangs of women" were "daily engaged" collecting 'altises', beetles which feed on vine leaves.

Inevitably the contrast between the relatively well-capitalized major estates and the wretched peasants grew greater. Land values as a whole plunged—the Gilbeys' diary for 1886 describes one property of 113 acres, valued "a few years ago by a notary at 380,000 francs, and in 1878 at 200,000 . . . recently the price asked was 185,000 francs and it is quite possible that at the present time it could be bought for below 50,000 francs".

Under these circumstances it was not surprising that the land round Loudenne 'resembled a wilderness', or that the rural

4*

population of the Gironde started to leave the land and flock to Bordeaux (whose population rose by a quarter). Nevertheless the acreage of vines in the Gironde did not decline all that much— the lowest recorded level was in 1900, at 320,000 acres, and ten years later it was back to 336,000 acres, just above its pre-oidium level. But, because the land was being cultivated with increasing intensity, the yield was two or three times greater than fifty years before. And the merchants had no way of moving that quantity at a reasonable price. Indeed they seemed stuck in the grooves they had so profitably occupied in the 1860s. It was useless for the Gilbeys, through the pen of Beatty Kingston, to complain that "the Bordeaux shippers and their agents in England should increase their outlay in such directions as commission to retailers and advertising, in order to push their wines in the United Kingdom". The Chartronnais, seemingly, had neither the capital, nor the entrepreneurial flair, to copy the hard-selling of brand names then being pioneered by the great houses of champagne and whisky distillers of Scotland.

The initiatives that were taken involved the promotion of individual châteaux, rather than reliance on the merchant's own name. Typically, Campbell's friend, Albert Schÿler, took the white Graves, Château Carbonnieux*, and "produced an ornate label in white and gold, a distinguished-looking capsule and, with instinctive genius, a small neck ticket bearing the mystic words 'this bottle should be slightly iced' ".

But it was the Cruses who carried the promotion of a single name furthest with Pontet-Canet. Because of its very large production (even today 400 tonneaux, or nearly half a million bottles) and the Cruses' powerful position, especially in the English market, it became a 'brand' in its own right (indeed the Gilbeys justified the purchase of a very large quantity of the wine "because of the popularity of the latter *brand*"). Until the early 1970s the Cruses were quite prepared to let other merchants bottle it. In the 1930s one important English client, 'Eddie' Harvey, used, apparently, to rush from cellar to cellar in a cab keeping the previous firm's version of Pontet-Canet in his mouth

* A well-loved Bordeaux legend, repeated by Campbell, tells how the Benedictine monks who owned Carbonnieux before the French Revolution allegedly contrived to sell their wine even to the Muslim Turks by labelling the bottle "Mineral water from Carbonnieux".

until he arrived at the next on his list, the better to compare the two. Because of the wide spread of the name, its use got rather out of hand—Jean Theil of Château Poujeaux remembers calling on Belgian village priests between the two world wars and finding a cask of what they (or their merchants) claimed was Pontet-Canet in every well-stocked parochial cellar.

Only the Calvets tried another strategy. But then they had always been different—their founder was French, they have never gone in for buying estates, and they remain a staunchly Catholic family in a largely Protestant trade. The brother of Jean Calvet, the present head of the firm, is a Benedictine, and a cousin is also a monk. Until the 1880s the family seemed content to follow the classical pattern: Octave, the son of Jean-Marie, the founder, spent eight months of the year selling his wines in England. But, when he died in 1886, his son Jean, then only twenty-five years old, showed a dynamism and a sense of future marketing patterns unique in Bordeaux. Some of his steps were orthodox enough. He had his brothers divided the world between them according to their aptitudes: Emile, the one who spoke German best, was despatched to cover Central and Southern Europe—much of which was then within the German-speaking Austro-Hungarian Empire; George was despatched to Latin America (he greatly boosted sales in what was still a good market for Bordeaux—and eventually settled there after marrying an Argentinian girl); Jean reserved the English market for himself, and he established such a dominant position that the professional wine market would dry up if he were delayed on one of his regular annual visits.

But he tended to sell a wider range of wines to the English than other Bordeaux merchants for he did not confine his purchases of wine to the Médoc. He was a pioneer in buying the wines of St. Emilion.

But Jean Calvet's major innovation—although it was, in a sense, a return to an older tradition—lay in his insistence that the members of his family, in his own words, "were not selling St. Julien or St. Emilion, you're selling the name of Calvet". It was this policy—symbolized by the famous eagle label he devised for all the wines sold under the Calvet name—which made the house the most famous in Bordeaux. The proof of the financial success of the policy came in the otherwise unpropitious year of 1894, only eight years after he had taken over, when he had to extend the family's cellars.

These, typically, were not actually on the Quai des Chartrons, but were, indeed still are, conveniently placed on the Cours du Médoc, just behind the Quai—whose inhabitants, unlike the Calvets, seemed to have lost the vital spark that was required to bounce back from the troubles of the late nineteenth century as resourcefully as they had done from earlier problems.

10

The Chartronnais in fact
and fiction

"Polished floors and even more polished conversation . . . billiard tables and afternoon tea."

SOMERVILLE AND ROSS

At the very time the Chartronnais seemed most secure, most formidable, most united to outsiders, they were, like many another aristocracy, becoming fossilized, and simultaneously seized with a certain fatalism. This was inevitable: throughout the ages sentiment in the Bordeaux wine trade has swung, like the most predictable of pendulums, from an exaggerated optimism to an equally unbalanced gloom. It was Allan Sichel, himself a Chartronnais (his family arrived from Mainz in 1883), who wrote of one vintage, "The vegetation is about three weeks behind, the hysteria is about normal."

Campbell remembers how "many a time did my friend Albert Schÿler tell me that the taste for claret would soon be a thing of the past and Bordeaux a ruined city. Pictures of Troy and Carthage and ill-fated Pompeii crashing over the heads of their devoted citizens were conjured up, and the outlook for a young man going into the Bordeaux business seemed bleak and unpromising".

Yet the world of the Chartronnais survived, and still retains an enormous fascination. For two and a half centuries a mere handful of families, almost all of foreign origin, decided the fate of some of France's proudest products while living in a style which seemed to outsiders exclusive, snobbish and disdainful, an aristocracy living in France but increasingly self-contained and aloof from their fellow-citizens. They were, as François Mauriac wrote in his famous novel *Préséances*, "an aristocracy of the cork . . . whose titles are almost invariably authentic, and who sustain a modest but precise function in modern life. Since the Tuileries were burnt down, the nobility of France has lost its role; but the cellars of Bordeaux are everlasting and our truly royal wine carries with it the right to ennoble the families who serve it".

This 'aristocracy' was always few in number and, in strict terms, included only two French families, the Guestiers—who speedily reverted to their former Protestant allegiance—and the Eschenauers. And, once the MacCarthys had sold up their business in the 1820s only three Anglo-Irish families remained, the Bartons, the Johnstons, and the Lawtons then, as now, the only aristocratic brokers. They were soon outnumbered by Germans like the Schröders and Schÿlers, Swiss like the de Luzes and the Mestrezats, and the German–Danish Cruses. It is a tribute to the formidable and continuing influence of the British market that the style of the Chartronnais was so Anglo-Saxon, though, until the end of World War II, petrified in a life-style which the English call Victorian.

And, of course, they intermarried. Indeed, in the absence of any other local Protestant families they married almost exclusively amongst themselves. The pattern was set at the end of the eighteenth century by the Bartons, the Johnstons, the Lawtons and the Guestiers. The de Luzes were soon involved when Baron Alfred married one of the daughters of William Johnston (a sister had married Pierre-François Guestier). These marriages created family problems over dowries more typically French than English: Daniel Guestier conducted a particularly long vendetta with his Lawton in-laws, though this did not stop further intermarriages between the two families.

But it was the Cruses who entwined themselves most firmly into the clan system. Hermann's son, another Hermann, married Sophie Lawton, his son Herman III married Gabrielle Guestier. Two of his nephews married into the de Luze family, a third married Anne Lawton, one of whose family, Henry Lawton, married two Cruse girls, one after another. The habit continues: the present Mme Hugues Lawton was the widow of a member of the Cruse family.

Even today the survivors still talk in terms of 'mon oncle Eschenauer', 'mon cousin de Luze', for, as so often in such a closed community, everyone feels sufficiently close to everyone else to call even distant relatives 'cousin'. Mauriac put it more spitefully. "Like kings", he wrote, "the scions were all, notionally at least, of the same blood and always called each other 'cousin'."

The word rendered here as 'scion' is, in Mauriac's original French, 'fils', literally 'son', an echo of the correct name of most of these firms, as in 'Cruse et Fils frères'. But he used the word more precisely: the essential quality of these 'fils' was that they, and everyone else, knew that they were the legitimate heirs to a title in the 'aristocracy of the cork', and behaved with a superiority which, conscious or not, could not fail to grate on the sensibilities of those around them who were not of the blood royal. The variety of ways in which this superiority was expressed provided Mauriac with magnificent material. One young broker remarked innocently to the narrator that " 'coming into your office I bumped into the fils James Castaingt. You know that I was introduced to him one evening at the Lion Rouge. I greeted him but he seemed not to notice me. He's short-sighted, isn't he?' I replied that all the fils were afflicted, as part of their birthright, with intermittent myopia".

The Chartronnais were indeed unlucky that a novelist of genius should have picked on them, should have thus provided the world with one of the most maliciously unforgettable of all pen-portraits of a social group observed from outside. For Mauriac came from a world diametrically opposed to that of the Chartronnais. Where they were ostentatiously Protestant, subscribing largely to a new 'English Church' built in mid-century through the initiative of Daniel Guestier, he came from a sternly Catholic background. Where they were 'aristocrats of the cork', his family money derived from the timber business—another of Bordeaux's vital commercial props based on surrounding rural riches but, in the world's eyes, decidedly less ennobling.

He later claimed that the venom he displayed was general, that he kept 'innumerable tender memories' of Bordeaux, that the picture he painted was interchangeable with any other provincial society (indeed, in a later edition, he quotes the compliments he received from a lady from Marseilles for his perfect grasp of the social nuances of her native city).

Of course, no novelist as morally pretentious as Mauriac likes it to be thought that his writings derive directly from closely-observed spite. But in Mauriac's case they obviously did.

In the novel, the narrator's aunt is the worst sufferer from the stings of Chartronnais snobbery. She had been brought up in the same convent as 'Madame John Martineau', who used the familiar 'tu' when they were alone, switched abruptly to the more formal 'vous' in the presence of a third person, but totally ignored her in a drawing-room where questions of precedence were all-important. Indeed, because Mme Martineau was merely a lawyer's daughter, she had to exaggerate the correctness of her deportment and not to "indulge herself in any of the little familiarities permissible to a Madame James Castaingt, wife and mother of wine merchants". In one typical incident, "Mesdames Willy Durand and John Martineau did not return my aunt's greeting. These ladies excelled in translating shades of scorn, benevolence, contempt, into ways of tossing their heads imperceptibly, smiling or not, giving the impression all the while of not having seen the person involved".

No wonder in the novel the narrator's sister, Florence, a blonde calculating creature, had but one ambition, to marry into the Chartronnais, to be no longer humiliated, but "to be able to humiliate in her turn".

Mauriac's grasp of the atmosphere conveyed by the Chartronnais (he was writing of Bordeaux at, or just before, the turn of the century) extended to their names: Willy Durand, Percy Larouselle (who picked his teeth, but preserved his social correctness by retaining his monocle while he did so), Willy Dupont, and the ineffable Harry Maucoudinat, victim of sister Florence's ambitions. Maucoudinat, who looked like a turkey-cock, was by no means brilliant, indeed had been the victim of one immortal exchange ("I, sir, am Harry Maucoudinat Junior", "and I, sir, am the examiner in Greek, and I am awarding you no marks").

Despite some surface idiosyncracies "the scions of the major businesses were in many ways interchangeable, all correct, all dressed by the same tailor, all sporty types, liberated from their offices at five o'clock", and all, like their female counterparts, "exempt from the common laws of politeness, masters of the art of whether to greet or not, incorruptible distributors of scorn".

The effect of the scorn dispensed so liberally by these young bloods was increased by the English influence visible in their names—Mauriac's Willys, Berties and Harrys are echoed in real life by the Williams, Daniels, Nathaniels and Arthurs still living in Bordeaux—the five sons of the present Nathaniel Johnston are called Denis, Archibald, Anthony, Eric, and, for reasons his father refuses to disclose, Ivanhoe. The discomfiture of the lesser breeds was the greater because the English, and those educated in England, are so very good at displaying an effortless—if often groundless—superiority. The influence rubbed off on the Chartronnais, some of whom, in Campbell's phrase, "even spoke French with what I should call an Oxford accent".

Campbell shows us the other side of the coin: the families as they appeared to themselves and to the handful of English and German youngsters who spent short periods in what Campbell describes as 'the wine trade's university city'. These well-connected students were destined to return to their countries as fervent supporters of the wines of Bordeaux and, more particularly, of the families they had stayed with. The same sort of education was not available elsewhere, which is why other merchants must have echoed Campbell's honest admission that 'I have never been able to acquire such an intimacy with burgundy as with claret'.

A peculiarly English cosiness was the dominant feature of the Chartronnais scene as perceived by the families themselves and their young guests. Other observers—even those less spiteful than Mauriac—may have regarded the regular weekly 'at homes' given by the Chartronnaises as occasions designed to instil the maximum social unease in those present—especially when, as at the Calvets, only English was spoken for the benefit of visitors. Campbell merely remembered how Mme Schÿler, the widowed mother "of Oscar and Albert, had all her family of sons and daughters with their spouses and elder children round her every Thursday evening—a real jolly family gathering. We drank our 'thirst-quenchers' of light claret and one or two others at the identity of which members of the family all made shots"—even Mauriac shows some respect for the educated palates of the 'fils'. They all wore boiled dress shirts and used the shirt-cuffs as memo pads. Campbell used one such jotting to prove that one of his guesses was correct. As a result the others began to take the young Englishman seriously and he was invited every Thursday.

There remains intact at least one example of the sort of intimidating setting in which Campbell scribbled his furtive and uncertain notes on his shirt-cuff. A recent visitor to the Cruse mansion just off the Quai des Chartrons has described "the wide staircase which leads up from the marble vestibule to the first floor suite of reception rooms which stretch across the width of two streets. The first houses a collection of priceless Louis XV furniture, escritoires and cabinets remarkable for their delicate inlays. A priceless tapestry carpet covers the floor and a matching set of tapestries is hung on the walls—a set so magnificent that it has been exhibited in London . . . through the double doors is what in the old days used to be the 'family drawing room' . . . among the lavish furnishings and heavy teak pillars, the family portraits and miniatures provide a touch of homeliness. The exotic woods for which Bordeaux is renowned are wonderfully displayed in the intricate floors which stretch through the whole of this part of the house". The only jarring note was struck in what used to be the winter garden where, among the elaborately-carved formal furniture and tapestry chairs, "the distinguished formidable widow of Emmanuel Cruse has installed a long, comfortable sofa facing a television set".

Despite the terror naturally inspired by such displays of wealth (in 1913 the Protestant Cruses even managed to carry off a magnificent medieval altar-piece from a Médocain church to one of their houses), a privileged visitor like Campbell seemed relaxed enough when he "dined with my kind patrons and cut capers after dinner to the tune of Ta-ra-ra-Boom-de-Ay (then the furore) and 'You should see me dance the polka' ". This sort of intimacy was extended to other foreign guests. Indeed part of the sales pattern of the Chartronnais, as with other purveyors of luxury beverages, consisted in their ability to capture a visiting importer or merchant and immerse him in their hospitality. (The recipe for this type of high-level, high-pressure salesmanship had been given earlier in the century to Madame "Veuve" Cliquot, of champagne fame, by her partner, Herr Bohne. He told her to lavish on one visiting wine-person "every civility and pleasure that Rheims can provide. Take entire possession of his person, ensure that you and your friends occupy every hour of his day. He must have all his meals with you, or your competitors will get hold of him". Although someone like Campbell was a genuine friend of the family, the treatment could be pretty cold-blooded: Bohne remarks of one important client that he was "a man entirely without education, a former tinker, if you cling to him like a spider to a fly he will buy".)

For selling luxury drinks has always been a matter as much of social contacts as of the inherent quality of the product. Somerville and Ross recalled gentlemen met while hunting who turned out to be professionally enthusiastic about one firm of claret shippers, and even today an advertisement in the *Financial Times* for a promotional job with a well-known brand of champagne demands of the successful applicant not only 'commercial awareness' and 'an affinity with the product', but 'an impeccable background' and 'high level social contacts'. In the sociocommercial war at this elevated social level, the champagne houses, purveying a single product backed by considerable financial resources, were at a decided advantage.

The Chartronnais, however, could use outside directorships and contacts which allowed them to influence the shipping and railway lines which were such valuable clients. The Cruses were particularly well-connected in this respect, but Barton and Guestier managed to ensure that those travellers drinking half a bottle of wine before they slept in their Wagons-Lits were offered Langoa-Barton. This contract—which took half the château's production—was kept up for over fifty years thanks to the fact that Daniel Guestier was a director of the Paris-Lyon-Midi Railway Company.

The competition between even the most distinguished families to "take entire possession" of visitors still exists, and is the source of many of Bordeaux's best stories—it was also extremely profitable for the hall porter at the Hôtel Splendid (note the English spelling of the name) who, allegedly, made a fortune tipping off rival hosts of the arrival of a potentially lucrative customer. Immediately after the repeal of Prohibition, a later visitor, Charles Walter Berry, remembered the porter "asking me if I knew of a certain American gentleman of the name of . . . most of the representatives of the Bordeaux houses had been making enquiries of his arrival".

Naturally legends grew up about the efforts made: the classic being the success, attributed to the late Emmanuel Cruse, in seizing possession of the head buyer of the state-owned Swedish liquor monopoly, still one of the most discerning and largest buyers of claret. At that time, just after World War II, he used to arrive by train, to be greeted on the platform by a veritable delegation of distinguished Chartronnais. One year, Cruse went one better: he took a train to Angoulême, then the last stop of the Paris express before Bordeaux, joined it there and thus captured the undivided attention of the Scandinavian buyer.

The systematic use of domestic hospitality by the Chartronnais stands in stark contrast to the normal habits of the French bourgeoisie, whose tables are usually closed even to the closest of business associates. The Chartronnais, of course, enjoyed the advantage of some exceedingly agreeable residences. Today, many them still live in the châteaux they have inherited—Peter Sichel at Château d'Angludet, the Cruses scattered up and down the Médoc, at du Taillan, Dame Blanche, and at Issan (one of the few Médocain residences of any real historical interest), Ronnie Barton at Langoa, the de Luzes at Paveil, the Schÿlers at Kirwan.

It was *de rigueur* for the Chartronnais to spend the vintage supervising the product of their châteaux. But, otherwise, these were treated largely as country estates (even Ronnie Barton, a serious viticulturalist, remarked to Cyril Ray that he could not see any vines when he was pruning the roses in the garden behind Langoa). In the 1930s the Cruses boasted to Charles Walter Berry that at Taillan 'one of our properties . . . not only good wine is made but some of the land is used for excellent pasturage', and at Parempuyre he "wandered through the park, admiring in particular the Dutch cattle which provided excellent cheese". Indeed, the mere fact that a major family owned a particular cru was no guarantee of quality.

But, at their best, the Chartronnais followed a healthy English tradition in being genuine improving landlords: the seemingly omnipresent Pierre-François Guestier brought new types of implements into the Médoc and encouraged better use of the 'palus' for keeping sheep for their wool and mutton (the 'pré-salé' from Pauillac, meat from the sheep which have grazed on the salty pastures near the river, is famous). He also introduced better strains of oxen—the basic Médocain beast of burden until well into the twentieth century. It was the Gilbeys, however, who introduced shire horses from England. They plodded at twice the pace of the oxen they replaced, thus, they noted, incidentally but approvingly, forcing the ploughman also to double his output.

The horses were at first imported—to be, unsentimentally, killed off once they were deemed too old for further use—but the Gilbeys soon started to breed their own (an early, and apparently successful, stallion bore the now incongruous name of Gay Wonder).

Not that the Chartronnais were the only landlords who loved the Gironde. Pierre Bert, the self-confessed villain of the Winegate affair, gives a lyrical picture of life on his grandfather's estate in Barsac. The three-storied Château Camperos, itself "of vague Renaissance style", was no more remarkable than hundreds of other French country houses, but Louis Bert, according to his grandson, expressed an unusual and imaginative love of "luxury, of the rare and the beautiful" in the park, which was "filled with magnolias and, apart from an avenue of fir trees, included only unusual species, whose names, intoned by the gardener, took on legendary shape to my childish ears. Cedars of Lebanon, gingkos [Maidenhair trees], Indian lilacs and other fragrant day lilies seemed to us to constitute the base of some enchanted forest".

Louis Bert was known to many of the Chartronnais as a lovable, rogue supplier of sweet white wines of dubious origin ("when one bought from old man Bert one knew jolly well what one was getting" was one veteran's summing up). But an enormous gulf separated him from the Chartronnais, not least in their attitudes to their estates. Louis Bert and his son could not resist buying more and more vineyards, even during the ruinous 1930s, to the despair of their accountant, who alone seems to have grasped how this "almost gut need to add to the family estate" would prove a fatal drain on the capital needed in the business. By contrast, the Chartronnais have always been prepared to sacrifice their châteaux —however long they had been in the family—to preserve their businesses. Many, of course, have remained in the same family for generations, but the Guestier sale of Beychevelle in 1875 was an early example of a tendency followed in hard times by the Johnstons, when they sold Dauzac and Ducru-Beaucaillou. In the 1930s, the Delor family were forced to sell all its eight properties in the Médoc. After Winegate, the Cruses had to sell Pontet-Canet —though, typically of that prolific clan, a brother-in-law, Guy Tesseron, was found to take it on. And in 1976 the Ginestets, forced to choose between their family firm and the family estates, sold their proudest possession, Château Margaux (in some of these cases, the families had no real choice, since the businesses would have fetched only a derisory amount). In good times, however, like the middle of the nineteenth century, the properties could be exceedingly profitable: of twelve merchants analysed by one historian from their tax returns, ten possessed properties outside Bordeaux, and seven of the ten derived the bulk of their income from them.

Nor did their sporadic sorties into the countryside make the Chartronnais any more popular. Somerville and Ross recorded how their talk with the peasants "had a pleasant tendency to drift into confidential calumny of our mutual neighbour, perfidious Albion"—for the Irish pattern of a tiny alien Protestant aristocracy dominating a resentful Catholic peasantry found an uncanny echo in the Gironde. And in a recent novel about nineteenth-century Bordeaux, *The Chateau*, the English author, Stephen Coulter, conjures up a Médoc full of brutal feudal landowners and wicked and conniving merchants, forever plotting to take their inheritance away from the proprietors. In the novel their plots are thwarted by the spunk of the American wife of a Médocain landowner. She has to combat every sort of suspicion and hatred and double-dealing, from her husband's family, from their advisers, and from the control exercised by aforesaid wicked merchants over any grower foolish enough to get into their clutches.

Visits to the châteaux were usually reserved for the autumn. To pass the winter the Chartronnais often possessed houses on the Pavé des Chartrons, which even now retains the English peculiarity that traffic is directed down the left hand side of the street. Guy Schÿler and Daniel-Georges Lawton still live on the Pavé, Hugues Lawton and Jean-Henri Schÿler on the Quai. Their ancestors usually had houses in the nearer suburbs, in Bouscaut or Cauderan, or delightful, unpretentious pavilions in Cernon and Floirac, on the slopes (the Côtes de Bordeaux) on the other bank of the Garonne. (These, long swallowed up in the growth of the city, are the subject of much sentimental reminiscing. Daniel Lawton still has in his office a charming painting of his family's residence.) Other houses were more pretentious: Cocks, writing in the mid-1840s, singles out Nathaniel Johnston's 'mansion in the park of Lescure, a handsome model of Italian architecture', the 'Château and grounds' at Floirac belonging to Pierre-François Guestier, and the woods and pastures which surrounded the residence at Cauderan of Fred Cutler, the English vice-consul.

These establishments were on a fairly lavish scale—census

returns show Pierre-François Guestier living at 39 Pavé des Chartrons, with his wife and their five children, attended by eleven servants, a teacher and a music master. Nathaniel Johnston, not to be outdone, had fifteen servants to wait on the nine members of his household—though, even at this early date, the masters and more particularly the ladies of the house could be found complaining of the difficulties caused by the disappearance of servants as loyal as those of the old school.

Town houses were of little use in summer, when the Bordeaux climate was hot, steamy, and generally agreed to be unsuited for children. This is where the pioneering and unprofitable railway across the marches of the Landes west to La Teste came in so useful. It was extended to the seaside village of Arcachon, with its oyster beds within the lagoon, and its immense sandy, piny, beaches on the Atlantic coast. By mid-century, Arcachon had become the smartest seaside resort in the south-west of France, thanks to the Chartronnais, who built their summer villas there, even improvising a makeshift 'temple' in a village hall nearby. (Mauriac realistically has Florence capture the attention of Harry Maucoudinat fils while bathing in the relatively care-and-status-free atmosphere of Arcachon.)

Harry Maucoudinat's regular swimming was the least of the Chartronnais's sporting activities, though Campbell "regularly swam in the fast-flowing chocolate-coloured river opposite the Chartrons". The most obvious was their horsemanship. Until recently the Cruses had their own pack of hounds (and were only too happy to equip a stray, horseless English wine-merchant for an exhilarating day out); but most notable in the last century were the stables, the steeplechases, the flat races.

It was Pierre-François Guestier who started the habit. He founded the 'Ecurie Guestier'—the family stable—at Beychevelle in 1821, and fourteen years later brought over a thoroughbred from England called 'Young Governor' (if only Mauriac had known that) who 'proved prolific'. Guestier's name, according to one memoirist, is 'intimately linked with the history of the turf in France'—he even received the accolade of membership of the Jockey Club in Paris, the most exclusive in France.

His brother-in-law, Nathaniel Johnston, was not far behind—he was 'one of the founders of horse-racing in the Gironde' and had a famous stud-farm at Lescure. The colours of a relative newcomer, Frederick Eschenauer, 'shone for many a year on the race-courses of the South-West'.

But probably the rural life found its most complete expression at the Château of Malleret at Le Pian just north of Bordeaux formerly owned by another merchant family, the Clossmanns. This estate of nearly a thousand acres is now owned by Roland Duvivier, who runs the family firm of de Luze, which took over the estate with the Clossmanns' business. It was their founding father, Fritz-Philippe, who bought the estate in 1855 and built up a magnificent vineyard together with a stud-farm and stables, winning numerous races with horses charmingly called Equinoxe, St-Hubert, Arnold and Master-Albert. Typical of this class of sporty landlords was Henry Lawton, the President of the Merchants' Federation during the German Occupation, described as "a great sportsman, passionate hunter, infallible shot, ornithologist and, when in the mood, a delightful versifier".

Although many of the Chartronnais went to school in Bordeaux (which is how Mauriac made his brief, presumably painful, certainly fruitful acquaintanceship with them), others went to private schools in England and brought back sports strange to France but relatively widely-played in Bordeaux. At the end of a long list of other clubs, Cocks mentions "a choice reunion of an essentially English character, lately established, under favourable auspices, by Nathaniel Johnston and J. P. Judd Esq., and termed the Bordeaux Cricket Club"—the game, not surprisingly, was played in the grounds of the Johnston establishment at Lescure. "Strangers," Cocks informs us, "are admitted to the game provided they be accompanied by a member of the club."

A similar pattern was established fifty years later with the new-fangled game of lawn tennis, first played in France in the grounds of the Lawton home—and Bordeaux still possesses one of the very few courts in France, or indeed in the world, where it is possible to play the original 'real' or 'royal' tennis, the infinitely more subtle ancestor of the modern 'lawn' variety. At the end of the century Edouard Lawton (father of the 'infallible shot') and his friends founded a proper lawn tennis club, the 'Société Athlétique de la Villa Primrose' at Balaresque, then in the outer suburbs, now a clearing of sporting activity in the thickets of suburbia. It was there that Albert de Luze, who had played with modern-minded English champions, introduced a more up-to-date style of tennis—including the widespread use of the volley—into France. And, almost inevitably, the first French Lawn Tennis championships were held there in 1909.

The next year Bordeaux's sporting facilities were completed by the foundation of a golf club by Albert de Luze, Daniel Guestier, the British consul and his deputy, and a mere seventeen others— even by Bordeaux standards, the golf club was reckoned to be 'très fermé'—highly restricted in its membership, for even by the outbreak of the Second World War it still had only forty members (it has more now, but is still run, reportedly in a pretty autocratic fashion, by Nathaniel Johnston).

But Bordeaux's clubs were by no means all devoted to sporting activities. For it was, in general, a very clubbable city—Stendhal was told "there were even clubs for servants; a club for servants who were not coachmen, and a club for coachmen". Further up the social scale came the clubs immortalized by Mauriac as the 'Cercle London and Westminster'—for one of the great advantages of Florence's marriage to Harry Maucoudinat was that the narrator's guardian and uncle was immediately accepted into a club too exclusive for a mere timber merchant.

Stendhal, Mauriac and the historians are all agreed that Bordeaux was a city in which wives were neglected in favour of a club life which included a great deal of gaming (in this respect the Chartronnais' Anglo-Saxon habits were perfectly compatible with those of Bordeaux's other merchant classes).

A few of the other clubs had legitimate political origins. The Union Bordelaise was founded four years before the Revolution, and remained loyal to the Bourbons even after they were finally expelled in 1830. By contrast, the Philharmonique supported the Orleanist King Louis Philippe. More typical of the Chartronnais —who were not, in general, political animals—was the Club Bordelais, founded in 1840, and almost certainly the model for Mauriac's 'Cercle'. (Not surprisingly, Daniel Guestier was President for thirty-five years.)

It was an important day in the social history of Bordeaux's upper crust, as, by then, there was room only for one 'aristocracy of the cork', when, in 1926, the Club Bordelais—of which a Lur-Saluces was chairman—merged with the Union Bordelais, to form the Union Club. This still has premises tucked away under the noble portico of the theatre, still has a Chartronnais chairman (Roland Duvivier of de Luze), and all the atmosphere of one of its London counterparts.

But in the nineteenth century the clubs were innumerable (Cocks mentions, besides the Cricket Club, the Comedy Club and Bordeaux's version of the Parisian Jockey Club). Even more typical was the New Club, founded in 1850 with only fifty members. Twenty more could be elected each year, but the application had to be supported by five existing members: its membership list included many familiar names like Schröder and Cayrou, and it was famous for the seriousness of the gambling there.

Not surprisingly Stendhal provides a frightening picture of the average Bordeaux businessman who "sees his wife only at meals. On rising he goes to his office; at five o'clock he goes to the Exchange which he leaves at six and goes home for dinner. At half-past seven, he is off to his club where he spends his time reading newspapers, talking with his friends and gambling. Not until midnight does he go home and often not till two o'clock in the morning". Since many of these absentee husbands kept a mistress, "whose house they visit from seven to nine o'clock in the evening", and since many of the Chartronnais were away for months at a time—often spending the first four months of the year travelling, selling the wines they had bought the previous autumn—the women led a pretty miserable life. If they, in their turn, tried a little gentle marital infidelity, then they were well advised to keep it within the charmed circle of the family's friends—Florence Maucoudinat's downfall comes when she is seen with a vulgar, loud-mouthed outsider, whose attentions damn her in the eyes even of the drunken tooth-picking Percy Larouselle.

But for the husbands, life, as usual in nineteenth-century France, was much more conveniently arranged. They had their mistresses (Stendhal says they were often fonder of them than of their wives; certainly Harry Maucoudinat was too exhausted by his 'cinq à sept' to retain any enthusiasm for the joys of the marriage-bed). Mauriac wrote that, even while still at school, the 'fils' "believed they were talking of 'love' when they were calculating, to within a few francs, the upkeep of a future mistress whom it would be flattering to show off on leaving school"— he also hints that the 'Lion Rouge', where Mauriac's young broker friend encountered James Castaingt, was some sort of brothel.

In fact, as the social historian J. P. Poussou remarks, there is not much reliable evidence on Bordeaux's morals. He quotes Camille Jullian, writing at the end of the nineteenth century about the Chartronnais as models of domestic virtue, held in check by a typically Protestant moral discipline. But he notes with equal disbelief the gossip writing a hundred years earlier who claimed that 'there were few cities in the world where habits are as corrupt' as in Bordeaux, thanks to the influence of the Duc de Richelieu.

In any case, the life of the Chartronnais outside business hours was by no means confined to horses, gambling, mistresses and cricket. The story of Charles-François de Luze, son of the founder of the firm, stands as a noble reproof to the Mauriacian legend. True to the family's Swiss origins, he organized the first ambulance from the Gironde paid for by private subscriptions to set out for the Franco-Prussian war. It was attached to the 3rd French division, and tended over a thousand wounded French soldiers, before de Luze died of meningitis contracted on the battlefield.

This de Luze was an exception—as he would have been in most societies—though the Chartronnais were, seemingly, more charitable than was usual in France, though not in England. Mesdames Guestier, Lawton and Edouard de Luze (née Dupeyron) are remembered for their good works as supporters of maternity homes, and there are local clinics in the Médoc bearing names like Johnston. More substantial help came from a childless member of the Johnston family. In 1846 he generously bequeathed a substantial slice of his fortune to municipal charities and in particular to the town's biggest hospital.

But the greatest impact of the Chartronnais was on the Chamber of Commerce. Again it was Daniel Guestier who established the tradition, soon after the Bourbon restoration—he had already been President of the Commercial Court for several years. Between then and the end of the World War I, during which his descendant, another Daniel, was president, the Chamber was dominated by the Chartronnais for whom it was an extremely useful power base. It was, after all, to the Chamber that Prince Napoleon came in 1854 to obtain his definitive list of the finest wines of the Gironde; and the Chamber acted as an excellent sounding-board for the Chartronnais' free trade opinions.

After these beliefs had triumphed in the 1860s, they had to be defended—it was Armand Lalande, founder of the firm of that name, who, with like-minded colleagues in other trading centres, started the free-trade paper *L'Economiste Français*.

Lalande, who was a deputy in the French Parliament during the early years of the Third French Republic was one of the last Chartronnais to be actively—or at least publicly—involved in national political life. (He was a clan-member only by marriage, however; his family was French but his wife had been a Miss Cruse.) Here again the tradition had been set by the Guestiers— by Daniel's son Pierre-François who was elected to the Chamber of Deputies in 1834 while he was in Ireland on business. Guestier had been brought up in Britain, and had thus "seen the great development of constitutional ideas in Britain"—which culminated in the Reform Bill of 1832—and these developments seemed linked to Britain's enormous commercial and economic success in becoming 'the world's warehouse'. This set the tone for the political attitudes of the Chartronnais over the succeeding half-century. They were 'liberals' in the nineteenth-century sense of the term, socially conservative, but considered, in France at least, economically 'progressive' because of their expansionist free-trade views.

Here again the contrast with the older-established landowners was complete. The Chartronnais played an active part in politics mainly during the Orleanist period when the Lur-Saluces, who had been active politicians during the Bourbon restoration, retired into private life. Comte Ferdinand-Eugène, a prominent deputy until 1830, refused the oath of loyalty to Louis-Philippe, and even resigned his honorary colonelcy because of political scruples. (His son seems to have deserted the family cause. As a young man he had resigned his commission in 1831 rather than serve the Orleanists. But he later became a liberal deputy, and ended up as a senator under the Third Republic, standing as a 'left-wing' Republican.)

More typical was his cousin, Amédée, who remained loyal to the 'Legitimist' Bourbon cause even under the Third Republic and tirelessly rallied his few supporters throughout the Gironde with innumerable speeches and meetings. Another member of the family, Eugène, was the leading courtier of another pretender to the throne of France, the Duc d'Orléans (who was so sensitive that he 'could not bear the mention of democracy'). Lur-Saluces was not as absurd a figure as his royal master: in the 1920s and 1930s he led Action Française, the extreme right-wing successor to the Royalists, to considerable political success in the Gironde. In this he was supported by the rural middle classes; Louis Bert for example, enjoyed the privilege of at least one long interview with the Duc d'Orléans' successor, the Duc de Guise, who, he claimed, greatly appreciated hearing his views.

The Chartronnais' allegiances were also, in time, sorely tested by changes in the political climate. Pierre-François Guestier, whose father had been honoured by Louis XVIII, reconciled himself to his Orleanist successor through his "devotion to monarchical traditions and the fear which the republican alternative inspired in him". After over a decade as a deputy he proved the solidity of his political base in being able to nominate his own successor and, in an unlucky stroke of timing, was made a peer of France by Louis-Philippe in 1847, a year before that monarch was himself overthrown, an event which 'so disgusted' Guestier that he retired entirely from politics—as did another Orleanist deputy, Jean-Edward Lawton, son of the William who had so terrorized the Médoc in the early years of the century.

Not that the arrival of Napoleon disconcerted all the Chartronnais. He visited Bordeaux in 1852 (including the traditional tour of leading cellars—in this case those of Hermann Cruse). Moreover his Chamber of Deputies included Jean-Henri Schÿler, and —for the last year of his reign—yet another Nathaniel Johnston, who bridged the gap into the Third Republic as a conservative deputy until he was beaten in the elections of 1876.

For the past century, however, the Chartronnais seem to have largely lost their zeal for politics on a national scale, though they, and their rich landowning counterparts in the Médoc retained the occasional local mayoralty—Lawton's partner Tastet had been Mayor of Blanquefort, and today Bernard Ginestet remains Mayor of the village of Margaux even though his family has sold the château of that name.

But the Chartronnais have retained one other handy semi-political tradition. Because of their origins, they have often represented foreign countries as their consuls in Bordeaux. The most notable case was probably Harry Scott, the early nineteenth-century English consul. His daughter married a Johnston, he himself nominally owned Lafite at one point (the real owner wishing to conceal his identity from his creditors), and his son inherited the job. In some other cases the connection of a particular family with the consulate was natural: the founder of the house of Mähler Besse was for half a century consul for his native Netherlands, and the son of the founder of Mestrezat was for a long time consul for his father's native Switzerland. In the middle of the nineteenth century the Cruses were consuls for a whole horde of small German states—a precedent set by Hermann himself when he became consul for Hamburg in 1842. But, in other cases, the connection was more obviously commercial: for three generations, covering nearly a century and a half, the Hanappiers have been consuls for Sweden, which cannot have hurt their extensive Scandinavian business. And the connection of that ardent defender of free-trade, Armande de Lalande, with Austro-Hungary, of which he became consul in the mid-1860s, seems pretty remote. In a sense, it could be said, these and similar consulships were part of the intangible assets of the Chartronnais, capital on which they needed to draw with increasing frequency in the twentieth century.

I I

Survival in peace and war

In the first half of the twentieth century, it seemed that Bordeaux was trapped in a vicious circle. If the wine was not good, it was unsaleable; but if—as happened in 1899 and 1900—the Gironde was lucky enough to have two great vintages in succession, then the market was too restricted to absorb them. Canny buyers like the Gilbeys could gloat that "the 1900s have one great advantage over the 1899s, as coming second in two successive years, the prices at which they can be bought are less by 33 per cent. Under these circumstances they can be purchased of the Bordeaux merchants to sell at lower prices than high-class clarets have reached the public for many years past". But the converse of these prices was the seeming permanence of the growers' misery.

These prices, like the unexciting state of the markets, and the apparent rigidity of the Bordeaux trade, persisted for nearly sixty years. But all the time the outside world, its values, legal restrictions, its capital and, above all, its new and dynamic personalities, were closing in on the Chartronnais, their suppliers, and their customers. Even before World War I, the outlines of some of the new forces were beginning to emerge.

In one sense the new stirrings were internal: whereas, during the nineteenth century, the trade had been fiercely individual, with merchants joining only in an eternally shifting series of temporary alliances to support their manœuvres against the growers, with the twentieth century collectivism and the law reared their heads.

The pioneers were the growers, banded together in the Gironde, as elsewhere in France, to fight back against the terrible mixtures being sold to the public in their name. The fight concentrated on ensuring that all the wine sold as French was 'honnête, loyal et marchand'. These apparently vague and innocuous words—literally translated they mean simply 'honest, loyal and marketable'—have, in the wine trade, very specific connotations: 'honest', that the contents are truly described on the label; 'loyal', that the wine is of exactly the same quality as a previous sample; and 'marketable' implies that it is, chemically, legal.

The battle was long and arduous. The depths to which phylloxera had reduced the French wine trade in general were shown by the first steps. In 1884 all taxes were removed from the beet sugar used to strengthen the alcoholic content of wine—a procedure popularly described as 'the beetroot coming to the help of the vine'. Then, five years later, came the Loi Grippe, the first of many passed by the French Parliament through the power of the growers' lobby. Its provisions were modest, declaring simply that 'wine is the product only of the fermentation of fresh grapes'. Two years later the Loi Brousse marked the first attempt to restrict the numbers and quantity of the chemical additives so freely used in wine-making.

Then at the turn of the century, at another Paris Exhibition, came the revelation of the full extent to which French wine names were being abused: 'Médocs' from California vied for the consumer's attention with those from Bessarabia, and from the Crimea came a 'Laffitte'. For, in the absence of château-bottling, the better the wine, the greater the profit in counterfeiting it. In England a supposed 'Château Lafite' sold by one Baruch Ehrmann at 29s 6d a dozen (a fraction of the price of the real stuff, even in those depressed times) was exposed in *Vanity Fair* magazine by Frank Harris—himself no mean confidence trickster. And from Belgium, the origin of most of Bordeaux's subsequent true-life horror stories, came the first of many tales of fraud.

The same year, the first serious steps were taken to improve the quality of wine, when taxes were slapped back on the sugar used in wine-making. This and subsequent attempts to discourage the use of sugar were—like the repeated attempts under the Ancien Régime to restrict the area under vines—honoured more in the breach than in the observance. In Bordeaux permission to use additional sugar is now given almost automatically, and in wine-growing areas in the Midi supermarkets send out loud-speaker vans proclaiming that wholesale supplies of sugar have arrived in good time for the harvest.

Other restrictions were pretty minimal. The first 'code du vin' allowed dozens of additives, including tannin, tartaric acid, and a carefully regulated dosage of plaster or potassium sulphate, 'any clarifying agent habitually previously employed', as well as a host of semi-industrial processes, including pasteurizing and refrigeration.

Nevertheless the law of 1905 was fundamental to half a century of attempts to start improving the quality of wine. For the first time, the law laid down a procedure confining the use of specific names to wines of a certain district.

The procedure was finally applied to the Gironde in 1911. It withdrew the right of a few outlying areas in the north and west of the Médoc to call their products 'Bordeaux', but its overall pattern, based on 'local usage' was greeted with relief. (By contrast in Champagne there was virtual civil war when the growers of the Aube department suddenly found themselves excluded from the official Champagne district.)

Official legal interest in the wine business was accompanied by the first stirrings of joint action. In the ultra-individualistic Gironde no one organization could embrace the interests even of all the growers. In 1906 the peasants, maddened by the ubiquitous frauds of the time, formed their Ligue des Viticulteurs—their Growers' Union. This, by no coincidence, was of the same right-wing political persuasion as the Lur-Saluces' Union Girondine. The rights of the Médocain growths honoured by the 1855 Classification—and dishonoured by imitations the world over—were defended by their own trade body, the 'Syndicat des Crus Classés en Médoc en 1855', founded in 1905—though this, like so many such organizations in Bordeaux before and since, confined itself at first to propaganda and lavish lunches.

Normally it was left to individual estate owners to pursue their rights. There was a frightful row in 1912 when a leading Paris grocery chain put on sale some wine labelled as 1900 Latour. This was duly pronounced fraudulent—too weak, too much glycerin— by two independent experts. Latour took prompt advantage of the recently-passed legislation providing for the 'repression des fraudes' and sued. The grocers then turned on their major suppliers, Eschenauers, and told them they would buy no more wine from them unless the action were stopped. The wretched merchants swore blind to Latour that *they* had supplied only wine which was 'honnête, loyal and marchand'. Latour took advantage of the position by forcing Eschenauer to agree to take the 1914

5

and 1915 vintages on very favourable terms which, unprecedentedly, included a share of the profits for the growers. The action was then called off. But that did not help Eschenauer: the grocers still did not resume ordering; and the 1915 vintage was so bad that the estate manager refused to allow any of it to be sold under the Latour label.

For the merchants had their troubles too. Indeed much of the official activity was clearly aimed at them because of their increasing use of Algerian wines. The Gilbeys acknowledged their "splendid quality and extremely low price", which "with the gigantic quantity approaching two hundred million gallons annually would completely revolutionize the French red wine trade, its suitability for the daily beverage of 'vin ordinaire' being far superior to anything now produced in the Midi, the Hérault and other parts of France". This opinion was shared by a visitor to Loudenne: "Mr. Johnston . . . remarked . . . that Algerian wines were never so good or so well-preserved as now and, he added, it simply shows what science can do."

The Gilbeys also perceived the threat from the legal activity of the first decade of the century. "It is to put a check on the ever-increasing trade in Algerian wines, that is the cause of the bills and/or projects now before the French Parliament in connection with wine. As we understood the project it will not be permissible to blend the wines, not only of Algeria, but of two provinces or departments without stating that they are a blend, and it is suggested that wines not produced in a province must be kept in a separate store. It is thought that the proposed measure will be for the benefit of the inhabitants in each department of France and increase the price of the native product."

The growers in the Gironde were, however, fully aware that they relied on regular injections of Algerian wine into their own product to make it saleable. They were obviously not keen to have this bruited abroad. In 1906, at the general assembly of the Department's Agricultural Society, the growers said there was no need to publish the fact in the papers, adding that until 1860 it was possible for the merchants to market their own brand of judiciously blended claret under their own names. This balance of interests resulted in a series of top-level conferences in September 1913, bringing together, probably for the first time in history, representatives from the trade—through the chambers of com-

merce and the two trade associations representing the merchants
—and the growers. The result was the famous 'Bordeaux agreement' which assured the growers of a continuing outlet for their
wines, yet provided some freedom for the merchants and even,
nominally, ensured that the law was obeyed, or rather that it was
not broken in too public a fashion. It was the growers' representatives themselves who "stated that it would be dangerous for
everyone concerned to aim at including the question of mixing
wines in any projected law: they believe that, taking account of
the quantitive controls being exercised over wines from a
particular area, the whole question can be considered resolved by
the mere silence of the law, and the growers agree, on their
honour, not to create any difficulties to the trade on the subject".

In commercial reality, this delicate piece of wording permitted
the merchants to sell as the produce of Bordeaux no more wine
than they bought from the growers. This compromise protected
the latter from the over-enthusiastic use of those marvels of
scientific viticulture, Algerian wines. At the same time it allowed
the shippers to blend them judiciously, provided only that any
excess were not allowed to flood the market for 'claret'.

This agreement also helped greatly in the formulation of the
whole idea of 'appellations d'origine'—the label guaranteeing
that a particular wine was indeed the produce of a particular
area, while at the same time forcing the growers to limit the
quantities of wine they could produce per acre.

For most years their efforts still required reinforcement. One
Bordeaux veteran remembers sending samples to England in the
1920s with varying admixtures of stronger wines, and finding that
the English buyers invariably preferred the strongest blend—the
one with ten per cent or more of Algerian. A good strong colour,
which Bordeaux could not supply unaided in bad years, was
especially important for customers in Northern countries like
Britain, Scandinavia, and Canada. Experts, like the late Ronald
Avery, the legendary head of the Bristol shipping firm of that
name, could easily detect wines which, as he put it, had 'been a
little touched up'. For the merchants were quite open about their
work. One told Campbell just after the last war that "we cannot
sell you any cheap claret because we are not allowed to import any
wine from Algeria." Even in the early 1970s growers making
sanctimonious noises about the supposedly disreputable practices

of the merchants had to be forcibly reminded that they had been quite happy to sell to the trade a great deal of the thin, flabby wine which was an almost inevitable product of the rainy summer of 1968, knowing very well that it would need reinforcing —'touching up'—to be saleable.

By the time the growers and merchants had agreed that silence was, indeed, golden, their financial prospects were less bleak than had appeared likely at the beginning of the century, a time plagued by over-production. Exports of the Gironde's wines were, slowly, recovering from the slump of the 1880s and 1890s. But the contrast with the palmy days of the 1870s was still very marked: whereas the Gironde had exported a quarter of the record 1875 harvest, Bordeaux succeeded in selling abroad only one gallon in eight of the 1900 harvest, which was slightly bigger than that of 1875. Nor were the long-term trends all that encouraging: the 19 million gallons exported in 1910 remained an export record for half a century.

Although Bordeaux's exports shared the problems of French wine in general—they remained steady at about two-fifths of France's total—nevertheless there was some movement in the market for the better wines. This was relatively so narrow that it could be—indeed was—galvanized by a single financial operator. In January 1907, a notorious local financier, Mario Petit, who was best known for his deals with Latin America and who had not previously shown any interest in wine, staggered the market by buying over half a million gallons from the estates of a well-known grower M. Charmolue—who owned, among other well-known growths, Montrose and Cos d'Estournel—for a mere 910,000 francs (about £500,000 in modern money).

M. Petit paid the equivalent of only 28 centimes per bottle, though his purchase included, besides the well-fancied 1906s, a great many of the two previous—and unremarkable—vintages, which Charmolue had previously been unable to sell.

The Bordeaux trade, acting through the brokers, immediately went round assuring the growers that business was still appalling, that really the 1906s were, on reflection, rather hard and unpromising, and trying generally to play down the effect of Petit's speculative move. They did not succeed. In March Petit exercised more pressure through his eagerness to back five- or ten-year 'abonnements', and by the end of May at least sixty such agreements had been concluded. All three 'premiers crus' were tied up, Mouton, and at least two-third growths, Kirwan and Cantenac (now Brane Cantenac). What is more, the agreements represented a marked step forward in the prices previously paid: Calon-Ségur, which had fallen into a miserable state, extracted virtually double the previous price, many others obtained half as much again as the average for the previous decade.

The names of the houses taking on what was a considerable risk give an excellent idea of the trade's pecking order at the time. Jean Calvet was clearly the dominant force: on its own his firm took on two second crus including Mouton (which, as usual, occupied a somewhat indeterminate place between the firsts and the seconds) and four lesser growths. It also took a share in the groups backing two first growths, two more seconds, a third and a fourth. Somewhere behind the clear leader trailed Barton and Guestier, Eschenauer, Schröder and Schÿler and, slightly behind them, Cruse and Nathaniel Johnston. And among new buyers of the better wines was the previously little-known house of Ginestet.

Many of the 'abonnements' were for only three or five years and, since they included the 1906 vintage, they finished with the 1910s, still reckoned to be one of the most miserable of the century. As so often, a small harvest of dreadful quality helped the growers for a couple of years. Jouet, Latour's estate manager, sold his 1913s in early September at what he considered a decent price, taking advantage of the rivalry between the two leading firms of brokers, Tastet and Lawton and Damade and Moreau—the latter being rather more straightforward than the Lawtons, who were apt to be somewhat vague when talking about figures. Indeed the following months saw a real burst of speculation. When the Gilbeys went to see Daniel Guestier on 2 October they "discussed the prospects . . . and the large purchases that had already been negotiated by the trade, and which extraordinary movement had been instigated by Mr. Guestier himself, as we had heard and which he now acknowledged. How it will turn out depends much upon the weather of the next few days, although a large number of re-sales have taken place in limited quantities, so that the prime movers may make a profit whatever the quality may be"—a classic picture of a speculative market small enough to be activated by a single speculator and sufficiently flexible to enable nimble operators to move in and out quickly enough to avoid any long-term problems.

In 1914, as so often in Bordeaux's history, the outbreak of a major war had, at first, only the most indirect of repercussions.

Obviously firms like Cruse and Eschenauer, which had depended on their Belgian and German clientele to absorb at least part of the production of the estates where they had taken on 'abonnements', were severely strained financially. But, although two of Jean Calvet's sons were killed, few of the Chartronnais lost any children (typically, the eldest Lawton served in the British army, although the family had been French for over a century). The lack of manpower through the war, together with shortage of vital chemicals, made it difficult to control diseases—contributing greatly to the problems with the 1915 vintage. And in 1917 there was even a suggestion that the cellars of the major estates should be commandeered to hold the mass of wine required to keep up the spirits of the French Army—a notion which sent shudders through the Médoc, and led to fears that the largely Spanish wine involved would taint the precious casks with a pervasive 'taste of goat-skin'. The matter was taken up in Paris 'at the highest level' by the Rothschilds, and nothing more was heard of it.

The demand for wine grew so intense that even the most ordinary product of the Médoc was, by the end of 1916, fetching the sort of price commanded before the war by a second growth. But, because so many of the better wines were tied up in long-term 'abonnements', they could not share in the general prosperity. Indeed at one point Lafite and Margaux were getting only 60 per cent more than were growers of the most basic wines.

Indeed the top three made life much worse for themselves when they were panicked into renewing their 'abonnements' for five years in early 1917. They should, in theory, have known better. Already, the previous year, Charmolue's stocks of claret, rebuilt after the previous purchase by Mario Petit, were again bought wholesale by outsiders—this time by a group of merchants from the north of France, acting through the up-and-coming house of Latrille and Ginestet. Latour, which had been free since its five-year 'abonnement' had ended in 1911, was able to sell its 1916 vintage for a price better than 'any obtained for twenty-seven years', and many other owners were able to sell their wines before the end of the year.

Nevertheless the owners were still suffering the effects of forty miserable years, unconvinced that any improvement would be at all lasting and, in some cases, so desperate, like the majority of their lesser brethren most years, that they needed cash in hand before the harvest to be able to pay for the grapes to be picked. Furthermore spring 1917 was the low point of the war so far as the French were concerned, for they were caught up in the 'Chemin des Dames' offensive, arguably the bloodiest and most futile of a war replete with such idiocies.

As soon as the contracts were signed a wave of speculative buying broke out which recalled the palmy days of the 1860s, and was to last long enough for everyone in the wine business to be accused of profiteering. The rush started with the 1917 vintage, which turned out far better than anyone had dared to hope after an exceptionally cold and wet August. The speculation started with the Sauternes, with claret following soon afterwards, and, as so often when many of the better growths were already tied up through 'abonnements', the resulting shortage of freely-available wine forced prices still higher. Before the end of the war in November 1918, merchants were paying double the 'abonnement' price for the first growths and, the following year, the 1919 vintage was eagerly bought 'sur souches', and the 'free' wines, like Mouton Rothschild, were selling at three times the 'abonné' price.

The burst of speculation was not, of course, confined to Bordeaux, its inhabitants or its products. Just after the war André Simon, the great Anglo-French wine merchant, used to instruct students in the English wine trade. In one of his prepared lectures he mentioned that "there is a dealer in antiques in the Brompton Road who offered a friend of mine last week 2,000 dozen of Champagne free on rail Paris; there are tea importers and soap refiners who have barges of Lisbon wine in the Thames now; there are ever so many banks holding warrants for thousands of dozens of sparkling and other wines now lying in bond and imported by people who have never been in the trade, who are outside the trade now, and the great majority of whom will never belong to our trade."

This hysteria was merely an offshoot of post-war inflation

which, so far as Bordeaux was concerned, quadrupled the price of timber, and vastly accelerated the cost of employing an increasingly-restless labour force. For once, the lesser proprietors could afford to pay, but the 'abonnés'' estates were actually losing money while everyone around them seemed to be making their fortunes, and they were being lumped with the 'merchants and other speculators' as war profiteers.

In late 1919 they tried to rebel: the Comte de Beaumont of Latour contacted the Duc de la Trémoïlle of Margaux at the Jockey Club in Paris; the Rothschilds of Lafite agreed to stand up at the same time and ask the merchants to vary the conditions of the 'abonnements'. But such was the continuing power of the Chartronnais that the firms involved were able to send away with fleas in their distinguished ears even the rich, aristocratic and well-connected owners of Lafite, Latour and Margaux. Indeed the only crumb of comfort the merchants were prepared to offer was to say that they would examine the estates' accounts for the two last years of the 'abonnement'—1920 and 1921— and 'consider' financial help too if the owners actually made losses in those years.

But by then it was too late: the post-war boom turned out to be a delusion, in wine, as in so many more important aspects of economic life. The slump of late 1920 and early 1921 was signalled in Bordeaux by an unprecedentedly sharp rise in interest rates, which by itself would have been quite enough to damp down any speculative ardour. (Simon, for one, would not have been surprised. He had compared the bout of speculation to a flood "natural after heavy rains but it is an abnormal condition: it does not last and sooner or later the flood subsides and the river returns to her bed". Moral: stick to normal trade channels, and do not let amateurs stampede you.) In Bordeaux the reversion to the 'normal channels' was the more dramatic because so many of them had dried up. For the jump in exports in late 1918 and 1919 which had fuelled the boom had been largely made up of sales to neutrals like the Danes, the Norwegians and the Dutch, and of former steady customers like the Belgians and the English renewing their stocks. In 1919 these five customers alone accounted for nine-tenths of the wine exported from Bordeaux in cask, and eight out of ten of the higher-value wines exported in bottle—double their pre-war market shares. Within a couple of years these sales had reverted to their pre-war level, and no alternative outlets could be found.

The reasons were various: the most obvious was the onset of Prohibition in the United States—which had never previously ceased to be a substantial buyer of the better wines (when the great J. P. Morgan died in 1911, 3,000 out of the 11,000 bottles in his cellar were of claret, very little of it dating from after the 1870s). Other nations, like the Swedes, the Finns and the Canadians, either banned or restricted sales of liquor or, like Britain, increased taxes on drink. The Russian market (which was never enormous) shut tight; more importantly, sales to Latin America virtually disappeared for ever for simple economic reasons—a serious blow since, before the war, Argentina alone accounted for nearly 15 per cent of Bordeaux's sales.

The collapse in 1921 was further accentuated by the inability of the Germans, shattered by a couple of years of hyper-inflation, to take up the slack—and the Germans had accounted for a fifth of Girondin exports in 1913.

Once German finances were re-established, wine sales re-started—jumping from a negligible quantity in 1923 to a ludicrous 4,650,000 gallons the following year. But after the excitement of re-entry into the market, sales settled down at well below the two million gallons or more Germany had taken before the war. Indeed, the only outlets which appeared to show any growth were France's colonies which, by the middle of the decade, were taking one bottle in three sold abroad. A final blow to Bordeaux's hopes came in 1926 when the franc, which had been extremely weak, was suddenly strengthened by the stiff financial discipline imposed by Poincaré.

The most dramatic change was in the value of the franc as against sterling. In July 1926 one pound bought 240 francs: by November it only purchased 135, and by January 1927 a mere 119. The result was that the promising recovery in sales seen since the German re-entry into the market was abruptly checked, and exports for the three years 1927–9 (before such calculations were rendered totally irrelevant by the world slump) averaged a fifth less than in the three previous years. Moreover the English market was badly shaken—because of the currency upset the 1926 vintage became famous as the 'most expensive

5 *

in history', although the Cruses were supposed to have done very well out of the exchange rate change. For the Chartronnais were unable to adapt their general attitudes: Campbell grumbles at the way they "made a mistake in sending us crude red wines at extravagant prices, after the First World War, and pushing their more commonplace cheap white wines on the British market"—a short-sighted policy which was to have serious long-term effects for the white-wine makers of Graves, Entre-Deux-Mers, Barsac and Sauternes, by associating these names with cheap wines, seemingly either reeking of the sulphur used too freely in the cheaper drier wines, or sickly-sweet without the character of a properly-made dessert wine.

For Bordeaux, the 1920s had none of the pleasurable associations conjured up anywhere else.

12

A revolutionary called Rothschild

The Northern French merchants who had spent so much on—
and profited so greatly from—M. Charmolue's wines were not
the only newcomers who used their profits from the war to try
and establish a position in Bordeaux. Another consortium
approached Jouet, the estate manager of Latour, hoping to
enlist his support for the take-over of five or six of the major
classed growths, and their exploitation on a 'modern scientific
basis', the sales to be assured by—necessarily anonymous—
Bordeaux merchants.

This sort of reverse did not deter more persistent outsiders.
Between 1918 and 1920 twenty or so major estates changed hands,
an upheaval sharper even than that experienced at the height
of the euphoria of the 1860s. Many of the estates were bought by
local merchants: the rapidly rising Ginestet family bought Cos
d'Estournel and Pomys in St. Estèphe; the Cruses bought
the historic château of Issan. But their 'cousins', the Lawtons,
sold Léoville-Poyferré for a mere 1.3 million francs—the
franc had much depreciated after the war so this famous second
growth fetched the modern equivalent of under £200,000—
to the Cuvelier family, then wine merchants in Lille in Northern
France who had bought the curiously-named Château Le Crock
in St. Estèphe before the war. Brane-Cantenac, a second growth,
and Giscours, an enormous estate which included a vast acreage
of woods as well as a rather neglected third growth, both went
rather more cheaply than Léoville-Poyferré.

The biggest buyer, however, was the very epitome of an
outsider, Désiré Cordier. He had started as a wine merchant in
Toul, in Northern France, in the 1880s. Like many of his brethren,
he had made a fortune supplying wine to the French army
during the war, and was a natural candidate for diversifying
into Bordeaux. At the end of the war he started investing seriously

in properties. In St. Julien alone he bought two major estates. The biggest was Talbot, with 250 acres of vines in a total of 400—a château always popular in Britain because the name commemorates the last commander of the troops who defended England's possessions in France in the middle of the fifteenth century. Talbot was classed only as a fourth growth in 1855: but Cordier's other purchase, Talbot's neighbour, Gruaud-Larose, was classed as a second growth at the same time. In the early nineteenth century it had been divided into two estates, with 190 acres of vines between them, as a result of one of the many divisions resulting from French laws of inheritance: Cordier had enough money to buy up both halves of the estate within a few years.

Unlike the Cuveliers, Cordier did not confine his activities largely to buying estates. He also set up in a big way as a wine merchant, but in a style and situation totally opposed to that of the Chartronnais. Where the latter still huddled together on their historic site, in offices of almost ostentatious scruffiness, he built a marbled pile in the monumental style characteristic of the headquarters of big businesses at the time, with echoing halls (and a flat upstairs for the family), situated just the other side of the centre of Bordeaux, a mile upsteam from the Quai des Chartrons on the Quai des Paludates. Indeed, since the 1920s, this stretch of river bank has come to symbolize the brash newcomers specializing in the wholesale trade, as surely as the Chartrons expressed the exact opposite.

Moreover, where the Chartronnais specialized in selling to foreign buyers, Cordier was the first major trader in Bordeaux to look seriously at the home market. In fact, although the majority of the French have never been either keen or knowledge-able followers of claret, there are exceptions, notably in the north of France, a market which extends into Belgium. Although the sales figures are separated by the Franco-Belgian frontier, the market is effectively a single one and Cordier was in a position, unprecedented on such a scale in Bordeaux, to satisfy it. His firm was one of the first in Bordeaux to sell seriously to the chains of co-operative stores in the north.

Cordier was not unduly concerned about the quality even of the famous châteaux he had bought. He was a lonely man, spending most evenings at the house of a neighbour, Henri

Martin, whose father was a barrel-maker at St. Julien. Martin remembers him knocking timidly on the door, and then sitting silently by the fire. Martin, even at that stage a keen wine-grower, could never persuade him to reduce production and thus improve quality: Cordier would simply bring out his account books to show how costly, and therefore how unthinkable, this would be.

The Cordier family have always been loners, and remain to this day deliberately aloof from Bordeaux, socially and officially —although Désiré Cordier, like many other owners of major châteaux, was a conscientious mayor of St. Julien. Otherwise the family has concentrated simply on building up a firm which is now the biggest in Bordeaux still owned by a local family.

The contrast with the Ginestets could not be more absolute. Where the Cordiers have always been outsiders, indifferent to wider economic, social and political considerations, the Ginestets have, since World War I, been constantly in the public eye. Indeed Fernand Ginestet, the founder of the house bearing his name, set an example of public-spiritedness which was a living reproof to the Chartronnais. They had notably failed to follow one upper-class English example—a willingness to take on the responsibility for speaking on behalf of everyone engaged in a particular trade or profession. 'Noblesse' never did 'oblige' the Chartronnais to help the rest of the wine business.

Ginestet's origins could not have been less Chartronnais. He came from a poor local family, and was the youngest of eight children. His mother was widowed soon after his birth, and earned her living through selling Singer sewing machines, then, in the 1870s, a miracle of modern technological achievement. Ginestet started working in both Bordeaux and London for the famous house of Rosenheim—which constantly crops up in the history of Bordeaux until it, like so many others, went out of business during the great depression.

In 1899, when he was only twenty-eight, he went into business for himself, without partners, and, as he was fond of saying, without any capital either. While Cordier was still based in Toul, Ginestet was showing the way by selling his wares in the north and west of France—and only turned his attention to foreign markets, almost entirely in Belgium, Holland and England, a few years later.

During the war, when he merged his firm with the small house of Latrille, northern merchants naturally turned to Ginestet to help him with their purchases. It was also natural for him to buy estates, as he started to do at the end of the war (though less usual to buy a property—Clos Fourtet—in St. Emilion). It was less inevitable, indeed unprecedented, for a successful merchant to realize that growers and merchants had more in common than they had dividing them: more unusual still, he succeeded in founding the first organization in Bordeaux's history which embraced both sides, and found at the same time 'his natural vocation as a mediator and conciliator', in the words of a Bordeaux memoirist. His organization, the 'Union des Propriétés et du Commerce'—the Union of Growers and Traders —was purely voluntary, for his son Pierre remembers that "there was never very much money in the kitty".

Ginestet soon demonstrated in the most dramatic fashion the practical utility of his idealism. In 1922 the French government tried to impose a fifteen per cent luxury tax on the better wines: much to the horror of his fellow-merchants, Ginestet mobilized 30,000 growers in a demonstration which he led through Bordeaux. The government was impressed, Ginestet was received by President Poincaré, and the tax was duly repealed (his enthusiasm was catching—he later persuaded the various organizations involved in another notoriously individualistic business, the film industry, to found a—highly effective—joint trade organization).

Ginestet's visionary sweep formed a total contrast with the normal habits of his fellow-merchants, whose ruthlessness, when confronted with the pleas of the growers trapped by their 'abonnements' into losses immediately after the war, triggered off another series of initiatives which were to have as long-term an impact on the Gironde as Ginestet's. In 1923 the trade found itself outmanœuvred when it tried its traditional ploy of refusing to pay for wines until their quality had been agreed by the buyers —a process which could be infinitely prolonged and thus delay even the first down-payment on them. Jouet of Latour was so angry that he sold his whole vintage to the well-known Paris wine merchants, Nicolas—and followed up his gesture by selling his next two vintages to the Paris grocery chain of Félix Potin and then to some Dutch merchants.

By a happy coincidence the angry mood of the leading growers
was matched by the ambitions of a new owner of a major estate.
This was Philippe de Rothschild, poet, visionary, and publicist
of genius, a man who has dominated the Médoc socially for over
half a century. He still lives much of the year at his beloved
Mouton, dressed during the day in a painter's smock and rope-
soled sandals, designing new labels for his wines, brooding over
new improvements to the view from his windows, the landscaping
of his estate, the very reincarnation of the aristocrats who
reshaped the landscape of so much of England so happily in the
eighteenth century.

He is the great-grandson of the English-born Nathaniel who
had bought Mouton eighty years earlier. His father, Baron
Henri, was no orthodox Rothschild: he qualified as a doctor
(and, in a typical gesture, founded his own small hospital in
Paris). He then turned to writing plays—under the name of
André Pascal—built his own theatre, the Pigalle, in which to
present them, and spent a great deal of time cruising round the
Mediterranean in his yacht, aptly named the *Eros*, with some
of the actresses in his company. But neither he, nor his mother,
who had been widowed in 1881 and owned the château for a
generation, visited the Médoc very often. Philippe de Rothschild
says that his grandmother came only five times in the whole of
a long life. As he wrote, "It produced wine, but no one went
there, never a visitor. The suspicious peasants locked the gates
behind them which hid their cows and rabbits and the washing
hung up to dry."

For, in these days, the accommodation was squalid enough
even by non-Rothschild standards. The family had built an
unremarkable little house—called 'Petit Mouton'—in the middle
of what was no more than a farmyard. The Misses Somerville
and Ross were told that it "had been built in imitation of an
English villa, but we did not dare to ask why she should have
chosen the square modern type, dear to the heart of a retired
solicitor". For the house does, indeed, resemble the sort of villa
built by the prosperous middle classes all over the world in the
late nineteenth century.

But it was not the style of the house which ensured that the
Rothschilds of Mouton, like their 'cousins' of Lafite (a much
more Rothschildian house, though too overwhelmingly crammed

with red satin furniture to suit modern tastes), so rarely visited the Médoc. It was the distance and the discomfort. Philippe de Rothschild remembers the all-night train journey from Paris to Bordeaux, the early-morning breakfast followed by a cab ride to change stations in the town, the further hour and three quarters in the slow train up the Médoc to Pauillac, and the final couple of miles in a horse and cart—for there were virtually no cars in the Médoc in the 1920s. On arrival there was no electricity (it reached Rothschilds only in 1935), no running water, and primitive drains—he still recalls the stench when the men came to drain the cess-pit every three months. It was not surprising that it was virtually unheard of for any serious Paris-based aristocratic proprietor to spend much time at his place in the Médoc.

But Philippe de Rothschild changed all that. He had happy memories of the house—where he had been evacuated as an adolescent during World War I from a Paris suddenly threatened by the Germans' heavy guns. And, as a very young man, the first true love of his life spent her summers at Arcachon, and was brought to Mouton, which the young lovers found a total wreck, though he felt even then "the place deserved to be taken care of". He was only twenty-one when he was given the estate by his father—his estate manager believes as a reward, or bribe, for giving up the dangerous sport of motor-racing to which both father and son were addicted.

Until then, the estate had been "the equivalent of a yacht or a stud" and had been losing money for decades. Philippe told his father that "it would be worse under me, and that if it ever did make money, it would not be in his lifetime"—he was right, although his father did not die until 1946, the estate did not begin to make money until the 1950s.

But only a Rothschild could have done what he did—and only at Mouton. "I could never have had so much fun with Lafite," he says, for the bigger property was very much a family possession, whereas Mouton was a personal asset of one branch of the family. The first step was obvious: to ensure that the wine made at Mouton would be amongst the best the Médoc could produce. Even before he arrived the prices Mouton had been fetching were outstanding (since the first growths were largely subject to 'abonnements' it was for a couple of years after World

War I, far and away the most expensive claret on the market) and, although opinions vary about the Baron's actual wine-tasting skills, his wine can be criticized only because it takes so long to develop—so that, for instance, the outstanding 1961 vintage will probably not be ready to drink until the turn of the century.

But, from the beginning, Baron Philippe was never going to be merely another semi-anonymous owner of an estate producing outstanding wine. It would, from the start, be his wine, and seen as such. He was only twenty-two when, in 1924, he made what he still believes was the single most important decision of his half-century at Mouton—to ensure that every drop of wine he produced would be bottled at the château. "I was horrified," he says, "I had no control over my own wine." By the 1920s, the merchants' names were no longer all that familiar, so they "gained fame and fortune from selling our products". It was not surprising that the trade took the decision as "an act of mistrust vis-à-vis the Bordeaux merchants". But Rothschild proceeded to rub it in.

In December 1926 he assembled the owners of the five 'premiers crus', including Haut-Brion and Yquem with the three from the Médoc, and induced them all to convert simultaneously to compulsory château-bottling, and to form an informal association to help combat frauds and to talk over prices before they offered their wines for sale. The only hesitation—a warning of conflicts to come—was from his 'cousins' of Lafite. They had been so badly hurt by the return by the purchasers of the mildewed specimens of 1884 which had been bottled at the château that they were still unwilling to embark on any such initiative again (they had imposed the absence of château-bottling as a condition of their 'abonnement' before the war).

No one but a Rothschild could have got away with it: he was only twenty-four, newly arrived in the Médoc and, moreover, Mouton was not officially a first growth. The same wave of enthusiasm for collective action among the leading proprietors led to the reinforcement of the association which had hitherto represented their interests only in the most languid fashion. Haut-Brion, and the owners of the châteaux in Sauternes and Barsac, joined in and it became far more integrated with other growers' organizations—an action which, in turn, triggered off the first attempts by the leading owners in St. Emilion to assert themselves.

But Rothschild's action was the most positive and revolutionary. Like many of the Baron's contributions to the Gironde, it has been under-rated because he was a Rothschild, a showman and, by Bordeaux standards anyway, an eccentric. It was a declaration of independence, proclaiming that some, at least, of the wines of Bordeaux did not need help, 'touching up', and existed in their own right independent of the trade.

Typically, Rothschild then added style to the substance. In 1927, when the 1924 wines were due to be bottled, he commissioned a new design for the label by an architect and stage-designer friend, Jacques Carlu. The design is described by Cyril Ray as "a highly nineteen-twenty-fourish pattern of the Mouton ram's head in black and grey, with a pale brown formalized chai and the five arrows—representing in the family's arms the five Rothschild brothers who set out from Frankfurt in Napoleon's time—in brown and red. Date, name and the pronouncement about château-bottling were all in the sans-serif lettering of the time".

Inevitably, the label startled the whole world of wine. The late Maurice Healy, a much-loved Irish barrister and connoisseur, exploded, only half-jokingly, that "the Bolshevist influence procured for itself a surprising manifestation at Château Mouton-Rothschild, the familiar thunderbolts were blazoned forth in all the colours of the rainbow and nothing except the labels under which inferior sherry is sometimes shipped to Latin America could give any standard of comparison whereby to appraise the 'jazz design' ".

The shock was quite deliberate. To complement the bottling of *his* wine at *his* château, Baron Philippe wanted "my wine with my label, not a vague anonymous label, I realized it was the sign of the place". He had, instinctively, grasped that the selling of wine at the level of a fine Médoc required the flair normally associated with the advertiser, or the showman—no one needs to spend that much on a bottle of wine, the competition is fierce (and in the 1920s champagne was still the dominant drink in the luxury trade) and only a touch of magic could lift claret above the ruck.

He certainly achieved his object: the label (which now looks merely an unremarkable period-piece) provided world-wide publicity for him, his wine, and—even his enemies were forced to admit—for the Gironde in general.

13

Stirrings in the slump

But not even the skills and capital of a hundred Rothschilds could have helped Bordeaux in the following quarter of a century. In the three years from 1930 to 1932 all the woes that in the late nineteenth century had been spread over a decade or more hit the Gironde within a few months. The Great Depression was more sudden and sharper than its equivalent in the 1870s. The restrictions imposed by foreign governments were tighter. And, although no particular pest is associated with the 1930s, the Gironde did suffer, between 1930 and 1932, from three successive vintages of dreadful quality, a run of bad luck unprecedented since the mildewed 1880s.

Worst hit were exports: between 1933 and 1935 when Bordeaux was trying to get rid of the appalling wine made in the three previous years they sunk to a mere one-seventh of Bordeaux's foreign sales at the peak of its prosperity in the 1870s and only a third of the figures reached around the turn of the century, not a period remembered with any affection in wine-growing areas.

First to slump was Germany—where the Nazi government introduced wide-ranging protectionist measures—though the drop was almost as great in Bordeaux's other traditional markets, Belgium, Holland and Britain. The only market to show any promise was, naturally enough, the United States. Although the figures show a trickle of sales right through Prohibition they soared from 1933 on. However, even in the peak year of 1934, only a tenth of the Gironde's exports went to the US before falling back to the pre-Prohibition level of roughly one-twentieth. For Prohibition left behind a legacy of controls and taxes which posed severe problems for wine salesmen more aggressive and well-organized than the Chartronnais. Each state imposed its own, very different, regulations designed to keep undesirable characters—like former bootleggers—out of the business, and to extract as much revenue as possible from liquor sales. Some states even set up their own monopolies.

The result was to fragment the market and to create a three-tier system of distribution: the 'national' importer, who actually brought the wine into the country; the 'state' importer, responsible to the individual state authorities for payment of their taxes; and the retailer. The system was expensive and for a long time it effectively confined sales of Bordeaux's wines to New York and a few other major cities.

Possibly the least helpful government of all was the French. It kept increasing internal duties on wine at the very time when the home market was having to absorb much larger quantities, for production barely changed, continuing to average over eighty million gallons a year. And increasing duties led to retaliation by foreigners. As Fernand Ginestet lamented, exports of French wines "are completely sacrificed to the protection of a few French industries, those whose voices are more powerful and therefore taken the most notice of by our governments."

Inevitably prices slumped to under a fifth of their, unremarkable, 1929 levels. And even though productivity actually increased slightly, the average grower saw his income reduced by nearly three quarters between 1929 and 1935, to a level well below the cost of production. This had jumped nearly ten-fold since 1914. Most of the growers were, in fact, peasants with tiny plots: of the 60,500 growers in the department in 1924, only 285 had more than 75 acres under vines, and the bulk—over 50,000—had under 7½ acres.

The peasants were used to extracting some form of subsistence economy from the soil, growing their vines around the other products which at least kept the family alive. The growers further up the scale fared relatively worse. They suffered an additional squeeze because so many wines which would previously have attracted a premium price were now being sold under the pernicious system of the 'degré-hecto' by which wine prices depend on their strength ("they've stopped tasting wines, they only weigh them now", was a bitter comment at the time).

Even today the basic price of wine is still expressed in terms of average strength and quantity, the 'degrees' of alcohol multiplied by the number of 'hectolitres'. This bureaucratic over-simplification puts a premium on the high-yielding high-strength wines produced freely in the South of France and, more especially, in Algeria. The system might have been expressly designed to humiliate and ruin any small grower struggling to produce relatively small yields of a rather better product, and in the Gironde, then as now, more than half the acreage of vines was devoted to making wine better than 'vin ordinaire', a proportion far higher than in anywhere else except Burgundy.

One typical grower in Loupiac on the beautiful Côtes de Bordeaux south of Bordeaux managed to get an average of 3·3 francs per bottle during the decade from 1923 to 1933, including the first four years of the slump. But, because of the operation of the 'degré-tonneau', system, his 1934 vintage—universally agreed to be the best for five years—fetched only 1·6 francs.

Further up the scale the figures differed only in their size, not in their proportion. The cost of a share in Latour, for instance, fell from 28,000 francs in 1929, to a mere 8,000 four years later. Not surprisingly a great deal of land in the better wine-growing areas was left fallow—in Margaux alone a million vines were pulled up. In 1934 the English merchant Charles Walter Berry noted that in the central Médoc "around Cussac could be noticed much waste land. Owing to the bad years the proprietors had scrapped their vines, but when they had done this they were at a loss to know what to do, for nothing else will grow". To this day the landscape of the area reflects the neglect of the 1930s: the pine trees growing in the scrubland all seem to be of a universal size and age. Even at classed growths like Pontet-Canet and Mouton-Rothschild's neighbour, Mouton d'Armailhacq, land was left fallow, and cultivation became relatively casual at Rausan-Ségla. Berry noted "a number of small pegs in the vineyard indicating that certain rows belonged to other vineyard proprietors; for example here and there we found inscribed on these pegs . . . Château Latour, Château Beychevelle, etc".

The price of an acre of vines in the Gironde plummeted to a quarter of the price paid for wine-growing land in the Midi—or a fifth of the going market value in Algeria—a direct result of the system of paying for wine by its strength and not by its quality.

Under the circumstances it was not surprising that virtually every estate was for sale—although in most cases there were no takers (the owners of Latour would love to have sold but concluded in 1936 that the estate would fetch only a 'derisory' price). The biggest sale of the decade was of Haut-Brion. Its seventy-five acres of vines were sold in 1936 for a mere 2,350,000 francs (not much over £100,000) to the American millionaire Clarence Dillon. Legend has it that the purchase was casual: that the day was rainy, that Dillon, on a flying visit to Bordeaux, had a cold and was unwilling even to look at a vineyard. It was Daniel Lawton who supposedly saved the day by buying a large rug for the shivering millionaire and inducing him at least to go and see Haut-Brion, most conveniently situated of 'grands crus' only a few miles from the centre of Bordeaux. In reality the purchase was far more premeditated: Dillon already owned a luxury hotel in Paris, and Seymour Weller, the American in charge of his French interests, had been on the look-out for some time for an estate to buy (he could have bought Cheval Blanc, the finest estate in St. Emilion, for about a tenth less than he paid for Haut-Brion, but at the time St. Emilion, though no longer the outcast of former times, still did not have the réclame of the Médoc or Graves).

The only beneficiaries of these miserable circumstances were those buyers of fine wines who still had a little money left. Charles Walter Berry's family firm of Berry Brothers and Rudd had done very well during Prohibition, when great quantities of its Cutty Sark whisky had been shipped through the Bahamas. He jumped at the chance he saw opening up by the ending of Prohibition and bought up the whole 1933 vintage of such famous growths as Beychevelle. But, in England, he lamented, "it is so frequently said that 'I cannot find anyone to drink claret'."

In fact the 1930s did see a small but noticeable effort to publicize claret, though in a strictly amateur and exclusivist fashion. In 1920, George Saintsbury, a Professor of English Literature, had published *Notes on a Cellar Book*, regaling the reader with details of the wines he had drunk—though he had to admit that when, just before 1914, he left Edinburgh (once a claret-loving city) it was difficult to find enough claret drinkers at a dinner party for fourteen to empty a magnum. Saintsbury became the model for a whole school of author-gourmets. These were characterized by Cyril Ray as the 'baroque school' of English wine writers, and indeed the style of such oenophiles as Warner Allen, Maurice Healy and André Simon does now seem excessively florid. Titles like *Stay Me with Flagons* or *Blood of the Grape* are reminders that Thurber's famous caption "It's a naive domestic Burgundy, but I think you will be amused by its presumption" did less than justice to the convolutions of their style. Yet there was sound sense, and a deep love of wine, buried under the titles (my many quotes from Ian Campbell come from his *Wayward Tendrils of the Vine*), and the fame of Thurber's remark is a tribute to their success.

These apparently absurd and snobbish gourmets had their serious side. The unequalled level of expertise in the British wine trade owes an enormous amount to the pioneering efforts of André Simon in particular and—to use a modern phrase they would thoroughly have deplored—they did 'raise the level of consciousness' of claret—though not unhappily of Sauternes—on both sides of the Atlantic.

For the general level of ignorance was appalling and symbolized by some famous old jokes—the restaurant menu with "vin ordinaire 2s 6d, vin très ordinaire 3s 6d" or the conviction, held for generations in London's clubland, that Mouton-Rothschild tasted of wool because of the sheep ('moutons' in French) previously kept there.

The trade itself had become so fossilized that it was not capable of any missionary endeavours. The heirs to the Gilbeys' business had been unable to sustain the momentum engendered by their direct-selling forbears, and in general, sales passed through the hands of the importers. These firms were often linked to the Bordeaux houses by unalterable ties of friendship—symbolized by Ian Campbell with his apprenticeship under Albert Schÿler. The Cruses, for instance, dealt for fifty years with Rutherford Osborne, who were even more famous for their Madeiras, and even those upstarts, the Ginestets, became intimate friends of the Dents of the City importers, Dent, Urwick and Yeatman. (This sort of link was not confined to England: the record is, supposedly, held by Eschenauer's agent in Denmark, the same firm for over a hundred years.)

Harry Waugh, a veteran wine trader and writer, remembers

of the importers how "business automatically came their way, few if any firms were so ungentlemanly as to break the sacred rule and to buy direct from the growers. I remember it was useless to try to telephone the principals either before 10 a.m. or after 4 p.m., for of course they were not often there". Waugh himself lacked adequate social contacts and had to wait for years before being allowed to serve the nobility and gentry, not to mention the all-powerful butlers who could so easily "shake up the bottle of claret or vintage port before it was decanted and to tell his employer that so and so are not so good as they used to be and to suggest another merchant of his, the butler's choice".

To break out of the stifling limitations imposed by this type of market required a major effort which could not be left to the Healys and the Simons, an awareness of the requirements of the market from the growers and an adventurousness on the part of the merchants. The pioneer was none other than Philippe de Rothschild. "Having created my product" with his château-bottling and the sensational label for his 1924 vintage—"why," he thought, "not be a merchant too?" The idea slowly took shape in discussions with M. de Marjerie, then his estate manager, and a friend, André Wisner, but it was the terrible vintages of the early thirties which, paradoxically, provided him with his opportunity. During the 1920s Rothschild had sold his second wine under the name of 'Carruades de Mouton', using the name of the small plateau called 'Carruades' between his estate and Lafite (the name 'Carruades' has been used by both châteaux at various times during the past century to sell their second wines). All the time he was looking for a way of broadening the range of wines he was selling, to help strengthen his position vis-à-vis the merchants. For some time the three of them played around with a new name for the second wine, and in 1931 came up with the name 'Cadet de Mouton'— Mouton Junior. This was swiftly changed to the simpler 'Mouton Cadet', a name which had to be employed the next year when it came to bottling the 1930 vintage. None of this was good enough for selling under the château's own name, and much was sold in tanker-loads as simple 'Pauillac' to Nicolas, the Paris wine merchants; but some was bottled under the name Mouton Cadet, given a label (which the present management

freely admits would today have had them sent to prison, because
it was so close an imitation of the normal Mouton label), and
two salesmen were hired to sell it. For Rothschild knew that
"from the day I had Mouton Cadet . . . I had a very remarkable
name".

From that time on the bandwagon started to roll: during the
dreadful years Rothschild was gradually buying control of his
neighbour, Mouton d'Armailhacq, and this brought with it a
tiny merchant's business, the "Société des vins de Pauillac"—
the Pauillac Wine Company. When the 1933 vintage proved
reasonable, and the 1934 magnificent, Rothschild was equipped
with a merchant's business and two salesmen to keep occupied.
To satisfy the demand, he and Marjerie had to buy 'Pauillac'
from other growers in the village and blend it to resemble the
rather hard, impersonal, but still very solid wine made by the
parent château in an off year. The barrier had been breached,
and in this modest, semi-accidental fashion, Bordeaux's first
brand name was born. Once wine not made at Mouton was
used, it ceased, in Baron Philippe's words, "to be a by-product,
it became a brand". Later changes in the wine were less important. In 1947 Rothschild had to change the name of his
shippers to 'La Bergerie'* because the fraud squad ruled that
under his former name he could sell only wines from Pauillac.
For that year the wines of the commune were too hard to be
sold young, so they had to look further afield, jettison the
appellation Pauillac and become a simple Médoc. Two years
later the vintage was small and the Merlot, which provides the
softness in the wine, failed completely in the Médoc, so they
had to look further afield and downgrade the appellation still
further to simple 'Bordeaux'. (Even now, of course, the wine
includes some of the surplus production of the Baron's château
wines.)

But for forty years Mouton Cadet remained an exception.
For Bordeaux is a brand manager's nightmare with its two
thousand château, many of them with lesser names attached
(Henri Martin of Château Gloria has three other names he

---

* Literally 'the sheepfold'. This name, and the rams' heads on so
many Mouton labels, help perpetuate the legend that the name derives
from 'mouton'—sheep. In fact, 'mouton' is a linguistic corruption of
'motte'—mound.

uses for his wine). And the names are thoroughly confusing. In the Gironde there are two Château Lafites (as well as two Laffittes), half a dozen estates entitled to employ variants on the name 'Latour', a further seventy-five incorporating 'La Tour' on their label—not to mention a Château Eyquem.

Inevitably the wine business is schizoid about this plethora of names. The infinite number of variations—from vintage to vintage as well as between the thousands of estates—ensures that buying claret is totally dissimilar to the purchase of any other drink. In other areas the choice is either restricted to the names of a relatively small number of merchants, or, as in Burgundy or Germany, by certain very strict rules. In Bordeaux because of the plethora of choice "the amateur", in the shrewd words of Maurice Healy, "may venture to compete with the professional . . . and buy according to his own instruction". This idea conforms with every consumer's desire to know better than the experts, to outwit those trying to foist on him a standard product, to be 'one up' not only on your neighbours, but on the trade as well.

The first step in the creation of a brand name, in Bordeaux terms, was to use wine not from a specific vineyard, but from a wider area. This, after all, had been the principle behind the merchants' use of their own names in the previous century, and behind the Gilbeys' brand policy. But Mouton Cadet was different. The initiative came from the proprietor, and the brand name relied not on the name of an intermediary, but of an estate.

Other attempts were made to break out of the system—though none on the Rothschildian scale. When Latour was 'abonné', for five years at the end of the 1930s to a Parisian entrepreneur, the agreement provided that the château could share any 'excess' profit and could sell the wine to the local trade if it offered a fifth more than the abonnement's price—which itself was indexed to the cost of living.

Given the temper of the times, more ambitious schemes were doomed. In 1929 Fernand Ginestet—who had just split with his partner Latrille—organized a small group of his fellow-merchants (none of them well known or Chartronnais) into a 'Société des Grands Crus'—a 'Great Wine Company'—and managed to buy control of a number of estates. But, after the disastrous harvests of 1930–32, Ginestet's partners fled the scene, leaving him to pick up the pieces, keeping some of the châteaux and selling the others.

He was more successful in another rescue attempt. Starting in 1934 he gradually bought control of Château Margaux which had fallen into a parlous state. It had even abandoned château-bottling in 1930. Ginestet pulled up seventy-five acres of vines on sub-standard land and, because this would inevitably lead to reduced production in the future, the price rose and he was able to revalue the stocks of earlier vintages he already had in stock.

But Ginestet was exceptional. Most of the merchants were sellers. The Delors were forced to sell their eight châteaux by the bankers who controlled the business through their nominee Robert Duten. In 1928 Arthur Johnston had already been forced to sell Château Ducru-Beaucaillou, and during the 1930s had to dispose of his precious stocks of vintages dating back to the 1870s. Naturally there were fabulous bargains available. One speculator managed to buy a major estate at a price so low that he recouped the entire purchase price by selling off the woodland and pasture, leaving him with the vineyard and château for nothing. Yet, surprisingly, at this their most depressed moment, the initiative seems to have passed to the growers—and not only the Rothschilds and the owners of Latour. In other wine-growing areas in France, there was a long-standing tradition of wine being made and sold by peasant co-operatives. But it was only early in the desperate 1930s that the growers of the Gironde studied the efforts of their fellows and started to imitate them. Inevitably there was some initial opposition from the merchants, who deliberately preferred to avoid the co-operatives and look to smaller, weaker producers. It was only in 1955 that the merchants and the Co-operatives' Union signed a peace treaty, by which the merchants agreed to take regular quantities from them. Nevertheless the co-operatives flourished—by 1954 there were sixty in the Gironde, accounting for two-fifths of the department's production. All have problems of quality control, since they are bound to accept all the grapes produced by their members, and it requires an unusual level of discipline to sustain an acceptable level of quality year after year—and the Bordeaux merchants are only too ready to spread the word of any problems encountered by the co-ops.

Inevitably, therefore, many of them—especially across the Gironde in Bourg and Blaye—werc and remain mass producers, selling their wine by the degree for blending by the Chartronnais. But increasing numbers are producing wine entitled to the 'appellation' label—they account for probably a quarter of Bordeaux's 'named' production, and a few have established a brand name of some consequence, notably in St. Emilion, in St. Estèphe ('Marquis de St. Estèphe') and in Pauillac itself. Even in a village dominated by three first growths room was found in 1932 for a co-operative which today makes up to 175,000 gallons of wine annually. Much of it used to be sold as 'Château Pauillac', but it is now known as 'La Rose Pauillac'.

The same impulse which produced the Co-operatives—the desire to avoid the historic marketing intermediaries—lay behind the impulse given by the slump, and, like the Co-operatives, never lost since then, to selling wine directly to French customers. There are virtually no specialist 'off-licences' or liquor stores in France (even today there are only a dozen or so in Paris), a lack of specialized outlets compounded by the historic French suspicion of the honesty and competence of their wine trade and by what Peter Allan Sichel* describes as the "romance of buying direct from the grower". Even the most amateur form of this sort of selling—the 'vente directe', direct sale of a few cases to passing motorists—now accounts for a great deal of wine. Slightly more professional are the lists kept by many canny cellarmen ('maîtres de chai') at individual estates of customers through the years, lists which form a useful reserve of contacts in bad times. Such is the snobbery of these customers that, in Sichel's words 'It's horrific how easy it is to sell privately'. These customers extend right through

* There are two Peter Sichels active in the companies representing the family's wine interests in France, Germany, Britain and the United States. Peter Max Sichel lives in New York selling mostly Blue Nun Liebfraumilch. Peter Allan Sichel—who has lived in Bordeaux since 1961—is the son of Allan Sichel, one of the most distinguished of the band of author-merchants who helped to explain the delights of drinking wine to a steadily growing audience in England after the Second World War.

the social scale: Jean Theil of Château Poujeaux, who sells all his wine direct, has for the past fifteen years supplied a great deal to the Matignon Palace which houses French prime ministers (his first customer was the late M. Pompidou, the very model of the rotund French bourgeois gourmet who would, classically, delight in buying direct).

But the majority of the growers, then as now, were not sales-minded: 'they didn't sell their wine, they got rid of it,' as the saying goes. And, because they were so indifferent to their customers, they found it very difficult to work with the merchants. Even with the transformation—largely as a result of initiative by Fernand Ginestet—of the pioneering 'Union des Propriétés et du Commerce' into the more official CDVB (Comité du Défence des Vins de Bordeaux—the Committee for the Defence of Bordeaux's wines) the growers' attitude did not change.

In 1934—when the CDVB had got into its stride after some early hesitations—one irascible proprietor exploded that "the committee ought to be a committee of growers. If there are to be any merchants on it, they ought to submit to the growers and their interests ought not to be confused."

Nevertheless Ginestet and the chairman of Gironde's agricultural union, a lawyer called M. Roquette-Buisson, provided the growers with a complete mechanism to create, if they wished, a name for their wines. The 1905 legislation had left numerous gaps which were steadily plugged between the two world wars, largely thanks to legislation introduced by the right-wing senator for the Gironde, M. Capus, guided by Ginestet and Roquette-Buisson.

In 1919 the merchants were forced to keep a record of the delivery and despatch of all wines entitled to the name of Bordeaux. A 1925 bill introduced the notion of quality into the idea of 'appellations'—a concept applied for the first time two years later for the benefit of the incomparable blue cheeses made only in the caves at Roquefort. But it was only in 1935 that the idea of 'appellations d'origine contrôlée' was finally defined, and provided with the requisite mechanisms of control and policing.

The law was to be supervised by the Committee—later renamed the National Institute—of 'Appellations Contrôlées'. This body—universally known as the INAO and composed

of representatives of all the interested parties—had the power
to lay down far more than the mere districts in which the
appropriately-named wines could be produced. The varieties
of grapes that could be used for any particular appellation
were strictly controlled. Previously control had been largely
negative and designed to eliminate certain notably over-
productive hybrids with euphonious names like Isabelle, Noah
and Othello. But the 1935 law was more positive, laying down
the few types that could be used. In the Gironde these were
largely confined to three or four each for claret and for sweet
and dry white wines. The yield of an acre of vines was limited,
a minimum level of alcoholic content decreed for each appellation, and standard procedures laid down for growing and
harvesting the grapes and making the wine (for instance, to be
entitled to the appellation of Barsac or Sauternes, a grower
had, in theory, to wait for the 'pourriture noble').

Within the commune there was, however, more liberty for
individual estates. During the Depression, many of the estates
were not cultivating all the land entitled to produce their wine;
and their production could be further boosted if their owners
bought the 'right' sort of land—the privileged plots deemed
to be worthy of the château's name. The law merely confirmed
the old Médocain tradition: that the crucial element in a château's
name was not the exact plots whose products went into the wine
(although all the better-known estates have always been based
on particular slopes) but the particular quality of the wine.
Within limits, it was up to the owner and his 'maître de chai'
to blend the products of many different fields to achieve the
expected standard.

These regulations were far more important for the Gironde
than for any other wine-growing area in France. For, although
the Département contains only an eighth of France's wine-
growing acreage, and accounts for only a twelfth of the country's
wine production, yet two-thirds of its production is entitled
to a precious AOC label, and it produces a third of all the French
wine entitled to that description.

Unfortunately the Girondins allowed local pride to sabotage
the chance that the new regulations could lead to orderly marketing. Every little village applied for its own appellation in an
obsession with restricting its name to the smallest possible

area. By the time the boundaries had been defined, the consumer was overwhelmed with a choice between forty-seven different brand names before starting to choose individual châteaux. The basic 'appellations', Bordeaux and Bordeaux Supérieur, alone accounted for nearly half of the 1976 AOC red wine crop, and two thirds of the white wines produced in the Gironde in 1976. At the other extreme were tiny appellations like the Graves de Vayres, and the smallest of the seven appellations which include St. Emilion in their name, accounting for a hundredth as much, a mere three-tenths of one per cent of the Gironde's total production.

In other cases the 'appellations' have barely been used at all. Many producers—especially in Blaye, on the Côtes de Bordeaux and in Fronsac—have remained passive victims of the trade, selling their wines by 'degree' and not under the name to which they were legally entitled, and even now unable to use their new-found rights to any commercial advantage.

Their passivity was in marked contrast to the active and detailed supervision exercised—for the first time—by the Fraud Prevention Squads and the inspectors policing the collection of indirect taxes. These were for the first time entitled to inspect growers' cellars and wine-making equipment, as well as to supervise the very detailed controls over every aspect of vine-growing—not just the type of vine to be planted but where they could be planted, and how they should be pruned.

This supervision was not confined to the growers. It extended also to the merchants (including the many in Bordeaux who had no cellars but operated from their homes and relied on suppliers from the cellars of larger firms who would bottle and label the wines for them). The merchants had to keep all the documents relevant to the purchase or sale of AOC wines for five years, and a refusal to make these available to the inspectors from the Fraud or Tax squads on their regular and routine visits would constitute obstruction of justice. Fortunately for the Chartronnais, the Bordeaux agreement of 1913 was extended to include the new regulations and it was tacitly agreed that the authorities would give the merchants proper notice of their forthcoming arrival—a thoughtfulness traditionally reciprocated by the merchants who would leave a case of wine in the boot of the official's car during his inspection.

This sort of formality was not entirely the result of the 1913 'gentlemen's agreement', for inspectors and merchants alike had to cope with the inevitable concomitant of this complex web of controls—a mound of paperwork. Wherever it went, wine entitled to call itself AOC had to be accompanied by an 'acquit vert', a green piece of paper to that effect. The result, in the words of Peter Allen Sichel (himself recognized throughout a notoriously bitchy trade as a model of honesty), is that "if the regulations are applied to the letter, you can't do your job".

But the convolutions were inevitable, for the gaps the new laws were trying to bridge were enormous—one government survey reckoned that there was thirty times as much wine circulating in the 1930s bearing the name of Bordeaux as was actually produced in the Département. And the temptations to fraud were enormous. For over twenty years after the new laws came into operation the prices paid for the 'smaller' châteaux, the solid aspiring middle classes among the estates, were not sufficiently higher than those paid for basic wine to encourage any attention to quality among the growers. There was, by contrast, every incentive to add sugar surreptitiously to boost the alcohol content, and to tamper illegally with the product.

Furthermore the measures were designed to help the grower, not by enlarging his market, but simply by laying down certain minimal conditions. These were worth fulfilling only because they enabled producers of AOC wines (provided they did not produce too much per acre) to avoid the various quantitative limitations placed on ordinary wine producers during the lean years.

But, contrary to received opinion, the regulations in no way guaranteed the quality of the wine: they simply provided a framework within which it was possible for those producing better wine to operate with some security. Because miserable wine can quite legitimately be made and then sold under even the most distinguished AOC labels, the idea has become somewhat tarnished. The real test of a wine is its taste, and it has taken a generation or more for the INAO and the more conscientious villages to impose this form of discipline in an effective—and even now by no means universal—fashion. In

6

the meantime the notion of AOC had fostered a double delusion: the grower thought the label would automatically sell his wine, the customer that the same label would, equally automatically, guarantee its quality. The combined weight of disillusionment growing out of this mutual deception has been immensely harmful.

14
Black comedy

The effects of external upheavals on the Bordeaux wine business have always been unpredictable. The French Revolution had consolidated the power of the merchants whereas the First World War had produced only some minor stirrings and, at the time, the Second World War—even the four years during which France was occupied by the Germans—seemed merely the blackest of comedies, carrying with it no particular long-term resonances.

During the Occupation a minority of merchants—a member of the de Luze family, the Pallières, father and son and Henri Binaud of Beyermann's—played a heroic part in the Resistance. Another small group enthusiatically welcomed the Germans, shared their Fascist beliefs and collaborated enthusiastically with them. But most growers and merchants behaved in exactly the same unhappy and unheroic fashion as the majority of their fellow-countrymen. They simply survived.

The only outwardly dramatic events occurred with the arrival and departure of the Germans. For a few days in June 1940 Bordeaux became the capital of France, as it had been on other dramatic occasions in 1870 and 1914. But this time the drama ended in the installation of the government led by Marshal Pétain, prepared to surrender to the Germans, and their subsequent arrival.

For two nightmarish months order collapsed. The English Chartronnais fled—merchants like the Sichels selling off their stocks of the excellent 1937 vintage at derisory prices. Langoa was pillaged by the Germans even of its kitchen utensils and crockery and left in a dreadful state. Everywhere the Germans started by looting wine from the cellars.

But soon order was restored, and the comedy began. For the commanders of the German troops in Bordeaux were more often than not wine merchants in uniform, or had some other connections with France. Kuhnemann, who commanded the naval base, had been head of a major firm of wine importers in Berlin. The Germans' requisition orders were signed by Feld Kommandant von Faber du Faur, the last survivor of an old Girondin Protestant family which had gone into religious exile in Germany at the end of the seventeenth century. The naval forces in Bordeaux were commanded by an admiral with the decidedly un-Teutonic name of Arnold de Laperrière. And when the Germans decided to regularize their purchases of wines and appointed a 'Weinführer', it turned out to be Hans Bohmers, a Bremen wine merchant whose agencies had previously included Mouton-Rothschild.

The Chartronnais' position was the worse because so many had their roots in Germany, or had intimate friends among the wine-selling community there. And these firms, especially Eschenauer and Cruse, flourished because the Germans proved to be massive wine buyers. Within eighteen months they had relieved Bordeaux of its previously excessive stocks—one purchase alone, in early 1942, totalled a million bottles of the most expensive wines. In theory the Germans dealt only through those firms which had sold wine to Germany before the war, but virtually all the firms benefited if only as sub-contractors (the Johnstons claim to be one of only four firms not to have been involved).

The situation inevitably became complicated by all sorts of peculiarities. The French government in Vichy tried to stop speculation by fixing prices and forbidding the purchase of wines 'sur souches' which carried with it considerable opportunities for tax avoidance. They succeeded only in creating a double market for wine. In individual cases French intellectual ingenuity came into its own. Although Langoa lost its crockery, Daniel Guestier, in Cyril Ray's words, "persuaded the German occupiers that Ronald Barton was an Irishman and therefore a neutral, which meant that the property—château, furniture, vineyards, and wines in the cellar—was saved from confiscation, though not from having German troops billeted in the house". Barton himself was serving in the British army as a liaison officer, but the issue of his 'neutrality' was "further clouded by letters from his sister in Ireland, who was in fact a citizen of the Irish Republic, addressed through the Ministry of External Affairs in Dublin to the Vichy government and the occupying power, asking for information about her family's property in France—information which, indeed, was dutifully vouchsafed to her". For the Germans behaved with the utmost correctness. Bohmers "did the least he could to harm the trade" in one observer's words, and after the war Ronald Avery found that his Paris bank account was actually in better condition than in 1940—for the Germans had paid for any wines of his they had taken.

Less comic was the position of the Rothschild properties, which had served as staging posts for the family on their hasty exit from the country in June 1940. Both were saved from destruction by the loyalty and courage of the Rothschild's staff and through a piece of legal cunning by which Lafite was sequestrated by the Vichy government. It thus ceased to be the property of a Jewish family and so was safe from the general confiscation of all Jewish possessions by the Germans.

The Rothschilds and the Bartons were at least sure of their position—Barton in the British army, Philippe de Rothschild in the sort of eccentric, courageous activity to be expected from him, his cousin Elie of Lafite in the French army. Life was more complicated for those who remained behind. Henry Lawton served as chairman of the merchants' trade organization until his death in 1942. Roger Cruse—who, in 1920, had put forward a plan for family benefits remarkably similar to that introduced by Vichy during the war and which continues to this day— served throughout the war as an assistant to Bordeaux's nominally socialist mayor, Adrian Marquet.

But the man in the worst personal dilemma was Louis Eschenauer, who had built up his grandfather's firm in a remarkable fashion since he became its effective head on the death of his cousin Louis Lung as far back as 1913. By 1940 Eschenauer was seventy, and thus old enough to be entitled to the title 'oncle' —uncle. This—or the equivalent 'Papa'—seems to be the spontaneous tribute of the Bordeaux trade to their outstanding figure, and in most cases the recipient is indeed pretty venerable.*

* The longevity of most people in the wine trade is a tribute to the truth of the saying of the ancient Greek doctor, Jalen, that "wine is the nursemaid of old age". Eschenauer himself lived to the age of eighty-eight, and his predecessors and successors as 'deans' of the business, Jean Calvet and Emmanuel Cruse, lived to much the same age. Daniel Lawton is still alive in his nineties.

Kuhnemann was Eschenauer's 'cousin'—indeed was one of those who naturally called him 'Oncle Louis'. Bohmers had been a close enough friend for 'Oncle' Louis to be godfather to his son. Even more awkwardly, Ribbentrop had been connected with the wine trade—and thus the Eschenauers—through his wife. So 'Oncle Louis' became the natural middle-man for dealings with the Germans, and inevitably had to receive the large numbers of Ribbentrop's friends whom Hitler's foreign minister sent to see him.

The Chartronnais's activities during the Occupation provided a rich source of material for social historians—and for future gossips—but more important things were happening. For, in the wine trade as in many other spheres of French life, the Vichy government, unencumbered by time-consuming democratic restraints, was able to initiate fundamental changes to old-established habits and institutions.

The impulse to change in Bordeaux was given by the visit in 1942 of Madame Vogüe, the president of the CIVC—the Comité Interprofessionel du Vin de Champagne—the joint committee of growers and merchants which controlled the champagne business. This had been established as a result of the disturbances which had greeted the delimitations of the 'champagne' district in 1911 and, ever since, had provided an example of peaceful collaboration which Ginestet and Roquette-Buisson knew Bordeaux would do well to emulate.

The next year a study group started work, and by Christmas 1943 the Vichy government had authorized the setting-up, subject to future legislation on the subject, of CIVB—a 'Comité Interprofessionnel des Vins de Bordeaux', originally intended to enjoy considerable powers over the business. But there the matter rested while Bordeaux was liberated, an event which provided

---

Over four hundred couples turned up before the war to a celebration in St. Emilion—a smallish town—confined to those married for over fifty years. And Jean Calvet told Charles Walter Berry that he "remembered four agents of his in England who had died at the ages of 78, 94, 88 and over 80, and further that his last four head-cellarmen had lived to the ripe old ages of 78, 84, 78, and the present one was 76 and still going strong". An even more remarkable tribute comes from the prevalence in the Médoc of septuagenarians like Jean Theil and Henri Martin sprightly enough to appear fifteen years younger.

yet another Bordeaux legend. The Chartronnais, anxious to protect 'Oncle' Louis' reputation, assert that he decisively affected the Germans' decision not to blow up the bridges of Bordeaux—which enormously helped the city's post-war recovery —when they finally retreated in August 1944 by pleading with his relation Kuhnemann. But this claim is disputed by Bordeaux's official historians who assert that Kuhnemann was too junior to have had a decisive influence, and would in any case have been bound to obey any instructions delivered to him.

Eschenauer's intervention did not help him after the war. His relations with the Germans had been close enough for him to be flung into the same cell as Adrian Marquet and another major collaborator, the Abbé Bergey, a priest who had been the Gironde's leading right-wing demagogue before the war. (Tradition has it that the old man—he was seventy-five at the time—burst into tears when he was led into the cell and exclaimed, "If only mama could see me now." Cynical observers say this remark, like his bewildered exclamation, "After 1918 they gave me a medal for selling wines to the Germans, now they fling me into prison for doing the same thing", were both part of the theatrical equipment of one of Bordeaux's finest natural ham actors.)

Most of the firms, including Eschenauer and Louis Bert's, which had profited to any great extent from selling to the Germans, were fined appropriately, and Eschenauer spent a couple of years in prison. But peace brought with it an apparent return to pre-war 'normalcy' enhanced by the curious way that export licences were granted. In the prevailing desperate shortage of wine, as of every sort of food and drink, sales were rationed —but, in the case of wine exports, the quantities were related to exports in the five previous years, a decision which effectively limited foreign markets for a couple of years to the very firms which had been most active in selling to the Germans during the war.

Amongst the most sensational survivors were the Cruses thanks to a 'cousin', Lorrain Cruse. He had studied for the tough examination to be an 'Inspecteur des finances' a year ahead of a young rugby football international, Jacques Chaban-Delmas. Both went into the Resistance, and Chaban-Delmas became a Brigadier-General before he was thirty. He was sent by de Gaulle to Bordeaux immediately after the Liberation to calm down a situation in which communist-led resistance leaders were too much in control and too set on revenge for de Gaulle's liking.

He returned the next year as a carpet-bagging politician, anxious for a power base in a city whose politics had been disrupted by the behaviour during the war of the city's former boss, Adrian Marquet. Chaban needed all the introductions he could get: and Lorrain Cruse provided an opening, not only to his family but also to Daniel Lawton. He was one of four brothers, a typical Chartronnais in his love of sport, a fine shot and a champion player at both lawn and 'real' tennis. But, more importantly from Chaban's point of view, as a young man he had been tutored by Marcel Cachin, one of the founders of the French Communist Party, and had been a very close friend of two leading socialists, Jules Guesde and his wife. He could provide Chaban with a range of contacts far wider than any other Chartronnais.

Although it was Lawton who provided the greatest help to Chaban's successful campaign to establish the position of 'Député-Maire' he has enjoyed for over thirty years the Cruse family remained very close to him. He encouraged Emmanuel's formidable wife, née Marguerite de Luze, in her determined attempts to put the city on the cultural map by founding the very successful musical festivals held in Bordeaux every year. For the Chartronnais had long lost any overt political ambition: even the ambitious Cruses were content to remain in the background, close enough to the mayor to drink with the tiny inner group which waited with him on election nights, while not occupying any public political position.

Chaban has never been overtly grateful for their early support. Although he has acted as an effective 'mover and shaker' in promoting his adopted city, he has never taken any public initiative to help the wine business—the city's biggest single employer and producer of its proudest product. Nevertheless, the Cruses' (and the Lawtons') closeness to Chaban was a public demonstration that a mere global conflict could not shake the power of the Chartronnais. What it did change was their marriage-patterns.

Before the war the marriage of Edouard Cruse to a Catholic had been enough to ensure that the children were automatically barred from inheriting any part of the family business; even in 1947 the marriage of Arthur Johnston's son Nathaniel to a Catholic created a major scandal. But, whereas before the war marriage away from the 'pavé' was the exception, afterwards it became the rule. More common than marriages 'out' of Protestantism were those with fellow-religionists from other parts of France. The present Mme Hugues Lawton showed the way when she married a Cruse: she came from the same sort of background as the Chartronnais—impeccable upper-middle-class Protestant owners of widely-respected major businesses, but from Eastern rather than South-western France (her mother was a Peugeot, of the car-making family). And, once the two small groups met, other alliances followed.

But their social and economic power remained cohesive enough to stifle at birth the dreams of co-operative activity expressed in the original plans for the new trade organization, the CIVB. This was duly authorized by legislation in 1948. But by then it had ceased to be a 'committee' and had become a 'conseil'—council. This change of name reflected a similar dilution in its powers. Where the original study group had envisaged that the new body would have the power to enforce the law and would be armed with the power to award professional certificates and levy compulsory contributions from growers and merchants, in the event—although the state did levy some money and pass it on—it was realized that no coercion was possible.

Paul Barailhé, one of its early directors, wrote that with a thousand merchants and fifty times as many growers "could one reasonably suppose that a simple ukase issued by this council would be adequate to constrain within one disciplinary framework this impressive and widely-spread mass of interested parties?" If the council had tried, why then, wrote Barailhé, "it would have become the scapegoat for all those not satisfied with their lot, and would sooner or later have fallen into disrepute, dragging down with it the only means of defending Bordeaux's wine interests". In plainer language, the original dreams had been effectively demolished by the resistance of the Chartronnais, who had no interest in working with the growers, and who took little part in the CIVB's activities. (Indeed the only element in the dream which remained intact was the CIVB's headquarters. In 1922, when he led 30,000 wine-growers through Bordeaux,

6*

Fernand Ginestet had pointed to the elegant eighteenth-century Hôtel Gobineau at the very heart of Bordeaux as the future home of the organization of which he was dreaming even then. After the war, the Hôtel, which had housed the Germans during the war, fell vacant, and was bought for the CIVB out of the excess profits confiscated from errant merchants.)

But the CIVB's wings were severely clipped, its activities limited. The CIVB acted with the INAO in controlling the whole question of Appellations, it acted as intermediary between the Bordeaux wine business and the state, it provided at least a nominal institutional framework within which growers, brokers and merchants could meet, and it acted as a propagandist for Bordeaux wine. But the modesty of its ambitions were exemplified by Barailhé's own depressive ideas: that the market, for the better wines anyway, was limited, and all Bordeaux could do was to seek to improve their quality and thus command a higher premium for the restricted amount it could sell.

In the few years after the war, this defeatist attitude seemed understandable enough. For, although the estates had been neglected during the war, production recovered too quickly. By 1950 it was back over the 100 million gallon mark first reached seventy-five years previously. But costs had soared and the customers—especially abroad—could not afford to pay or, if they could, were prevented by import restrictions from buying. Exports only returned to pre-war levels in 1950; and the price paid even for the better wines was miserable—in the four years 1948–51, the average 'bourgeois' wine, only one notch down from a classed growth, sold for only one and three quarters the price of the most basic Bordeaux, and even the second growths sold for only three times the basic floor price. (This led to some fabulous bargains, especially of the 1950 vintage which fulfilled all the conditions: a large, initially underrated harvest coming on to a market spoilt and saturated by widely-acclaimed vintages in each of the three previous years.) British buyers of the top growths were particularly well placed. In 1949 the Labour government had removed the fiscal discrimination against wines imported in bottle which had operated for over half a century.

Even the Chartronnais were pessimistic. At the end of the war Christian Cruse refused an offer from Pierre Ginestet, Fernand's son, to take a share in Château Margaux, because the '44s were

still in stock—an argument which assumed that they were a
liability and not an asset. And margins were so narrow that
Daniel Lawton could afford to take only one of his sons into
partnership with him. The other, Hugues, had to go and work
for the local aperitif company of Marie Brizard (Hugues Lawton
still remembers the tears in the old man's eyes as he woke his
son up the day he was due to start work).

Bordeaux, as so often, was out of tune with the rest of France
but for once worse off than its compatriots. In the post-war years
the Gironde slipped badly in the economic league table, so that
by 1953 its inhabitants' income per head had slumped to half that
enjoyed by Parisians.

The stabilization of France's economic position by Antoine
Pinay, and the increasing amount of free money in the world,
gradually helped Bordeaux's position—but at first only for the
cream of the crop. Prices for clarets entitled only to the basic
appellation had still not recovered to their 1948 level six years
later. But demand for the better wines (apart from the miserable
1954 vintage) suddenly increased the gaps between the different
classes.

This produced what Allan Sichel* described in his annual
report from Bordeaux as "a market of extremes . . . on the one
hand frequent examples of vineyards being abandoned in some
of the best territories of Bordeaux, and on the other, the firm
prices of the first growths". This, he thought, "was not a healthy
sign because we believe the reputation of Bordeaux to be firmly
based on the solid qualities of its bourgeois growths, now, like
other bourgeois, in danger of being squeezed out of existence
by economic factors". Growers of the solid middle-class wines
could not afford to let them mature and "Bordeaux finds an
excellent demand for wines at prices at or below cost of production and, as a result, is forced to abandon its vineyards, whilst
at the same time the occasional drinkers of two hemispheres,
presumably in order to be on the safe side, are prepared to pay
high prices for well-known names"—a classic restatement of one
of the most unfortunate and long-lasting results of the 1855

* Sichel continued these pithy and valuable reports until his death in
1965. His business, and the duty of continuing them, was inherited by
his son Peter, whose pen proved worthy of his father's—no mean
compliment.

classification, the ability of growths then classed among the nobility to command a premium price among the ignorant, the timid, or merely conspicuous consumers.

The lament for the 'bourgeois' growths (as for their human equivalents) was happily premature. The attractions of Bordeaux looked the greater because the Burgundians—chronically unable to supply enough wine—had been able to raise their prices to what the trade considered exorbitant levels. Bordeaux's exports for 1954 were the highest since 1930, and even the miserable vintage that year was snapped up. In the first half of 1955 the still-narrow, still-nervous Bordeaux market started to accelerate, and the speed brought with it the usual symptoms. Sichel's report that October remarked that "as usual the movement started with the first growths . . . and the spectacular prices, reached as the limited quantities first sold were resold and sold again, quickly induced a mild panic on the market. Some irresistible offers were made to owners of second and third growths". In late summer when it was clear that the vintage would be at least very good, the prices of the first growths, sold 'sur souches', were approaching double the, equally promising, 1953s. By October "activities have slackened off for the moment largely because bewildered growers are waiting to see what further pleasant surprises are in store for them . . . other growers are said to be tearing their hair out by the roots—and doubtless planting vines—because in their innocence they sold all or part of their 1955 crop in the early days at about the same prices as their 1953s". Sichel shrewdly concluded that "the present price level has been created by demand, speculative, strategic and partly genuine and *not* by growers".

The dawn was not false. The upsurge in demand first noticeable the previous year was to prove the beginning of nearly two decades in which the Gironde, like the capitalist world whose cycles it reflected, slowly, painfully, and with many hesitations, hauled itself out of the slough of despond in which it had splashed unhappily for the previous eighty years.

In Bordeaux it took a major natural disaster to consolidate the gains of the previous couple of years. In February 1956 the Gironde endured the worst frosts since the eighteenth century. The whole month saw a literally killing combination: deep frost at night with temperatures down to − 20C which froze the ground

round the roots, and bright sun by day which melted the earth. This froze again the next night, splitting and destroying the roots as the ice expanded.

Prices naturally climbed, but it was only later in the spring that the extent of the damage was fully appreciated even by close observers like Sichel: "There was something definitely wrong with the vines . . . in some areas there was no sign of sap movement; elsewhere a few buds appeared and died . . . Pomerol and Cérons appear to be unlikely to produce any wine; as do parts of St. Emilion, some of the best white wine areas on the left bank, and isolated parts in other areas; we have counted the buds at Château Climens with a moderately clear eye and a compassionate heart. The Médoc appears to be the least affected." The long-term effects were considerable. Many vineyards had to be more or less completely replanted. Production fell everywhere —the 1955 crop was not repeated until 1962.

The price of ordinary basic Bordeaux rouge, which had risen by fifty per cent during 1955 alone, jumped by the same proportion during 1956—ironically, because the 1956 vintage was so poor, prices of the better wines actually dropped. So the crus bourgeois, seemingly so threatened two years previously, were fetching prices approaching those of the second growths. For the surge of demand in 1955 combined with the frosts of the following February had made it possible for wine-makers to hope again, and no longer to be at the whim of a trade which itself had suffered through an eighty-year slump.

15

The new men

In the late 1950s casual travellers through the Médoc were occasionally greeted by the striking and unusual sight of a few vineyard workers, clad not in faded blue denim but in slacks or jackets bearing the unmistakable stamp of Brooks Brothers tailoring. This sight indicated, not that the famous New York shop had opened a branch in the Médoc, still less that the Médocain workers could afford to travel. For these were cast-offs, kindly donated by some of the United States' richest men, bankers, industrialists, hoteliers, to the workers on the estates they had bought.

The man who had organized the purchases—and thought of the charitable gesture—was Alexis Lichine, born of Russian parents who had fled to Paris at the onset of the Revolution, taking with them the then four-year old Alexis. From his teens he was an obsessed wine-taster; and his palate is reckoned outstanding even by the many people who dislike him. At an early age—as an advertising salesman for the Paris-based *International Herald Tribune* during the depths of the Depression— he also discovered that he had the gift of the gab and a flair for selling, a talent he soon found was better rewarded in the United States than in Europe.

In the late 1930s he exercised his talents for the late Frank Schoonmaker—one of the small band who took on the immense job of teaching the American people about wine after Prohibition had been lifted. Indeed until very recently most of the people selling French wine in the United States traced their business education back to Schoonmaker, Lichine, or to a handful of other pioneers like Bob Haas or to Colonel Frederick Wildman.

Even before the war, Lichine had established some valuable social and business contacts—including the banqueting manager of the Waldorf-Astoria and the owner of Antoine's, most famous of all New Orleans' restaurants. These contacts stood him in good stead: combined with his perfect French they enabled him to spend the war largely in intelligence work (and in arranging the wines for General Eisenhower's distinguished guests, a task he was to continue when the General moved to the White House). After the war, he worked for a short, unhappy period with Armand Hammer in United Distillers—an experience which taught him the sharp edges of selling. He then started on his own as an importer of French wines with the help of Seymour Weller, the American who ran Haut-Brion for its owner Clarence Dillon. Lichine's favourite stamping ground was Burgundy, partly for vinous reasons, and also, one suspects, because he so enjoyed haggling with the Burgundians to extract from them greater quantities of their wines, supplies of which, even then, could not match the demand.

But he soon realized that Bordeaux, in its run-down condition, offered ample opportunities for his talents, as a merchant (he early established his French headquarters in Margaux) able also to mobilize American finance. His first chance came with a fourth-growth, then called La Prieuré, a run-down property with an uninhabitable house (true to the name, it had been built in the sixteenth century as a Benedictine priory). His first attempt to buy it in 1950 was unsuccessful, but the new owner, a French woman, fell ill and Lichine snapped it up a couple of years later for the franc equivalent of a mere £8,000. A few weeks later a formerly outstanding second growth, Château Lascombes, came on the market for £25,000.

Given his reputation, Lichine had no problem finding the money from American investors who did not object when he turned La Prieuré into something of a showpiece, complete with floodlighting, even changing the name to Prieuré-Lichine. For Lichine, like Philippe de Rothschild, combines a decided flair for show business with an obsessive desire to improve his vineyards.

In the early 1950s, even the best vineyards were in a sad state. Cyril Ray describes how, at Léoville and Langoa after the war, "some of the vineyards had not been ploughed for two or three years; and it had been impossible to make new plantations or the normal replacements for vines that had died of old age or become unproductive, so that about one-quarter of the normal complement of vines was missing". It was not surprising that "other growers . . . took the quick, cheap and easy way out: they grubbed up sound but neglected vines in order to replant whole vineyards at a time although this meant reducing the average age of the vineyard and thus the quality of the wine". Ronald Barton only got "the old vines into good heart again . . . by repeated ploughings over two or three years to clear and clean the fields."

This combination of the hard work needed to reclaim the neglected land and the then prevailing low prices naturally discouraged many owners, and in the ten years after the war the area under vines in the Gironde fell by 50,000 acres to a level unknown for centuries.

The newcomers were few, but they were able to build up major holdings at relatively low prices, provided only that they were patient and aware, like Lichine, that, whereas the purchase of a major château like Lascombes could be concluded within a few weeks, buying the family plot from a peasant family could take years (Lichine shares this understanding with Philippe de Rothschild, another superficially impatient autocrat who realizes that "here things go very slowly, they take a generation to change").

Nevertheless Lichine took full advantage of the flexibility of the AOC rules. At Prieuré he bought 28 plots and more than doubled production from 30 to an average of 75 tonneaux. But it was Lascombes which he transformed most completely because it was a second growth and the increased production would therefore be worth more (in addition, La Prieuré is his home in France, whereas Lascombes was always far more of a business). When he bought it the château was producing a mere 35 tonneaux, but previously neglected parts of the estate, entitled to the name but which had fallen victims to the years of depression, enabled him nearly to double that amount. Then through an aggressive buying policy he increased production to the relatively enormous figure of 200 tonneaux—nearly a quarter of a million bottles a year—reckoned the limit that any major estate can produce while still retaining its reputation and sustaining the price appropriate to its class.

Lichine, still at nearly sixty-five a restlessly active publicist for himself, for his own wines, and indeed for wine in general, possesses the same mixture of qualities—the nerve, the taste,

the flair for publicity, the salesmanship—which had characterized
the founders of the Chartronnais' empires. But, by the time he
came on the scene, arteries had seized up and the coldness of
the welcome he was accorded froze deeper when he started
work on a personal revision of the 1855 Classification for his
book on French wines (this reflects the balance of his interests:
he devotes twice as much space to Burgundy as to the Gironde's
wines).

Nevertheless Lichine established his office in Margaux—up
the road from La Prieuré. At the time he was selling only
£200,000 worth of wine. But his importance was two-fold:
in the United States he was an incomparable and tireless propagandist, preaching the virtues of wine to audiences outside the
few cities where the habit of drinking imported wines had
previously been concentrated; in Bordeaux he was educating
a whole new generation of young apprentices who worked
with him and emerged to continue his work for themselves or
for other shippers. Previously the experience of working in
Bordeaux had been confined to the well-connected youngsters—
like Ian Campbell or Böhmers—who had worked with the
Chartronnais. Lichine founded another school, whose pupils
shared his decidedly more enterprising and aggressive views on
wine selling.

Lichine's initiatives were essentially long-term. They were
matched by similar moves among the French wine-growers in
Algeria. During the 1950s it steadily became apparent to them
that life there was never going to be the same again and they
looked to those parts of France where they could retire to
exercise their talents. Although the majority chose the South
of France, some hundreds did trickle into the Gironde over a
decade or more.

Their influence was beneficial since they were skilled, relatively well-off, and hungry to recreate in their native land the
immaculate estates they had supervised in their former home.
The pioneer was Nicholas Tari who in 1952 bought Château
Giscours. This is arguably the most beautiful estate in the
Médoc: over 175 acres of vines nestling in several hundred
more acres of lake and woodland, which had seen its best days
when owned by the Cruses before World War I. But when
Tari bought it, the estate was so run-down that it produced

only a thousand cases of wine. Tari restored it, planting vines on fifty previously neglected acres, and increasing production twenty-five-fold.

Tari was a rich early example of a trend. The only other major purchaser in the 1950s was very much a special case. In the mid-1950s the big English trading firm of John Holt— which had no apparent previous connection with wine—found itself with a great many francs in the Cameroons, then a French colony. The currency could not be brought back to Britain but could be invested in France. So Holt's bought Margaux's neighbour, the second growth, Rausan-Ségla, from the Cruses. (It had been brought into the family through Frederick Cruse, whose father-in-law owned it. The Cruses were famous for having a seemingly unfair proportion of sons among their offspring, and contriving to increase their patrimony through judicious alliances such as this.)

But these purchases did not conceal the fact that most of the Gironde was still a depressed area, for the rise in prices came only just in time to save the department from turning into one of those pockets of over-populated rural slum landscape which still disfigure the most surprising places in Western Europe. Indeed it has required a massive flight from the land—which has reduced the number of wine-growers in the department from nearly 60,000 just after the war to not much over 25,000 today—to permit the survivors to live in any sort of acceptable fashion. (Another factor has been the tractor, a piece of equipment which enables its possessor to increase the area of vines that can be cultivated by one family to nearly twenty acres, enough to provide a decent living if the wine is red and of acceptable quality. In 1952 there were only 3,000 tractors in the whole department: sixteen years later there were 20,000, and by now every serious wine-grower appears to have one, though there are still thousands of holdings where the owner is either old or has a full-time job and which should not really be counted.)

But until recently the Médoc, in particular, had a feudal appearance: the lords, many of them decidedly impoverished, lived in their castles, most of them distinctly decrepit, and the poor lived in hovels at the gates. This is no exaggeration: when two British groups took over Latour in the early 1960s,

they discovered that the workers' cottages still had earth floors—
and their condition brought tears to the normally unsentimental
eyes of the wife of the new managing director.

Another symptom of the class structure has been noticed by
every author and journalist to have visited the Médoc for the
past century and a half. The little towns and villages scattered
up and down the peninsula are grey and dreary; and, crucially
from a visitor's point of view, they lack the good restaurants
and small comfortable hotels which elsewhere are the minor
glories of rural France. Historically there simply has not been a
bourgeoisie numerous enough to support any.

Because the better wines did not sell for proportionally
higher prices in the 1950s, even the supposedly luckier owners
of 'crus bourgeois'—hundreds of which had been classified
as such in the 1930s—were hardly making ends meet. Even
at the end of the decade Allen Sichel spelled out the sums: it
cost £500 to plant an acre of vines, which produced no grapes
legally capable of being made into wine for three years. Subsequently they would earn only £50 for every acre of vines
out of expenses—assuming they could get the maximum
permitted yield from their grapes.

The marginal living to be derived from the better estates
even at the end of the 1950s was enough to deter any but the
most determined grower from building up his own estate.
Indeed the case of Henri Martin is outstanding because there
are so few like him in the Médoc, although elsewhere in the
Gironde there are a few growers of humble origins who have
built up proper estates, and a number of dynamic peasants
who have worked on building up the department's many co-
operatives. Martin, still, in his seventies, spare, sharp and
upright, is the son of a local cooper, descended from a long line
of local cellar-masters and labourers. Yet he shares many
attributes with Rothschild and Lichine—the biggest advertising
features in the Médoc are the giant wine bottle proclaiming
Henri Martin's home village, St. Julien, and the signs announcing
Lichine's Château Lascombes. He too is a showman, and a
patiently obsessional wine-grower. But there the similarity ends.
His first contact with a major château came at the end of the First
World War when his father used the cellars of the neighbouring
St. Pierre Bontemps at St. Julien to store his barrels. When

the owner proposed to sell the estate, Henri's father was forced to buy the cellars with the name attached. But later he had to sell the name, and his son's wine has always been sold as Château Gloria. His acquisitions came from outlying parcels of land belonging to his father's friend Désiré Cordier at Gruaud-Larose and Talbot and from other well-known names—the Léovilles, Duhart-Milon, Pichon-Longueville—eight different classified châteaux in all, four of them second growths. All his resources went into his wine: his home was a small flat above the ageing shed, and while there were vines to buy, it even remained uncarpeted. This frugality was rewarded; today he owns 120 acres of vines, producing 30,000 cases.

Martin is generally recognized in Bordeaux as a wine-maker of distinction (some would say genius). He is extremely selective with his own grapes—he used only a quarter of his harvest in the abundant but uneven year of 1973 to make Château Gloria, consigning the rest to his three lesser labels; and his reputation was good enough for him to be called on to rescue the estate at Château Latour where in the early 1960s he controlled for the first time the financial resources required to carry out the large-scale, long-term estate planning which had come so much more easily for Lichine—"I was offered the chance to win the Derby," says Martin.

Martin has come to symbolize the limits of the imagination and capabilities of a peasant—albeit one of genius—and the extent to which he could change the face of the Médoc. Martin's first step was to establish the name of his wine—one which even in the 1949 edition of Cocks and Feret was relegated very much to the 'also-rans', the tiny holdings not worth a separate description. Nevertheless, "to have my own wine", the same ambition which had spurred on Philippe de Rothschild, Martin started bottling all his own wine in 1950—at a time when virtually no château in the Médoc bottled more than a proportion. (Lichine was even more fanatical: he stampeded the tiniest growers in Burgundy into bottling their wine at their 'domaines' in his search for authenticity.)

But still the merchants would not pay more for Martin's wine (although it was carefully selected even then) than they would for any other St. Julien without a recognized château name. But Martin was lucky. Fonroque, the estate manager of Haut-

Brion, brought with him to Gloria the legendary Louis Vaudable, who ran Maxim's in Paris. Vaudable had just been awarded the contract for the catering on the first-class Pan-American flights to New York and was looking for a better-than-average claret to serve in individual quarter bottles. Gloria filled the bill admirably and a market in which the Chartronnais had always specialized suddenly demonstrated that it did not need them. Today Air France, reputedly the biggest single customer for claret in the world, buys a great deal direct from the Forner family, Spanish wine merchants who rebuilt La Rose-Trintaudon from nothing to a production of a million bottles a year.

Martin never liked the Pan-Am contract. Where a more sales-orientated wine maker would have been overjoyed at the opportunity to put his wine in front of some of the world's most frequent and well-heeled travellers, Martin was worried that the quality would not show up too well in bottles so small and in conditions so unlike those in which wine should, traditionally, be appreciated. But at least the Pan Am contract gave him his independence, and he has exploited it ever since.

Yet Martin has always managed to combine without undue strain the ability to sell his own produce in the course of his wider efforts as a propagandist for the Médoc (in the same way Lichine's enthusiasm for wine is general, not confined to, but always including, what he just happens to be selling at the time).

Martin's first step was pure propaganda: he had long admired the way the Chevaliers du Tastevin in Burgundy had set about popularizing their wines through a mixture of mock-medieval showmanship, combined with some serious wine-drinking. So, with an artist friend, he set about creating an entirely artificial, if historic-sounding, equivalent in Bordeaux. The result was the 'Commanderie du Bontemps du Médoc'—'Commanderie' because one of the medieval pilgrims' routes to the shrine of St. James of Compostella in Spain crossed the Gironde and the route was guarded by a company, or commanderie, of suitably militant holy men; 'Bontemps'—merely 'good time' elsewhere in France —because the same word is used for the small wooden bowl used to beat the egg-whites for fining the wine.*

The initiative was successful. Even the Chartronnais unbent

* When filled with wine, sugar, and thinly sliced fresh peaches it makes ideal afternoon refreshment for thirsty wine-bottlers.

sufficiently to turn up at the regular ceremonies—complete with trumpeters, red velvet 'medieval robes' topped by floppy tassled berets, orations extolling the virtues of the new 'commandeurs', generally people of some use, past or future to the Médoc, and terminating with the inevitable four-hour lunch, the courses interspersed with more speeches and song. Inevitably other districts had to follow suit: there are now a dozen or so similar fraternities in the Gironde, ranging from the Gentilshommes de Fronsac to the Connetablie de Guyenne. But then the Bordelais enjoy this sort of palaver. Pierre Ginestet founded the Académie du Vin de Bordeaux shortly after the war. This started as a body designed and dedicated to defending Bordeaux's wine and guarding its reputation in the same devoted fashion as the Académie Française watches over the purity of the French language. Over the years, the Academy has dwindled into a dining club meeting at increasingly irregular intervals.

As a grower who had already shown considerable independence and initiative, Martin was a natural choice to head the CIVB, whose president he became in 1956. For fifteen subsequent years he acted as a tireless and successful propagandist and, less successfully, as a link between growers and merchants.

The gulf between the growers and the merchants was still huge: when he organized tours of the Chartronnais' cellars for the cellar-masters of the Médoc, these vital craftsmen had never met their equivalents at the merchants', who in most cases were responsible for cherishing, ageing and bottling their wines. And he encouraged other obvious initiatives—like inviting the 'sommeliers' (wine waiters) from leading restaurants in Paris and the Riviera for regular visits to Bordeaux.

But the gaps were too big to be filled by one man, or one generation of men, and today Martin is bitter. "It was a waste of time," he says. "I was beaten by the Chartronnais." The bitterness is understandable, but there was another side to the argument: in their age-old suspicion of the merchants, even growers as outward-looking and sales-minded as Martin would not listen to harsh truths about the market if they came from the mouths of their historic enemies. Martin himself has to admit that the growers, conditioned by generations of servitude, had no compunction when dealing with a merchant, even one trying to help them. One year he persuaded his friend Désiré

Cordier to take his neighbours' wine at a guaranteed price, to encourage them to improve its quality. The next year most of them turned up with miserable specimens, relying on Cordier's pledge to take the whole of their production.

Martin would not have felt so isolated if his father had plied his craft in St. Emilion rather than in St. Julien. He would have been perfectly at home in the small hill-town and in the little village of Pomerol which stands between it and the port of Libourne. While Martin was embarking on his pioneering efforts the 'Libournais'—the wine growers who traditionally sold their wine through Libourne rather than Bordeaux—were carrying out the full programme which he could only realize in part.

The Libournais were lucky: for their historic social structure and their relationships with their neighbours and friends at Libourne who sold their wine favoured joint action as clearly as the feudal, individualistic structure of the Médoc, and its relationship with Bordeaux, fostered an individualism which bordered on anarchy. For the Libournais were small land-holders, with a long tradition of independence.

At a superficial level this meant that the 'traditional' institution Martin had to invent in the Médoc with his Commanderie had existed in St. Emilion for eight centuries. With the existence of a town of such antiquity came the legacy of the 'Jurade'. In the Middle Ages this expression represented the citizens of a town who had sworn an oath of allegiance to it, and subsequently formed the small group which then ran its affairs. It was resurrected by the St. Emilionnais after World War II as an entirely suitable title for the body which concerned itself with the quality and promotion of their wines. Even more appositely, the 'new' Jurade, like the original, consisted of a relatively small number of the richer citizens of the town, mostly those owning the better estates on or near the 'Montagne'— the summit of the hill. In every possible sense of the word they looked down on the lesser growers who owned land on the 'Côtes'—the slopes—and, even more completely, on those in the villages round the base of the hill away from Libourne, each with its own little 'appellation', none of any importance or distinction. But together they occupied a wine-growing area of 17,000 acres, bigger than the Médoc.

Even the better-off, like M. Manoncourt, who owned Figeac, one of the district's finest wines, and who dominated the town for years, were not major landowners, and there were few aristocrats—one of the rare exceptions was the late Comte Malet-Roquefort of La Gaffelière, who owned his own pack of deerhounds. Virtually everyone else—and there are seven hundred growers in St. Emilion alone—is of the same humble stock which is the norm in other French wine-growing districts. Where it is exceptional for the owners of an estate in the Médoc to live there, it is equally unusual for a St. Emilionnais or an owner at Pomerol to live anywhere else. These social origins are reflected in the houses, most of which are modest villas (Pomerol resembles a suburban market garden dotted with bungalows and sturdy if unremarkable grey residences). And the holdings are, relatively, tiny. Château Ausone, historically the most famous in St. Emilion, is still only 17 acres: and only thirty or so properties are over the 50-acre size which is the minimum for a decent holding in the Médoc.

The differences between the Médocains and the 'Libournais' are more than social. The wine is made very largely from the Merlot variety of grapes—against a maximum of fifteen per cent in the Médoc (a distinction noticeable in the 'fruitier', more Burgundian, less astringent taste of the Libournais wines). This variety ripens earlier, but is more subject to frost than the Cabernet Sauvignon which dominates the Médoc. So St. Emilion can flourish in a year like 1967 when other grapes tended to be unripe, or, like 1964, when the Gironde was affected by late rains; but suffered appallingly from the 1956 frosts. That year St. Emilion produced a mere tenth of the wine it had harvested in 1953 and production continued to average only two-thirds of the pre-frost levels until 1962—and, for ten years after the frost, apparently healthy vines would collapse from the long-term damage done that dreadful February.

The 'Libournais' tradition differs between St. Emilion and Pomerol. Before the war St. Emilion had been the fief of the Abbé Bergey, whose presence in the same cell had so much upset 'Oncle' Louis, and who formed the epicentre of the town's power structure. After the war much the same group, though now without Bergey, continued to dominate the town. In the early 1950s they were worried by the progress made by the lesser growers below them. They saw that the INAO had carried out a proper classification in Graves, the first undertaken in the Gironde since 1855. So they did not have to rely on the brokers, but called in the INAO to make their new grading system official.

The INAO found a fair degree of chaos, with owners deciding that they were 'first growths', 'exceptional' or classed in some other meritorious fashion almost at will. Even the new severely streamlined lists shocked the Médocains. For when the list was published in October 1954—to come into force with the 1955 vintage—it was found that there were twelve 'Premier Grands Crus Classés' in St. Emilion, two of which, Ausone and Cheval Blanc, were elevated on to their own mini-summit, and sixty-two other 'Grands Crus Classés', one more than the whole Médoc had been deemed worthy of a century earlier.

Even though some of the new aristocracy were from the 'slopes' yet the ruling class made sure that no wine unworthy of the name of their town should be sold. The INAO had already decreed that no fewer than 300 out of the 1300 or so vineyards that had previously been entitled to the name should be struck off the list of 'true' St. Emilionnais. Then, in a truly revolutionary step, the Jurades agreed with the INAO that for the first time in France the award of the precious 'Appellation d'Origine Contrôlée' label would be awarded only after a wine had been tasted—the only way that the 'AOC' label would actually mean anything to the customer. The St. Emilionnais have—in general—managed to avoid the temptation of being too kind to their neighbours' wines. Indeed in three years in the 1960s only basic St. Emilion was produced; not a drop was awarded a higher, narrower 'appellation'.

The new classification, not to mention compulsory tasting, should have showed the way forward to the Médocains. Instead panic set in at the thought of customers (especially Americans, to the Bordelais a word synonymous with a combination of money and ignorance) mistaking a mere Premier Grand Cru Classé from St. Emilion with one of the *real* aristocracy.

For the Chartronnais and their English customers had, for a century, largely ignored or underestimated St. Emilion and Pomerol. The traditional guide-books of the nineteenth century had followed the lead, so had the brokers in 1855 (a classification which, supposedly, included all the wines produced in the Gironde). Even the St. Emilionnais' triumph at the 1867 Exhibition only started to stir interest. Only a few Chartronnais—notably Jean Calvet and, later, Christian Cruse—made any effort to sell St. Emilion's wines. And none of the old guard bought châteaux in the district—the pioneers in this as in so many other respects were Ginestet and Cordier, both of whom purchased estates in St. Emilion as part of their balanced holdings representing all the worthwhile wine-growing areas in the Gironde.

If St. Emilion was underestimated, Pomerol was largely ignored. For it seemed an even less classy version of St. Emilion which was at least a town with a distinguished history, with a group of 'good old boys' running it, whereas Pomerol is a hamlet, not even a proper village, a mere 1,500 acres squeezed between the railway line and main road out of Libourne and the slopes of the St. Emilion hill. Never mind that a group of St. Emilion's most distinguished châteaux, including Cheval Blanc, lie on the boundary between the two, Pomerol was, and indeed remains, a largely peasant affair.

Indeed such is its social homogeneity that it still refuses to judge its neighbour's wines, has stuck out solidly for nearly a quarter of a century since St. Emilion went in for compulsory tasting, refusing to copy its neighbour. But then it never needed to. For Pomerol in the past half-century discovered the keys to success—though ones available only to small growers who, like the Burgundians, found themselves producing limited quantities of wines that were widely appreciated. The vital elements were: direct sales, Belgium, and Corréziens.

The three went together. The 'Corréziens', like their neighbours the 'Auvergnats', share a similar origin. The Auvergne and the Corrèze are both spectacularly beautiful and almost equally poverty-stricken departments in the Massif Central mountains hundreds of miles east of the Gironde. Traditionally their inhabitants have escaped from the poverty of their homeland down the Dordogne river which connects them with Libourne, loading their few worldly possessions on to small boats which they broke up and burnt or sold on arrival. After the First World War half a dozen established themselves as far down river as Pauillac, where they threatened to form a trade association of their own. This really shocked the Médocains, used to thinking of Bordeaux as the wine capital of the region. But they encountered no such resistance in Libourne and the areas round about. Many would buy small properties in Pomerol and begin by hawking their wares from door to door in the north of France and in Belgium, touring the region by rail. The Corrézians were so poor that they often spent the night in railway waiting rooms—or so they would tell their more cosseted children and grandchildren in later life. Very often they sold their wine door to door, not only by the case, but also in small barrels (each containing six dozen) which still fill many a chai in Libourne. The customers were, at first, professional men, prepared to bottle their own wine, eager for a bargain, but in the post-war years the more skilled workers have accumulated enough to become good customers—for in Belgium as in France wine and food are appreciated by all classes.

More ambitious Corrézians would sell to shops and to co-ops. There was room for everyone—the Chartronnais were never very interested in selling such small quantities retail, and even in Belgium the market was so splintered that the smallest seller could find his niche. The competition for the newcomers came mostly from the Belgians themselves—one of the half-dozen best châteaux in Pomerol, Vieux-Château Certan, was bought by a Belgian merchant, M. Georges Thienpoint, as long ago as 1924.

But for all the competition, there is now only one name which counts in Pomerol: Moueix,* a family (or rather two branches of a single family) which has established a firm grip on the district to an extent unequalled in the history of the Gironde. The senior branch has followed the orthodox pattern. Antoine floated down river in 1906 and bought a small property. His business flourished, and his heirs—his grandson Armand and his nephew, Antoine's great-grandson Bernard—now own a number of reasonably well-known châteaux, including two of St. Emilion's Grand Crus Classés. They still work fantastically hard 'peasants'' hours. Since his father died in early middle

---

* There are a number of Corrézian merchants whose surnames end in -eix, which means 'coming from' in the local dialect. Mou-eix means 'coming from the river bank'—the Palus.

age a few years ago, Bernard, for instance, has regularly got to his office before 5 a.m., works a seven-day week and cannot bear to spend more than a few days on holiday any year (the family still retains a feeling, almost a superstition, for its roots, and has never sold the tiny farm in the Corrèze from which they escaped not so long ago).

This devotion to hard work has brought its rewards. A few years ago they invaded Bordeaux and quietly bought a controlling interest in Schröder and Schÿler, the very heart of the Chartronnais (the purchase was less surprising because the firm had gone virtually broke in the Depression, and had since been riven by a bitter family quarrel).

The contrast was complete: the Moueixes lived and had their cellars at Taillefer, a modest enough château on the outskirts of Libourne—characteristically the vines are well-tended, but the lawns are rough. At the Schÿlers' own Château Kirwan, the opposite was the case, and the wine—a third growth—had fallen below its due standard.

But 'A. Moueix and Fils' has been overshadowed by the fabled success of one member of the other branch of the family, Jean-Pierre—though 'A' may still have a bigger business than 'J-P'. Jean-Pierre Moueix is undoubtedly the Gironde's most notable personality, a worthy successor to Hermann Cruse, Jean Calvet, and 'Oncle' Louis. He is a big man, of a lordly presence, florid, theatrical gestures and a deep, resonant voice which he uses to lull his listeners with a constant flow of elegiac French. Moueix can convey an impression that you are doing him an honour merely by listening, let alone buying from him. For he is a consummate salesman: he has been selling wine now for over forty-five years, but claims never to have failed to sell his wares wherever he has gone.

His manner, which critics might find somewhat unctuous, resembles that of the late Lord Duveen, the arch-salesman of works of art to American millionaires. But he had to start the hard way. During the depression his father bought the modest Château Fonroque in St. Emilion and, at the age of eighteen, young Jean-Pierre was despatched to Belgium to sell its wine. Within a couple of days he had disposed of the lot to the trade—for he has never, or so he claims, sold a drop to a private individual. He promptly became what the French call an 'agent multicarte'—a travelling salesman representing more than one company—and immediately after the war founded his own company, based on his strength in Belgium, where he is still the biggest supplier, Holland, and Northern France.

Moueix (now reaching an age where people are beginning to call him 'papa') differed from his Chartronnais predecessors not only in his social origins, but in his inherited love of the land, and in a quite remarkable visual flair. Within a few years of setting up on his own he had bought Trotanoy, one of the three or four best in Pomerol and, just before the classification of the wines of St. Emilion, he acquired Château Magdelaine— one of its dozen 'Premiers grand crus classés'. Later he added a number of others, mostly in Pomerol, and tied up the sales of so many others that his position was a virtual monopoly. Indeed, because of his insistence on quality—a passion fully reflected in his prices—he forms in a sense a one-firm classification system.

But his greatest triumph was in elevating the status of Pomerol's most famous wine, Château Petrus. The English had virtually ignored it before the war (although it had figured on several informal lists as Pomerol's outstanding product). It is a curious phenomenon: geographically, it was until the mid-1960s merely sixteen acres on a clay outcrop in the middle of Pomerol (the estate now includes another eleven of the best acres formerly owned, on the same tiny clay patch, by Château Gazin).

At the end of the war a M. Loubat finished acquiring the estate, but it was his widow who, helped by Jean-Pierre Moueix, built up its reputation. Mme Loubat herself came from a well-known wine-growing family. She was proud of her wine: in Edmund Penning-Rowsell's words she "never made the mistake of underestimating the value of her product". Women wine makers that determined can be formidable—Mme Fournier, a Bordelaise settled in St. Emilion, turned Château Canon into one of the best wines of the district—but Mme Loubat found a natural ally in Moueix, who sold the wine exclusively from 1947 on, and in 1961, on Mme Loubat's death, bought Petrus. Together they created a 'new' first growth, almost a cult. For the estate is so small that its price can now be held at, or above, that demanded by the top growths of the Médoc—cynics, denying that the price or reputation of a wine are drastically affected by its quality, should compare the rise in Petrus with the simultaneous fall in the value of the Château Ausone.

Moueix likes to put it about that he was forced to sell a number of Monets in order to buy Petrus. It is far more likely that he meant to sell them anyway, for he is a restless collector of paintings. His home, Château Videlot, is an unremarkable château on the outskirts of Libourne, remarkable only for its setting, a few hundred yards from the Dordogne, with a view through the water-meadows, properly framed with woods, in summer a shimmery landscape strongly reminiscent of the country childhoods allegedly enjoyed before World War I by nostalgic littérateurs.

The contents are extraordinary, a collection of modern art unequalled in the area, and remarkable for its quality anywhere in the world. Whether it be a Picasso, a Vlaminck, a Dérain, a Francis Bacon, a Dufy or a Warhol, it was chosen not for the name but clearly for its intrinsic quality, and in most cases bought before the artist acquired his present eminence. The selection has only one parallel in the Gironde: and that, inevitably, is at Mouton-Rothschild.

Immediately after the war, Rothschild had returned to his 1924 experiment and commissioned a different label every year from a well-known artist—the only exception was 1953, the centenary of the château's purchase by his family when, in an uncharacteristic fit of filial piety, he reverted to the sober old label which had served to promote the wine before his arrival at Mouton. The Rothschild labels are of varying degrees of quality and suitability (not every artist's talents can be expressed in the rigid format of a tiny oblong label). But, like everything else he does, the experiment was a personal gesture which was also good for publicity purposes.

A far greater success was the wine museum he devised in partnership with his second wife, the late Baronne Pauline, for Philippe de Rothschild's first wife had died in a concentration camp and after the war he married an American lady of charm, flair and enthusiasm, Pauline Fairfax Potter. He had inherited some rather heavy and over-decorated German seventeenth-century drinking vessels and together they dreamt up the idea of a museum. Given the characters involved, this inevitably emerged, not as an earnestly didactic affair, but an exhilarating demonstration of the very varied ways in which artists, tapestry-weavers, glass-makers, silversmiths and potters have celebrated the qualities of wine through the ages.

Collecting the objects and arranging them in the former cellars at Mouton took over a decade. But the result was unique: virtually every object—Chinese, Venetian, Italian, German— is beautiful in itself and arranged not to demonstrate the cleverness of the museum's creators, but to emphasize the inherent qualities of the items. The result, in Cyril Ray's words, is "an overall effect of light, space and elegance. Some glass cases are set into the walls, some are free-standing, at irregular angles to each other. Some are lined with coloured silks to set off Italian terracotta or Chinese blue-and-white. Some are lit from below to enhance the engraving of a Flemish or Venetian glass."

The museum was originally the most Rothschildian of private gestures. But inevitably it has also become a major tourist attraction, indeed the only real initiative taken by any estate owner to satisfy the artistic curiosity of the thousands of consumers, actual or potential, of claret.

Moueix is a great admirer of another aspect of Rothschild's talents—in his translation into French of the haunting if complex works of Elizabethan poets. Their collections have in common not only the underlying flair of the collectors, but their uniqueness. In a business, whose greatest pride is in collections made by grandparents displayed in houses acquired by the same generations, Rothschild and Moueix stand out as innovatory, not as mere inheritors.

But, for all the beauty of his collection, Moueix needed to sell a lot of wine, and for five years after the frosts of 1956 there was not enough for him at home, in Pomerol or St. Emilion. Fortunately for him, at precisely the moment he turned his attention to Bordeaux, he found ideal scope for his speculative gambler's temperament.

16

The Chartronnais' last stand

"In one of those inexplicable French economic explanations the price of wine will not go down because it has been a successful year. The previous years, 1956, 1957, 1958, were bitter and cold years for the wine growers, and very little wine was made. This is reasonable. But this year, with wine in quantity, the price is still going up.

We made the mistake of asking one of the growers why.

'Because,' he said, as if talking to a child, 'it's a great wine and everybody wants it.'

So much for the economics of wine."

Art Buchwald, like many Americans, was discovering the particular quirks of Bordelais logic in the autumn of 1959, a year which marked a major turning-point in the history of the Bordeaux wine trade. For seven and a half centuries the area's finest wines had been sold to the English. But in 1959 the Americans took the palm: that year, for the first time in history, they paid on average more for the wine they bought from Bordeaux than the English. In terms of total value the Americans, still a quarter behind the English level in 1960, had overtaken the traditional buyers in 1962, and kept the lead in 1963. Even though the relative positions altered later in the decade, when the American market stagnated while English buyers turned increasingly to Bordeaux, yet the principle had been established. In 1959 the Americans had taken over the historic rôle as principal buyers of the finest wines and, consequently, pace-setters for prices. For a decade, however, Bordeaux shut its collective eyes to the impact of this change.

Even without the arrival of the Americans, 1959 would have been a remarkable year. Its inheritance was an unhappy one: prices, which had soared as a result of the 1956 frosts, remained high, especially for the most basic wines, and the customers were apparently unwilling to buy at the increased levels. Even a devaluation of 20 per cent in the French franc in September 1957 only offset some of the increase, and did not prevent exports from slumping by a third in early 1958—at a time when sales of other French wines were soaring (during the last half of the 1950s the proportion of French wine exports accounted for by the Gironde dropped from a half to a third).

Within a few months the scene was transformed. It was probably triggered by a further devaluation of the franc in December 1958, which left it at only two-thirds of its 1956 level. French costs did not rise appreciably, so the combined devaluations restored prices—apart from those of St. Emilion and Pomerol, which were still short of wine—to near their pre-frost levels, at least so far as foreign buyers were concerned.

Because of the pioneering efforts in the USA of Schoonmaker and Lichine, because of the increasing prosperity of countries like Sweden (which for a time overtook Britain as a buyer of fine claret), because of the increasing conviction during a hot summer of a peculiarly fine vintage to come, the excitement mounted steadily, dissipating the frettish atmosphere of the previous year. Buchwald's article appeared in early October when, in Sichel's words, "Bordeaux is convinced that the whole world will want its 1959s, and Bordeaux may well be right. That is the dominant feature of the market today".

But they were writing before the final accolade was given to the vintage by simultaneous articles the following month in *Time* and *Newsweek*. These confirmed to the American public that 1959 was indeed the 'vintage of the century'. It was not, of course: 1929 and 1945 had both been finer, and in the following years the phrase became normal (in 1964 Allan Sichel reckoned that "out of the last six vintages, three have been hailed prematurely as the vintage of the century"), but 1959 was the pioneer.

More crucially, the market was still so narrow that it did not take many orders to cause hysteria. (Even in 1957, for example, Bordeaux's biggest market, Belgium, had spent only £1,150,000 on its wine). The effect of American interest was the greater because it concentrated on the few 'named' growths which had been for so long the favourites of, and often monopolized by, the English market, and so because little first-class wine had been produced in the two previous years. The 1958 vintage, indeed, was haughtily described by Sichel as "very useful to countries

7

with a large regular consumption and of considerably less interest to the UK."

The results were simple: the first growths opened at just under double the level they had fetched in 1955, the last comparable vintage; and lesser wines jumped even more—over two and a quarter times. But the demand was still confined to named châteaux, for ordinary 'Bordeaux rouge' was only an eighth up on its post-frost levels.

But if the quantity of wine bought by the Americans increased sharply, the pattern of trade remained relatively undisturbed. Even the prices were not remarkable by historic standards; certainly nowhere near those paid at the height of the boom of the 1860s. In October 1868 far more wine changed hands than in 1959–60, and at higher prices. The 6,000 francs a tonneau paid for Latour, Lafite and Margaux that month was in modern money over twice the 15,412 francs paid for the 1959 first growths.

These 1959 figures, however, conceal the rise of 50 per cent or more that took place immediately after the opening prices had been set early in 1960. Speculation continued unabated, naturally spreading over into the 1960 vintage. Sichel was reflecting the trade's worries when he wrote in May, "Vintage reports of the future may have to be written before the vintage, if present tendencies continue. The majority of the Bordeaux wine trade— growers and shippers alike—deplore the custom of dealing in wine that does not exist." He tried to pooh-pooh the trend: "The transactions in 1960 wines which have so far taken place are picturesque but insignificant. The fever may take hold and spread quickly. The principle is irresponsible and speculative—it only becomes a possibly justifiable risk about the month of August."

The blame was placed firmly on outsiders: "There are certain intermediary groups who, being without responsibility, are tempted by the general shortage of good wine to 'get in first' and there are a few sellers and buyers willing to gamble on the risk involved. Not all the buyers are French shippers. We do not expect the custom to continue, since by the very nature of the transaction either the buyer or the seller is eventually dissatisfied."

Sichel was right: but almost certainly did not guess the trick which nature played in 1961. Early that year many growers, emboldened by their success in 1960 (a year of no outstanding quality), were naturally prepared to sell what they thought would be about a third of the vintage. But then came a late frost, wiping out two-thirds of the potential harvest. The resulting vintage was of superb quality, the first to be truly comparable with that of 1945 (by that time the 1959s were emerging as excellent wines, though the vintage of a decade rather than a century), but the quantity was tiny and the prices correspondingly higher than those of 1959. But, thanks to the Americans, the demand was so heavily focused on the first-growth clarets that 1961 can be pinpointed as the year when their prices really started to escalate away from the Gironde's other products. In 1948 the first growths had sold for under five times the price of AOC Bordeaux Rouge; by 1959 the difference was fourteen times (far higher than the historical norm) and by 1961 it was a seemingly crazy twenty-four times. The lesser 'named' wines followed some distance behind: and although the owners of the big four liked to claim that the prices they demanded were for the benefit of the whole trade, this became decreasingly true throughout the late 1950s and 1960s as the demand increasingly polarized. (At the other end of the spectrum, there was consistent over-production of basic wines, and constant encouragement by the government to dig up vines. There was also a complex system of export subsidies—or rather a two-price system, higher for the French consumer, lower for the export market, but one which allowed the exporters to make a handsome profit. This lasted for only a couple of years after it was introduced in 1959.)

The growers who had sold 'sur souches' learnt a severe lesson in 1961 when they were helpless spectators, watching the prices of their wines escalate without being able to satisfy the demand. Most had very little wine to spare above the 'theoretical' third they had pre-sold. In a few cases the vintage was so small that the growers could not even deliver the amounts they had sold on the vine. They were not likely to sell before the harvest again in a hurry.

The amount of wine available in the open Bordeaux market was also diminished by a last Herculean effort to beat back the tide of outsiders. Roland du Vivier of de Luze and Emmanuel Cruse looked back to the days when the major shippers could control the market by taking abonnements between them of most of the major châteaux. This was the origin of what became known as 'Group A'—the eight shippers considered the most powerful in Bordeaux. Seven were names familiar for a century past: Calvet, Cruse, de Luze, Eschenauer, Ginestet, Delor, Barton & Guestier. But there was one outsider: Jean-Pierre Moueix had made so much money out of his happy speculation on the 1959 vintage, had become such a powerful force in Pomerol and St. Emilion, and these areas had emerged as so important, that Emmanuel Cruse insisted that he be admitted to the club.

The pecking order was clear: below the eight in Group A was another band, Group B, including Nathaniel Johnston, and Schröder and Schÿler, who were entitled to buy from Group A at prices fixed a few per cent above the basic purchase price.

The big eight brought with them a great many valuable châteaux; either because they owned them—Pierre Ginestet possessed the whole of Château Margaux as well as Cos d'Estournel and a number of other châteaux—or because of historic links. Some old-timers still hark back to Group A as the last attempt to provide an orderly market for Bordeaux's wines. If it had survived, claim its defenders, it would have slowed down or even prevented the speculative excesses of 1971–73. The (unspoken) assumption is that the ring could have continued to keep the growers down and prevented outsiders from influencing the market.

From the beginning, however, the ring had sizeable gaps. The Cordiers stayed clear of it, and a number of important estates—including two leading second growths, Léoville-Lascases and Ducru-Beaucaillou—refused to become involved; and even the members did not automatically bring all their production with them—the Cruses, for instance, reserved the right to sell Pontet-Canet. Moreover the member firms were not large or well-financed. As production climbed in the 1960s, following the replantings necessitated by the 1956 frosts and encouraged by the rise in prices since 1955, their narrow financial base was inevitably eroded, especially when they had to take on too much wine from poor vintages.

But the underlying problems were more serious: the ring members continued to compete, and the whole effort was an attempt to re-create a long-lost era, when the merchants involved could control the narrow world of Bordeaux. The competition remained real enough: "they made lots of rules and followed very few of them," is the summing-up of François Gardère, a leading broker. Two or three of the firms might be selling the same wine in the same market at very different prices. For although they were all working to an agreed price schedule the temptation to cheat was overwhelming, especially for members whose ideas of accountancy were pretty elementary, and who tended to overlook the importance of such elements as overheads and interest rates when calculating their profits. The system was also somewhat leaky—with constant allegations that members of Group B, assured of a supply of wine, were undercutting their bigger brothers in Group A, by selling wines soon after they were bought, reducing their own costs to a minimum.

Commercially the system could be by-passed: the state-buying monopolies of Sweden, Finland and Norway, who between them accounted for perhaps a tenth of Bordeaux's outlets, formed a buying ring far more effective than Group A. But, in any case, they were, as one observer put it "feather-bedding . . . the ring was turning merchants into mere commission takers . . . As merchants your living came from being quick on your toes . . . it was the nadir of Bordeaux commercialism . . . they were becoming rentiers, living off their percentages, rather than entrepreneurs." Indeed Groups A and B probably marked the start of the process which over the following fifteen years transformed the traditional 'négociant-éleveurs', responsible for ageing and cherishing the wine, into mere middle-men, financially and commercially unable to act as principals, but merely living off percentages, like better-paid brokers.

Nevertheless, whatever its inherent weaknesses, the ring held together, nominally at least, for some years admitting other houses as these grew more important. The basic dream was that two successive sizeable good vintages would suffice to demonstrate to the growers that demand had limits, in price and amount, a lesson which would be the more convincing if the second vintage were a very large one—in other words they were looking back to the vintages of 1899 and 1900 which had provided the world with such splendid clarets at such 'reasonable' prices.

They had to wait rather a long time—though only at the top end of their market. The big 1962 vintage fulfilled some of the conditions. But the world was so short of wine after the tiny vintage in the previous year that the prices of named châteaux fell only to their 1959 levels. Nevertheless the demand for more ordinary wine was so sensitive that the price of ordinary Bordeaux reverted to its 1956 levels. So a small grower had to sell just over forty hectolitres of wine for every hectare merely to recoup his costs—and in many cases this was the maximum yield he was allowed by the authorities. In the mid-1960s cost inflation made the situation even worse, and the contrast between the small growers, virtually forced to cheat in order to live, and the relative handful of major proprietors became more noticeable than for a long time—during the preceding seventy-five years, growers big and small had shared a common misery.

If the growers of ordinary claret could only just survive, the thousands of growers of white wine, big and small, sweet and dry, had fallen into a pitiable condition. Tastes had turned full circle. The days of free-spending Russian grand-dukes had long gone. So virtually all the makers of Sauternes and Barsac had to adapt to support prices based on strength rather than quality. Increased alcoholic strength meant adding vast amounts of sugar, so in the 1950s and 1960s they ruined their reputation by pumping out wines whose sweetness was obviously based on sugar rather than on the grapes themselves. Cheap, sweet, wines became the novice's introduction to wines, accessible syrups to be spurned when the consumer had more experience and more money.

In 1967 the growers, scared at the dreadful wines made under the appellations Barsac and Sauternes in three consecutive bad years, 1963, 1964 (those late rains) and 1965, resolved to apply the law and use compulsory tastings to eliminate poorer wines. The first year they did so, three-fifths of the 1966 vintage—a splendid one—was disqualified. This statistic points up how nominal and pointless the whole elaborate apparatus of 'AOC' could be if the growers involved lacked any pride in their wine, or any hope of selling it at a better price if they did insist on proper standards. (And, as Peter Sichel pointed out, once they were producing a wine of a quality high and consistent enough to warrant legal protection, they would no longer require the disciplines legally associated with the AOC regulations).

But by that time it was too late: the combined effects of fashion and a legacy of poor wines prevented any recovery for the 'Sauternais' and the 'Barsacins' for a decade to come. The situation was not much better where the growers, encouraged by the government, turned to making drier wines as they did in large numbers, for the same problems confronted them. During a decade when numbers of other dry or 'fruity' French white wines, from Chablis, Muscadet and Alsace, were enhancing their reputation and the prices they could command, the Gironde's Graves and Entre-Deux-Mers remained characterless, often associated with the sulphur used too freely to stabilize the wine. Indeed the lack of unity in the trade has borne most hardly on the white wine makers of Bordeaux, because of their historic separation from the market-place. Growers elsewhere felt confident enough to impose their own high standards and were able to conquer markets in France and abroad because the organizations selling their wine—the co-ops and the relatively small merchants—were trusted by the growers, and working closely with them.

In Bordeaux, despite the firmness of their grip on the vast majority of proprietors, the shippers had to wait until the mid-1960s to demonstrate to the select few that things had really returned to 'normal'.

For nature took a hand: the 1963 vintage was an all-time horror. Most of the châteaux did not sell any wine under their own name that terrible year. And some of the rest later recalled their wine from the customers, claiming without any great conviction that there had been such a sudden onrush of demand that they needed any surplus wine to satisfy the new buyers.

After a patchy vintage in 1964*—the year when a deluge descended on 8 October to ruin the chances of growers looking for that extra degree of ripeness and alcoholic strength which comes from picking later than your neighbour—stocks had risen to record levels. But much of the wine was from the virtually unsaleable 1963 vintage, and the situation was not helped by the poor vintage in 1965. "Even the ebullient optimism of the Gascon," wrote Peter Sichel, "is dampened by the September rainfall, which was more than three times the average and followed a heatless summer . . . the grapes . . . for the most part still green imitations of what a ripe grape should look like." It was only after the splendid vintage of 1966 and the bigger and

* This was acclaimed, prematurely, as yet another 'vintage of the century', most publicly by M. Pisani, the French Minister of Agriculture. When the skies opened, the weather was said to be committing "lèse Pisani".

rather less highly regarded 1967 that the shippers' historic conditions for controlling the market—large stocks of saleable wine from
two successive vintages of reputable quality—were fulfilled (for
the first time, curiously, since 1952–53). But 1968 proved to be
another problem year after nearly three times as much rain as
usual fell in August, and only the most disciplined growers—like
Cordier and Jean-Eugène Borie at Ducru-Beaucaillou—produced
wine worthy of their name.

So by the end of 1968 the members of the ring had to face the
fact that, in three out of the eight years since they started their
arrangement, they had been forced to take on wines which were
either difficult or impossible to sell. This, of course, was one of
the risks of 'abonnements' especially when practised on such a
large scale, but in the 1960s nature did seem to declare its dis-
approval of the system with especial clarity.

Nevertheless the Chartronnais still clung to the idea that life
was not changing fundamentally. And indeed Bordeaux as a
whole spent more of its time and energy in the 1960s examining
its own navel, scratching at its oldest sore, the classification of
1855 and its possible revision, than looking outward and learning
more about the rapidly changing commercial environment in
which it was operating. For, superficially, the figures seemed
reassuring. Exports rose steadily through the years and the prices
they had to pay the growers—apart from the first growths—
seemed finally to return to an acceptable level. So Bordeaux felt
it could indulge itself.

The arsonist who fanned the flames of a controversy which
had never been entirely quenched was, not surprisingly, Philippe
de Rothschild. Before the war he had been the man most responsible for the activities of the small informal group which represented the interests of first growths, and Mouton had regularly
sold for the same as, or even for more than, Lafite. But after the
war his status was challenged by his outspoken, undiplomatic
cousin Elie, who proved a worthy opponent. Elie, a man with a
disconcerting resemblance to a sardonic Jewish eagle, came back
from an unpleasant spell as a prisoner of war in Germany to
restore Lafite to its historic rightful position. His return was
memorable: he called the workers to a series of meetings at
8 a.m., and after a few days when none of them bothered to turn
up, the message got through and Lafite soon became a by-word

for its spick and span appearance and the absolute correctness of every aspect of its activities. He also ensured that the group of 'first growths' was placed on an officially correct basis, thus naturally excluding Mouton.

For Elie and Philippe made no secret of their mutual dislike, Elie saw no reason why his cousin should be included, however informally, in the ranks of the first growths, and being the man he is, he made the point bluntly and clearly. But—contrary to prevailing opinion in Bordeaux—he appears not to have actively hindered his cousin's long compaign to achieve official first-growth status.

So began Philippe de Rothschild's long march. Before he could even attempt to ensure that his wine was accorded its proper distinction, he had first to invent an official mechanism to carry through a new classification—no longer could he rely on charity as he had done before the war. His first impulse was to act through the wider association of all the growths classed in 1855 presided over at the time by the Marquis de Lur-Saluces (a man of considerable talent as a linguist, who acted as official translator when Kruschev visited France in the late 1950s). This merely led to a blazing row. Many of the other owners were angry with Lur-Saluces anyway because he had not fought against the official classification made by St. Emilion in 1955—a cleverly chosen date, easily confused with 1855, and bearing with it all the apparatus of 'premiers grands crus' (no one seems to have worried so much about the equally official classification of the Graves, presumably because the wines from the Graves did not represent such an obvious independent threat to the supremacy of the Médoc).

Rothschild accused Lur-Saluces of having automatically forefeited his job because he had not tried to protest against the St. Emilionnais' dastardly plot. And his retort, redolent with centuries of aristocratic disdain for Jews and other upstarts, that "if you can't inherit a title you can always buy one", confirmed Rothschild in his belief that any new classification must be done in the most official possible fashion. Two years later a motion was accepted to start on a new classification. The problem was that no official mechanism existed.

In 1959 the situation was further complicated by the publication of Alexis Lichine's own list of clarets (the argument throughout

7*

ignored Sauternes and Barsac). This was sensible: Lichine avoided numbers, substituting five of his own categories ranging from "Crus Hors Classe"—the nonpareils—through Crus Exceptionnels, Grands Crus, Crus Supérieurs, down to Bons Crus. Furthermore he included the wines of St. Emilion, Pomerol and Graves in what was the first rational list ever made of all the Gironde's red wines. The only quarrel anyone had with his eight 'hors classe'—which simply added Mouton, Petrus, Ausone and Cheval Blanc to the original four—was whether Ausone was worthy of a place.

Lichine's list was very similar to the more official list suggested in 1961 by the INAO—which, however, stuck to the Médoc. The INAO simplified things further by copying the categories it had used in St. Emilion. There were four 'premiers grands crus classés', Lafite, Latour, Margaux and Mouton (Haut-Brion, as a Graves, was excluded), compared with the two in St. Emilion, twenty-one 'premiers grands crus', against twelve in St. Emilion, and a mere thirty 'grands crus classés' against double that number in St. Emilion—where, however, the estates were infinitely smaller.

But the INAO list struck seventeen of the 1855 estates off the honours list. These were either châteaux which had been absorbed by others (Palmer, for instance, had swallowed up the tiny third growth of Desmirail, and Cordier had removed Dubignon-Talbot from the scene to protect the name of Talbot) or which were simply not good enough. There were also ten newcomers, all of them pretty obvious—including Henri Martin's Gloria, Jean Theil at Poujeaux, and Lanessan which should have been included in 1855 anyway.

But the 1961 list did demonstrate clearly how transitory can be the glory of a château. Thirty years previously, five 'courtiers' had conducted their own classification of the Médoc, on behalf of the Chambers of Commerce and of Agriculture. They had divided some 250 estates into three groups. The top class of 'crus bourgeois superiéurs exceptionnels' included only six châteaux. Yet only one of the six was elevated by the INAO in 1961: another, Angludet, was being replanted by the Sichels in the early 1960s—so it was 'in' in 1930, 'out' in 1961, and would assuredly have been 'in' ten years later. (All the talk of reclassification did lead to one useful initiative. In the mid-1960s a hundred of the 'crus bourgeois' banded together to promote themselves.)

The 1961 list naturally infuriated many of those who had been relegated or dismissed from the ranks of the nobility. A more surprising objector was Baron Philippe. The general assumption was that he was unhappy with the lowly rank of 'grand cru' accorded the wine from Mouton d'Armailhacq, which he had renamed Mouton Baron-Philippe. In fact he was surprised that this had got in at all, and his objections were more fundamental.

Firstly, he claimed not to be clear what precisely was being declassified. Was the—'terroir'—the soil and situation where the wine was being made—being deemed unworthy, deconsecrated as it were, or were the wine-making skills of one owner at a given moment in time being called into question? This question summarized the reasons why any classification should be a temporary affair. The transient skills of a particular generation of wine-makers combined with their freedom to alter the size, position and make-up of an estate ensure that no classification can be permanent. But because any change seems revolutionary, politics ensure that it will not be temporary either. (St. Emilion's 1955 classification was supposedly due to last only for ten years. But since then, not surprisingly, no one has had the nerve to suggest that it be up-dated.)

Equally fundamentally, many growers beside Rothschild were worried that the INAO had acted arbitrarily, had imposed an autocratic solution which the state could in future alter at will, thus changing property values. So, in the name of private property, Rothschild, Cordier and a number of other major owners walked out of the discussions. For the rest of the decade an immense amount of time and trouble went into devising the mechanisms through which a new classification—either of the Médoc, or preferably of the whole Gironde—could be agreed. Every conceivable regional or municipal institution became involved: the Chambers of Commerce of Bordeaux and Libourne, the departmental 'Chambre d'Agriculture' and the elaborately named 'Fédération des Syndicats des Exploitants Agricoles'*, Poor Pierre Ginestet, as Grand Chancellor of the Académie de Vin, tried to act as mediator: "If your Academy were not involved" in a new classification, he told the members, "it would be

* Literally, the Federation of Unions of Agricultural Cultivators.

rather as if the French Academy were not concerned with the Dictionary".

During the 1960s the only person who got anything out of all this effort was Baron Philippe himself. Not his precious rise in rank, to be sure, but an enormous amount of publicity, which he encouraged by his obsession, repeated to every journalist, to every official, to the humblest visitor, that 'it was a monstrous injustice that Mouton was not a first growth'. To express his feelings he even paraphrased a rhyme invested by a seventeenth-century French family which, debarred from the throne, still felt superior to mere princes. Rothschild's version:

> "Premier ne puis
> Second ne daigne
> Mouton suis" *

is (even he agrees) impossible to translate while still retaining the neatness of the French.

> First I cannot be
> Second I disdain
> I am simply Mouton

is as near as I can get. He also ensured that his wine should sell at least at the same price as his cousin's, a race which had a great deal to do with the increasing gap between the first growths and other clarets—in 1959 the firsts had sold for about two and a quarter times the price of the seconds, whereas by the mid-1960s they were four times the price.

His cousins, however, made life rather easier for him because of their absence and because, from 1961 on, the estate was run by an administrator, M. Nemès, who also looked after the family's scattered agricultural holdings elsewhere. His influence was unfortunate. He was an absentee manager based on Paris—boasting, shortly before his death in 1977, that he had visited Lafite only twice during the previous fifteen years. Moreover he was greedy for short-term profit. He maximized the yield of Lafite itself by stopping the sale of a second wine, 'Carruades de

* The original rhyme was:

> Roi ne puis
> Prince ne daigne
> Rohan suis.

Lafite', as had been the practice in the late 1950s, and, overruling local protests, he allowed a Lafite of dubious quality to be made in 1968.

One tradition he continued: the rivalry with Mouton. He hated admitting that Mouton's wine could be placed on the same level as Lafite. When taxed with leading the price spiral upwards he would reply that "Lafite was a simple producer, not a merchant". Not that the competition between the two was entirely a matter of price. It descended to trivialities: if a distinguished visitor was due at Mouton, he must needs be welcomed also at Lafite. If the wine of one were served at a banquet, the other must be represented. The results were sometimes petty in the extreme. At one imposing luncheon party Baron Philippe served the ritual Lafite (of an off vintage naturally) with a curried rice dish, thus ensuring that the subtleties of its flavour would inevitably be lost on the guests—who just happened to include former prime ministers of France and Great Britain. There was then a suitable pause, after which the Mouton '59 was served with the cheese. The gossip generated by the tension, and by the convolutions of the organizations wrestling with the new classifications—if any—were great fun, but, apart from Mouton, they did not help to sell claret.

There was, however, one well-placed observer in Bordeaux who understood the damage being done by this obsession with rank. At the very end of the decade Bordeaux was rocked when a confidential paper of about a dozen pages written for an economic study group leaked to the local paper, *Sud-Ouest*:

"The great growths," it exploded, "have been transformed into venerable and untouchable mummies . . . Bordeaux is a prisoner of the whole idea of a 'cru', the finest possible example of a museum of fossils." No wonder anyone who attempted to alter the arrangement of these "historic monuments" would "be treated like a maggot in a soup packet". Inevitably "anything which changes is regarded as suspect . . . the worship of tradition is the best possible excuse for intellectual idleness"—a vice which the author suspected the Chartronnais inherited from their English forebears.

He understood precisely that "the slow cycles of the vine and of wine" were difficult to adapt to the shifting whims of the consuming public. The mechanisms surrounding 'appellations controlées' bore their share of the blame for they were "designed to protect the producer rather than the consumer. Their origin reflects the traditional concept of French agriculture that the production of a given crop automatically entails its consumption, and that the more clearly the product is defined and the pro-duction protected at the outset, the better the conditions for selling it."

But above all there was the dead weight of tradition which precluded any effective initiative: "Whether it is a question of the control of 'appellations', of the changes in a product required to suit the market, labelling these products, the financial credits indispensable to complete the ageing of some qualities of wines, or of modern wine-making techniques which elsewhere are helping our competitors, any initiatives are destroyed by our antiquated social and political conventions."

These arguments were merely those which any intelligent outsider might have used, although they were expressed in a slightly hyperbolic form. Yet they created the most almighty furore. A deputation from the CIVB complained formally to the editor of *Sud-Ouest*, accusing the paper of sensationalism and of disloyalty to local business, proving that, as late as 1969, Bordeaux's heads were firmly in the sand—or rather stuck in the Gironde, brooding over the continuing injustices of the 1855 Classification.

17

While Bordeaux slept

The report published in *Sud-Ouest* stung the Chartronnais with especial venom because its author, Bernard Ginestet, if not precisely one of them, was decidedly one of Bordeaux's vinous aristocracy. Bernard, the second son of Pierre and thus the grandson of the revered Fernand Ginestet, is delightfully articulate, with sardonic good looks and an incisive mind. Like the Chartronnais he is fascinated by fine wine but, unlike most of them, also fascinated by the history of Bordeaux and by the Médoc's problems—he is still a much-loved Mayor of Margaux. As my quotations indicate, he understood clearly the real problems facing Bordeaux—the need to establish names able to compete in a modern market place, to adapt wines to the requirements of supermarket shelves, to stop looking backwards, to forget what happened in 1855. He was also, apparently, in a position to act. His father owned Château Margaux, during the 1960s he controlled the sales of the family's other châteaux including Cos d'Estournel. Even before the economic blast he had shocked Bordeaux, taking a leaf from the book of the Chartronnais a hundred years earlier, by marketing his wines under a family brand name. He advertised his wines 'signé' Ginestet in motoring magazines and even, horror of horrors, in *Lui*—the French equivalent of *Playboy*. To a marketing man, these advertisements were merely elegant examples of a standard package: an old family business (by marketing if not Chartronnais standards) establishing a brand image in the magazines read by well-heeled young male adults. It is difficult to convey the shock and horror such a routine exercise created in Bordeaux. The Chartronnais had always been reticence itself: if Barton & Guestier's American agents had advertised Barton & Guestier it was at one remove, and involved no personal publicity.

But Ginestet lacked consistency, staying power.* Brooding over him there was a severe family problem—an elder brother in constant need of psychiatric attention who later committed suicide. His death came after Pierre Ginestet had handed over the majority of his assets to his children—an attempt to minimize inheritance taxes which came badly unstuck.

But even in the 1960s, Bernard seemed unsure of his exact business 'game-plan'. He and his father infuriated the other members of Group A by trying to sell their poor vintage wines from Margaux and Cos 'non-millésimés'—without any vintage year on them, an ill-judged experiment which merely reduced the value of the name.

If Ginestet was Bordeaux's hare, then Jean Cordier, also a grandson of one of the newcomers of the first half of the century, was the unregarded tortoise, who has plodded through Bordeaux's tribulations and emerged as head of unquestionably the city's biggest French-owned wine business.

Désiré Cordier had died soon after the war. But at the end of his life he was joined by his grandson Jean—since all three of his sons had died young. Effectively Jean became sole head of the family firm in his early twenties, and to this day retains the stooped, withdrawn look of someone who has been burdened with responsibility too young. For a number of reasons—because his shyness appears the same as aloofness, because he is an exceedingly tough businessman, and because, like his grandfather, he has remained totally indifferent to the activities of the rest of Bordeaux—he has never been the trade's most popular figure. Naturally he excluded himself from the club. Instead he showed the club the directions in which its members ought to be moving.

Unlike his grandfather he was deeply involved in the quality of the wine produced by the nine estates he owned—these provided a representative spread unequalled by any other single firm since they included, besides the two major growths Talbot and Gruaud-Larose, another important Médocain property, Château Meyney, a first growth in Sauternes, Lafaurie-Peyraguey, and a trio mass-producing white wine in the Premières Côtes de Bordeaux. Jean Cordier himself added the Clos des Jacobins

* All his—considerable—qualities and his—irritating—faults show through in his book *La Bouillie Bordelaise* (*Bordeaux Mixture*).

in St. Emilion. He was one of the first proprietors to call in professional academic help. The Abbé Dubaquié, the first director of Bordeaux's wine research institute ('Station Oénologique') who had been his godfather, ensured that Talbot and Gruaud-Larose, in particular, produced wines of a very high standard, although in the past fifteen years Bordeaux's ever-eager critics assert that they have been allowed to become too fruity, too easy on the palate, to be truly characterful.

But Cordier's independence showed through as early as 1957, when he withdrew his wines from the open market, and allowed his agents everywhere exclusive rights over them. Four years later he even abandoned the historic-shaped bottle for his wines, containing them instead in shorter, squatter bottles, with the name embossed in an oval plaque on the shoulder, a design modelled on a much older type of claret bottle.

Cordier was also careful with his agents, spotting a number who were neither 'traditional' houses, nor fly-by-night newcomers. These included Percy Fox in England, and an exceedingly tough Belgian, 'Père' Fourcroy, now the largest importer of fine wines in his native country. Because of the control he retained over the sale of his wines, these agents could promote them properly, knowing that any money they spent would not be wasted on sales made through rival firms.

Cordier alone, it seemed, had found a consistent house style, bridging the theoretical gulf between the mass of individual châteaux and the whole idea of a 'brand'. For the Gironde effectively still only possessed one brand—Mouton Cadet—and this flourished during an era when its owner's energies were already occupied with battling to get recognition for Mouton-Rothschild, with his museum and with his translations of English poetry and drama.

Fortunately by then he had found a helper. In the mid-1950s he hired Philippe Cottin, a competent young executive from Burgundy—forbidden territory to lesser Bordelais—whose relaxed, pragmatic, professional attitude formed the perfect foil to Rothschild's ceaseless flow of ideas, his tendency sometimes to see the wine business through the eyes of a poet rather than a businessman. Rothschild and Cottin are like a prima donna and her indispensable manager, each appreciating the other's qualities, but each occasionally weary or impatient with them—Cottin born down by Rothschild's flood of ideas and eloquence, Rothschild by Cottin's failure immediately to grasp the long-term potential of some imaginative initiative, almost certainly not the first to have been put forward that day.

In the 1950s they were taught their business by their English shippers, Edward Young of Liverpool, who had taken the agency for Mouton when none of the bigger companies in the business were interested (it was a similar lack of initiative which ensured that Mateus Rosé, that other great success story of the time, was handled by another small firm, Rawlings). Until then one gets the impression that no one at La Bergerie really understood the realities of marketing a brand rather than a 'by-product, sold en primeur to the shippers' as Cottin describes much of the selling of Mouton Cadet before Young's arrival on the scene. Young's were used to handling major brands and taught Cottin how to set about establishing Mouton Cadet. Most of it was simple enough: Teddy Hammond, then the sales director, would spend much of his week ensuring that Mouton Cadet was on the menu of many of the better London restaurants, as the finest form of publicity. To men like Hammond the idea of promoting a blended wine of consistent quality and price was a perfectly natural one. Within the limits imposed by nature, Cottin and Rothschild thought so too, but the rest of Bordeaux was shocked to the core—the very essence of claret being to them its variety and unpredictability.

Rothschild and Cottin were lucky: for the majority of English importers were, by that time, taking no initiatives, merely advising their clients which wines to buy as they were being bottled. Harry Waugh recalls how, even before the war, few of them ventured abroad on business, and during the twenty years after the war they were steadily absorbed by the English brewers. These were themselves merging at a great rate to form, by the mid-1960s, a handful of giants, each controlling tens of thousands of pubs, thousands of 'off-licences' as well as wine merchants and importers. Young's were duly bought up at the end of the 1950s and by the mid-1960s found themselves part of the then-biggest brewery group, Bass Charrington. But, luckily for Rothschild and Cottin, the small group of marketing executives who had helped Mouton Cadet on its way remained in control of the wine side, in Britain anyway, of the merged business. Cottin recalls with gratitude how men like Hammond and Stanley Williams stayed loyal to the brand they had established—and BCV added its own refinements, like the annual 'vintage dinners', given, amidst a great deal of excellent publicity, to influential politicians, businessmen and journalists.

By the end of the 1950s, Rothschild and Cottin had enough funds available to expand Mouton Cadet's sales still further. For the fifteen years after 1955 most of the increasing profits made by the château itself were ploughed back into the brand. The obvious next market was the United States, where they had not seriously tried to promote their wine before. In 1962 they were lucky enough to be taken on by some 'serious' importers, Munson Shaw, who, like Edward Young, understood how to sell branded liquors, and had precisely the contacts in leading New York restaurants which the English had taught were so important. Then, only three months later, Munson Shaw were taken over by the much larger National Distillers. They were the agents for Calvet, and sold the then-immense quantity of 40,000 cases of his wine under the Jouvet label. But, in yet another happy accident, the then-boss of National Distillers went off to Grenada in the West Indies on a honeymoon with a new young wife. On the menu at the hotel where they were staying was only one wine—Mouton Cadet. The boss was impressed, and called Cottin to a meeting in London where, again, Mouton Cadet seemed to be on the menus of all the best restaurants. The policy of National Distillers was duly changed, and within a few years 70,000 cases were being sold under their umbrella through their wholesale network throughout the United States.

The take-over of Munson Shaw was an example of the way the American market was developing on similar lines to the British. In Britain the bidders were the brewers: in the United States major groups in hard liquor—or, in the case of Liggett and Myers, which took over Austin Nichols the old-established blenders and importers of tea as well as of wines in the mid-1960s, tobacco companies in a frantic search for diversification into what was clearly a growing market. For wine consumption in the United States, which had risen only by a tenth in the five years up to 1960, then started to accelerate, until it was growing at nearly 10 per cent a year in the late 1960s. Most of the increase—and thus most of the take-over activity—was accounted for by the cheaper wines from California, and imported wines of all kinds represented only a seventh of the market.

But in the late 1960s the growth seemed to be mainly in 'table' wines, where imports had their strongest position, rather than in sparkling or fortified dessert wines: so the impetus to establish a strong position in Bordeaux was greater than in, say, Jerez or Oporto. For marketing men would look forward to the classic pattern: new consumers would start with the cheaper local wines, but would, sooner or later, move up the scale. One prophet of this change was Ab Simon, hired from the textile business by Austin Nichols. Foreseeing that "it's the consumer, who starts out with a bottle of $1·49 wine, who before long will be trying the more expensive bottles", he led the way with early, massive and profitable purchases of the '66 and '67 vintages.

Even without the help of individual enthusiasts like Simon, the size of the groups involved meant that even a peripheral, and often indirect, involvement in Bordeaux was, in the Gironde's terms, so massive that a relatively minor investment decision by any one of them could easily upset Bordeaux's whole commercial balance. This was a new development: indeed the only important new factor which distinguished the 1970–75 boom from its predecessors. In previous booms outside capital had indeed been attracted to Bordeaux, but it was personal—bankers, financiers and speculators risking their own money. The new groups represented an unprecedented incursion of corporate finance: "they added two zeros to every order", in the words of one newcomer, Bill Bolter. He was a young academic, who originally came to Bordeaux from Edinburgh University in the late 1950s to write a thesis on Montesquieu. He soon drifted into working for Lichine, ostensibly on the latter's much-delayed encyclopedia of wines and spirits, in fact in the business. In the early 1960s he joined up with a rich young American, Steven Schneider, to found the first new 'Chartronnais'-type firm for half a century. For Bolter and Schneider were both Anglo-Saxons; and Bolter settled in Bordeaux, living in the next apartment to a Lawton on the 'Pavé' and, like his predecessors two hundred years before, concentrated on sales of the better-class châteaux to an Anglo-Saxon clientele—though in this case the buyers were mostly American, and not English.

Other young Anglo-Saxons were also proving to the Chartronnais that they could expand their American sales. But—even when they should have known better—the French attitude to the American market was equally compounded of greed and condescension. They assumed that the Americans knew nothing about wine and that their purses were limitless. Even Bernard Ginestet, most open-minded of Bordelais, found room in his book only for stories illustrating the supposed ignorance of the Americans. Even he avoided any rational discussion of this, the most exciting new market Bordeaux had seen for two and a half centuries. He and his fellow-shippers could never understand two basic truths about the market: that the consumer really was king, and knew it, and that the Americans tend to fits of enthusiasm, which lead them to learn a great deal about the subjects involved. Within a decade, indeed, the habit of drinking claret seriously, discussing it, comparing the different vintages and châteaux had spread more widely through the American social system than ever it had over the previous two hundred years in England, let alone in France. Henri Martin's 'Commanderie', for instance, had an active branch in New York, but none in England. He visited the United States fairly frequently, following in the footsteps of his colleagues in Burgundy: for the 'Chevaliers de Tastevin' had first visited New York in the inauspicious days of late 1939.

This enthusiasm owed a lot to the Lichines and the Schoonmakers, and a great deal also to the small band of pioneer growers in California who set themselves the task—which appeared impossible in the 1960s—of making wines, largely from Cabernet Sauvignon grapes, which could compare with the best clarets. The French ignored these developments—with a very few exceptions, like Jean-Pierre Moueix, who sent his younger son Christian to study viticulture at the University of California.

But in most cases the use of an intermediary ensured that the shipper did not come into direct contact with the final retailers. Furthermore the Chartronnais were unwilling to take a long-term view or to work in partnership with their importers. The problem in the 1960s was that the market was soft, and could profitably be supplied through the orthodox channels. The Cruses, for instance, employed a young American, Michael Buller, as an export salesman and, with the backing of yet another whisky firm, Brown Forman Distillers of Louisville, greatly increased their sales. But the distribution circuit this involved was extremely expensive, it trebled the price of the wine between the grower and the final buyer, as a French diplomat and ex-businessman, Jean-Pierre Gachelin, spelled out at a seminar:

"A case of French wine leaves the French port at a theoretical price of $15; if I add shipping costs and the payment of customs duty, excise duty, and the taxes in New York State, which total about $4 for a full container—the most frequent example—the case then costs $19. The importer's margin varies, but is usually between 30 and 40 per cent of the cost price. Fixing this arbitrarily at $7, which, added to $19, gives the selling price to the wholesaler: $26. The percentage taken by the wholesaler is at least 28 per cent of the price he paid, more often 30 per cent and sometimes even 40 per cent; in this case we shall take an average of $7·50, and therefore a selling price to the restaurant owner, or to the retailer, of $33·50. In New York State the retailer allows himself a margin of 50 per cent of his cost price, which in this case is $16·50. So the case which left France at $15, will be sold to the consumer at $50."

This 'normal' circuit was clumsier and more expensive than in Britain, where the importer did less and charged less, and where the chain was, in many cases, shorter because the importer usually sold to the final retailer, thus eliminating the wholesale link. So the temptation to shorten it was considerable. One pioneer was the firm of Dourthe—always an outsider because it was based not in Bordeaux, Libourne or even Pauillac, but in the village of Moulis in the heart of the Médoc. Moreover, during the 1960s, Roger Dourthe's daughter married a complete outsider, Jean-Paul Jauffret—whose only qualification for entry into the Chartronnais was his prowess at tennis (his brother was for a long time France's best tennis player). Roger Dourthe and Jauffret both encouraged a tough, confident young English disciple of Lichine's, Anthony Serjeant, to shorten the chain by selling their wines through importers based in one region or even one state. This policy not only cheapened the cost of marketing the wine, it also introduced Bordeaux's wines to new markets—for previously most of its sales had been concentrated in a few areas. The most important outlet was and remained New York, led by a handful of retail stores like Frederick Wildman and Sherry Lehmann (reckoned, even at the turn of the century, to be 'the only rival to Delmonico's' as an outlet, and one patronized extensively by the great J. P. Morgan). For the rest, a handful of cities, mostly on the East Coast, but also including New Orleans—because of its tradition of French culture and cooking—Chicago and San Francisco, accounted for the bulk of sales. Not surprisingly, Serjeant often found himself the first salesman from Bordeaux ever to visit many states and cities in the heart of America, even such potentially lucrative markets as Denver. The excitement of this direct contact with new markets obscured for a time the problems which went with it—dealing with customers less knowledgeable about the trade, less expert in divining customers' requirements, than the 'traditional' importers.

Ironically, at the same time as his disciples were showing their paces, their master, Alexis Lichine, had been one of the first sufferers from English lack of understanding of the American market. In 1964 his shipping firm had been taken over by Bass Charrington, though not by the British-based division which had handled Mouton Cadet so expertly, but by the International side. The take-over started with a major misunderstanding, and never recovered from its initial problems. Bass thought they were buying a well-established world-wide brand name; in fact they were getting an essentially American operation, and one which was, in any case, too overstocked for comfort or for profits in the years after the take-over when sales in the United States were relatively flat. Bass made matters worse by treating Lichine as just another executive, and not in his proper role as a propagandist and salesman. Then salesmen, used to the hard selling of hard liquor, moved in and ruined the brand's reputation through gimmicky pricing and undercutting the opposition—though they did hold on to a 10 per cent share of the market. Inevitably, by the end of the 1960s, Lichine had retired back into private life. He finally completed his encyclopedia, and went back to advising leading hotels and restaurants, to lecturing, publicizing his books on French wine, his encyclopedia, and even, indirectly, the wines which still bore his name, but over which he had no responsibility.

Lichine's fame was far more substantial than the business he had built up: the same contrast applied to many of the Chartronnais, who had never built up business empires of any stability (we have seen how the fortunes of even the Guestiers fluctuated from generation to generation, and there is a saying in the family that 'the Johnstons know bad times every four generations'). Mauriac had taken the point: in *Préséances* the narrator's uncle is startled by how small a fortune even the well-placed Harry Maucoudinat brought into the marriage with his niece Florence, whose substantial dowry, based on the solid if socially unpretentious timber business, clearly formed a greater attraction even than her blonde hair and blue eyes.

The Chartronnais, faced with increasing production, rising prices and the commitment to take on regular quantities of expensive wines through their membership of Group A, had no real defence against take-overs—and by foreigners at that. The French wines and spirits industry includes quite a number of groups with solid financial backing—the great champagne houses, the blenders of vermouth and liqueurs, the distillers of rum and cognac, the latter often based either in Bordeaux or in Cognac, a mere fifty miles away. Yet none of these was tempted into the wine business. For them claret was too cyclical a product, and in any case none of the major French liquor groups could add anything to Bordeaux's existing networks. English brewers and American whisky distillers emphatically could.

The first such take-over had started, quietly enough, in the 1950s. In 1955 Barton & Guestier's American importers, Browne Vintners, had taken an exact half interest in the firm, thanks to the influence of the last Danny Guestier, the archetypal Chartronnais (he was even educated at Harrow). Unfortunately Guestier met an equally archetypal Chartronnais fate when he was killed in a car crash one early Monday morning in 1960 on his way back from Arcachon. His death left Ronnie Barton partnerless—and also unable to cope with his American partners, since he himself had nothing to do with them, never indeed went to the United States until 1971. Barton & Guestier were a major prize: thanks to Danny Guestier they had taken full advantage of the regulations which ensured that virtually all the wine imported into the United States would be in bottle rather than in cask. This enabled Barton & Guestier to establish its wines under the name of the Bordeaux shipper rather than the importer, the retail merchant, or the château (even today Barton & Guestier Sauternes is still the market leader, and after the war American customers preferred their Pontet-Canet shipped under the Barton & Guestier label as proof of authenticity).

Guestier's death, and the increasing ambitions of Browne Vintners' owners, the Canadian giant, Seagram's Distillers, ensured that control would pass out of local hands. In 1964 there was a capital increase, with all the shares being taken up by the Canadians, a classic technique by which a bigger partner can impose its control over small, capital-short partners. Sam Bronfman, Seagram's tough, ex-bootlegger boss, promptly put his son-in-law, by the name of Ginzberg, in charge. Ronnie Barton, unhappy with the new arrangements, retired to Langoa—fed up, in particular, with Ginzberg's decision not to allow the Wagons-Lits company to continue the age-old (and exceedingly profitable) arrangement by which the railway company took responsibility for bottling the large quantities of Langoa-Barton they sold. He still allowed his old company to sell the wine from his two châteaux, an agreement terminated only in 1977.

But the first Chartronnais firm to be taken over completely had not been Barton & Guestier, but Eschenauer. After Oncle Louis' death in 1958 at the age of eighty-eight, it quickly became apparent that the firm could not remain independent much longer, and two years later John Holt's, the English trading company which had bought Rausan-Ségla in 1956, snapped it up. They put in to run it, not a wine man, but one of their own executives, Jean Roureau, who speedily followed the commercial policy being pursued by Jean Cordier, including a special bottle, concentration on the name of the firm as a brand, and rationalization of the distribution network within France. During the 1960s, indeed, the three outsiders, Cordier,

Eschenauer and Ginestet, tried to federate their business.* At
a personal level the three, supposedly 'impossible' principals,
understood each other well enough, but their employees succeeded in frustrating their bosses' intentions (Dourthe and
Nathaniel Johnston tried a similar deal, which also fell apart).

Roureau, unlike Barton & Guestier's new bosses, fitted in
with the Bordeaux scene. So did another bidder of the 1960s,
the English fine wine company of Harvey's. The profits from the
firm's famous sherries, especially Bristol Cream, enabled George
McWatters, an amiable, moonfaced Englishman who had
inherited a part of the Harvey business, to expand the business.
He, like Lichine, had encouraged a group of young men to
learn their trade with him, and does not seem unduly concerned
that they subsequently went on to higher things. McWatters
was a serious wine man and had been through the Bordeaux
apprenticeship traditional for English merchants. During his
stay with Calvet he had grasped two simple facts: "that there
was a jolly good cushion of profit between the grower and
the English importer . . . and you could never hope to get
into the business from outside." McWatters tried hard enough:
the veteran Harry Waugh spent years scouring Bordeaux for
unjustly neglected estates, and in the post-war years Harvey's,
and the other great Bristol shipping house of Avery's, provided a model for their lazier London brethren in how to
broaden the choice of wines available to the English drinkers
through an aggressive and sophisticated buying policy—behaving, in fact, like English-based Chartronnais. Fortunately for
Harvey's, yet another of the 'Big Seven' was for sale. Since
the 1930s, Delor had been in the hands of its bankers who
had put in Robert Duten—probably Bordeaux's first professional manager—to run the firm. He had kept Delor going
during the depression by selling off the eight châteaux the
family had formerly owned. But Delor, like Eschenauer, had
considerable problems immediately after the war resulting
from the levy on the excess profits allegedly made during the

---

* The technical device they used was a "Groupement d'Interêt
Economique", a type of organization which allows the participants
to retain their individual freedom, while sharing equally in a particular
project. It was used, for instance, by the consortium which builds the
European air-bus.

German occupation. So the take-over, in 1962, was not un-expected and painless, so friendly indeed that Duten's son Bernard still works for his father's old firm as chief buyer. The only change was that Harvey's put in another professional manager, Yves Pardes, a solid executive from the timber trade.

Fortunately for Pardes and Duten, they were sheltered from the take-over battles which engulfed McWatters in the mid-1960s. After repelling one bid, he found himself ousted by the Showerings, an exceedingly tough family of rural perry makers, who had transformed their sparkling drink 'Babycham' into a major brand. The Showerings reckoned, rightly, that they could make more money out of Harvey's famous brands than McWatters, who was a superb long-term strategist, but lacked a real interest in the detailed day-to-day administration of his business. Then the Showerings themselves merged with another large English brewery group, Allied Breweries, to form a business bigger even than Bass Charrington. Never-theless, Delor remained intact, acting as the local supplier, not only for Harvey's, but also for the other wine companies within the Allied Breweries orbit.

Much the same sequence of events restored a much older English bridgehead in the Médoc, Gilbey's empire at Loudenne. In 1962 Gilbey's, no longer a major force in the wine business, merged with Twiss, Browning & Hallowes, another importer, and United Wine Merchants. Despite its name this company relied largely on the profits from the J. & B. Rare light Scotch, named after its Justerini and Brooks subsidiary. By that time, Loudenne was decidedly shabby and run-down and Gilbey's own trade had, for some time, not warranted such a major operation. So the management of the combined group, which was named International Distillers and Vintners, very nearly sold it off, together with the enormous quantities of classed growth clarets stored in its grandiose Victorian cellars.

In the event Jasper Grinling, a descendant of one of the Gilbey's partners, persuaded the board to keep the château and to invest in it not only as a warehouse for storing and shipping wines, but also as a commercial business in its own right. To run it they sent out Martin Bamford, a bouncy, young, dedicated wine expert. He restored the château to its former glory and the IDV marketing network in Britain ensured that Loudenne reverted to its original role as a major centre for the purchase of claret. Indeed, by the end of the decade, Gilbey's was almost an honorary member of Group A, buying not only for IDV's merchanting businesses and off-licences in Britain, but also through a separate company for those in Ireland, Canada and the United States as well. Bamford and his colleagues were even working on their own brand to compete with Mouton Cadet. This, a second brand name for Loudenne wine, was originally called La Tour Pavillon, but because of French legislation, changed in the late 1940s to La Cour Pavillon.

So, by the end of the 1960s, two major British brewery groups, IDV, Seagram's, and, indirectly, a number of other major North American liquor groups were all physically present in Bordeaux. Every one of them was able to finance the purchase of more wine than the original owners of Group A combined, and each was instantly responsive to changes in the market, far more so than even ten years before. "We didn't have telexes in Bordeaux in 1964," said one shipper. Five years later their chatter was ubiquitous.

18

The growers stand firm

In May 1968 the whole of France erupted in the most serious strikes since the 1930s, but for once the effect in the Gironde was the same as in the rest of rural France: a massive increase in the wages paid to agricultural workers. This affected proprietors not only directly, but also because so much of what they bought —like casks—depended on rural labour.

There was a new generation ready to meet the challenge. Their influence was not yet dominant: for during the 1960s prices rose only enough to keep pace with inflation. Even at the end of 1968 the mood among the growers was still so pessimistic that they were asking the INAO to reduce the permissible yields, in a restrictionist attempt to force up the price of their stocks (a proposal dismissed by Martin Bamford at the time as "absurd, since undoubtedly poor wines would have an equal right to the appellations as the good, and the good would therefore be penalized").

Nevertheless a new generation was emerging, a process graphically described by Jean-Paul Gardère, a leading broker from Pauillac. "Formerly, the father would come back home saying simply that he had sold his wine. And nobody argued. Today the son has taken up the reins: he is well-informed and educated, he can do the sums his father never could, and he states that they need to get a certain price for their wines to pay their way. And because the mother stands by the son to keep him at home, the family stands up to the broker or the buyer, and prices remain firm."

Gardère was well placed to see and understand the problems of growers big and small. For since 1963 he had been responsible for the wine-making at Château Latour, scene of the most dramatic take-over of the decade in the Médoc. Early in 1962 George McWatters of Harvey's heard from his merchant bankers,

Lazards in London (who had themselves got the news from their French 'cousins' Lazard Frères in Paris), that Château Latour was for sale (many of the shareholders had, probably, been itching to sell on many occasions in the previous eighty years, but this was the first opportunity to cash in on a rising market for almost that length of time). The money involved—£900,000 for a controlling majority—was too much for Harvey's alone. So Lazard's owner, Lord Cowdray, became involved. He is no wine lover, preferring Scotch, and allegedly expressing his decision to buy in the immortal words, "All right I'll buy the place as long as I don't have to drink the bloody stuff." From the start Cowdray, the tough, one-armed grandson of one of England's richest men—a former contractor who at one time controlled Mexico's oil-wells—looked on Latour as a landed estate rather than a business.

At the time, Gaullist paranoia at the activities of 'Les Anglo-Saxons' was at its height and an elaborate political lobbying campaign had to be mounted to allow the deal to go through (despite the good impression created in Bordeaux by the Delor take-over). Fortunately Lord Poole, the Chairman of the Conservative Party, was a director of Lazards: he in turn induced Ted Heath, then in charge of Britain's first attempt to get into the European Common Market, to speak to Valéry Giscard d'Estaing, France's Finance Minister at the time. Eventually de Gaulle agreed, commenting simply that at least 'les Anglo-Saxons' couldn't take Latour's earth away with them.

Cowdray, who had taken 51 per cent control of Latour, leaving Harvey's with 25 per cent and the Beaumonts with 24 per cent, appointed David Pollock, one of his key executives, to run Latour. For their part Harvey's appointed Harry Waugh. He shocked Bordeaux by putting the estate into the hands of two experienced local men, Gardère for the wine-making and Henri Martin to supervise the growing of the grapes. They found the estate badly run down—still, for instance, using mules, donkeys and oxen instead of tractors. Some of the investments they made, like the installation of stainless steel fermenting vats which made it easier to control the temperature of the wine as it fermented, were hotly debated novelties. Others, like the purchase of small outlying portions of the estate still in the hands of peasants, were more usual. As a bonus, the new owners found that the estate retained the right to plant a number of plots of land, which had hitherto been neglected.*

Once these were replanted, there remained the problem of disposing of the wine made from the young, newly-planted vines. So, from the mid-1960s, Latour started to market a second wine, Les Forts de Latour,† at a price which many people consider excessive, as much as for a second growth (though the new owners were choosey enough to downgrade much of the estate's wine to simple 'Pauillac'). By the end of the decade, the new owners could show profits—reputedly as much as their original purchase price in the boom year of 1972—to encourage other outsiders to appreciate the profits that could be made through investment in a château.

Other foreign take-overs were much less spectacular than that of Latour. The only other classed growth to change hands was Bouscaut, one of the châteaux in Graves singled out by the INAO in their classification in the 1950s. In 1968 the château—together with a smaller neighbour, Château Valoux—was bought by an American syndicate, headed by an insurance broker, Howard Sloan, a financial public relations executive, Allan Meltzer, and Charles Wohlstatter, wealthy enough to have been able to buy up the Racquets Club in the smart desert resort of Palm Springs because he felt it needed refurbishing. Prices had escalated in the five years since the Latour purchase, and the syndicate paid $2 million, nearly as much as for Latour.

Their motives were, as so often, mixed. They were not strictly in the wine business—when local agents offered Meltzer other châteaux he replied simply that "if I wanted to be in the real estate business, I'd be in Minneapolis". Basically they were

* They also discovered trunks full of documents, including thousands of precious letters from former estate managers to the absentee owners. They handed these over to a team of local historians, headed by Professor Charles Higounet, who in 1974 produced far and away the most scholarly book ever written about the Médoc, two volumes which have been invaluable sources of information for this author, not only where Latour is concerned, but also in throwing new light on the relationships of merchants, brokers and rival estates.

† Like so many good ideas, this has several fathers. Henri Martin claims to have spotted the name on an old map of the parish. McWatters recalls thinking of the name himself. Most likely it emerged out of the general excitement involved in the rebuilding of such an estate.

wine-lovers who thoroughly enjoyed the possession of their own
vintage, their ability to call for it in smart New York restaurants.
But there the resemblance to the bankers who had bought
châteaux in the palmy days of Napoleon III ended. For one
thing, Meltzer and his friends enjoyed staying at the château—
which they reckoned to be second only to Beychevelle as the
most beautiful in the Gironde. Moreover they and the other
Americans who purchased châteaux—like Steven Schneider,
Bolter's partner, who bought the bourgeois supérieur growth
Fourcas-Hosten with some friends—expected their investment
to pay, or at least not to lose money.

But, for all the fun and fuss associated with the take-overs by
'les Anglo-Saxons', the majority of the developments derived
from the simple increase in the prices paid for better wines.

During the fifteen years after 1955 there was a double movement: tens of thousands of small growers abandoned their plots,
and the total area of vines in the Gironde slumped by a quarter
to under 260,000 acres, the lowest for centuries. Simultaneously
production of the better red wines entitled to the AOC certificate
rose sharply: in the last five years of the 1960s they averaged
nearly 30 million gallons, more than a third above the average
recorded in the five years before the frosts of 1956; and in the
succeeding five years they rose by a further quarter.

The increases were even sharper for the 'château' wines. A
comparison of the 1949 and 1969 editions of Cocks and Feret
shows clearly that most 'classed' estates had increased production
by a half, and on many the rise was even greater. At Mouton the
output had jumped from 75 to 250 tonneaux, at Latour from
100 to 300—though, in both cases, much of the increased production was destined for the estates' second wines. Other increases
were even more spectacular: at the relatively little-known La
Lagune production jumped ten-fold to 200 tonneaux, the same
sort of increase as that achieved by the Tari family at Giscours
and Lichine at Lascombes. At their family property of Pontet-
Canet, the Cruses doubled production to 400 tonneaux—nearly
half a million bottles, far and away the biggest of any classed
growth. The Dourthe family had taken on a number of unclassed
growths and built up production very substantially—from 20 to
120 tonneaux at Maucaillou, near their Moulis headquarters, for
instance.

The whole of the area round Moulis formed the centre for a number of new massive expansions in the twenty years following the price explosion of 1955. This was not surprising: the parish had nearly 2000 acres under vines at the end of the nineteenth century, a figure which had fallen to under 600 at the end of the war. And even when present planting plans are fully implemented the figure will be up to only half the nineteenth century figure— though production will probably be as high.

Typically the investors in the Central Médoc were a mixture of locals and outsiders: the Dourthes, M. Theil at Poujeaux (who nearly trebled his output to 180 tonneaux), other Frenchmen, who built up Château Lamarque by the river from 20 to 200 tonneaux, Algerians who did much the same at Duplessis-Hauchecorne in Moulis. In St. Laurent in the backwoods to the north behind St. Julien, the Forners, a family of Spanish shippers, bought up the fifth-growth Camensac and the unclassified Larose-Trintaudon and built them up to produce the same half-million bottles as Pontet-Canet. The Forners avoided the Bordeaux market, selling their wines directly to customers like Air France and Seagrams—for they were producers big enough not to be afraid even of the biggest customers.

Probably the two biggest investors were both French: a group headed by yet another Rothschild, Baron Edmond, started building up another major estate in Listrac at Château Clark; and, near the river, the major French wine merchant Jean Castel, famous for the Castelvin he sold through French supermarkets, bought Château Arcins and Château Barreyres, nearly 700 acres in all. By the end of the 1970s these will be producing well over a million bottles a year.

The Anglo-Saxons were represented by Steve Schneider at Fourcas-Hosten in Listrac, again in the backwoods, and by a young English graduate of the Montpellier wine school, Nicholas Barrow, who in the mid-1960s bought a small property, Château Courant, on the main road north out of Margaux. At the end of the decade he teamed up with a Washington lawyer, Russell Train, and a group of American investors looking for a 'tax shelter', an investment on which they could off-load some of the taxable profits they were making elsewhere. They were originally introduced to the Médoc by Jimmy James, one of the wine-loving wine merchants who, in the United States as earlier in Britain,

8

had done so much to spread the word to a wider audience. The new group was far more ruthless and businesslike than the Americans at Bouscaut. Barrow served them well: he developed Malescasse—a formerly run-down château with enormous cellars just south of Lamarque on the river—by a minute study of local vintage maps, buying only appropriate acreage and planting it.

Before he teamed up with the Americans, Barrow had made his living by offering a mobile do-it-yourself service for growers who wanted to bottle their own wine, but lacked the finance to invest in their own plant—and within a few years was ensuring that over one and a half million additional bottles could legitimately be called 'Château-bottled'.

The demand for his services was a prelude to the most important development in the Médoc in the 1960s—the agreement, made in 1969 but coming into effect with the 1970 vintage, that all classed growths should be bottled at the château. In this respect the locals needed no prodding from outside—even though Martin Bamford noted, in November 1968, that the "growths under contract" (most to Group A) "have done noticeably better than those that have kept their freedom on the market". As a result the leaders of the movement were not hereditary growers.

One was Jean-Eugène Borie, whose merchant family had bought the dilapidated Château Ducru-Beaucaillou in 1941. Borie himself is know as the 'golden boy of the Médoc'—even though his appearance and manner are not at all glamorous. In his neat business suit he looks like a friendly but precise bank manager, rather than a playboy or peasant. But he lives at his château, and his careful supervision of his wine has ensured that it is considered one of the most reliable in the Médoc. He had steered clear of Group A: and he was typical of other growers who found no difficulty in selling their wines at a handsome profit through the 1960s, who therefore felt more confident as it drew to a close, and who came to realize that they no longer required the safety net provided by Group A.

But the spark that lit the idea was the arrival of a much younger man, Bruno Prats, the first cousin of Bernard Ginestet. His mother, Pierre's sister, had married Jean Prats, who is now the managing director of a major aperitif company, St. Raphael. Prats, an earnest young man, looking for all the world like an intense, serious French doctor, complete with spectacles and neat pointed beard, had been sent, like so many of his generation, to learn viticulture. Unlike most others he had the chance to exercise his talents on a grand scale immediately after graduation. For, as a result of a family settlement, his branch of the family took over all the Ginestet family properties apart from Château Margaux itself.

The spread, which included Cos d'Estournel and half a dozen others (including one oddity, the island in the Gironde off Margaux called 'Ile de Margaux'), was enough to catapult Prats immediately into the front rank of growers. And, like the young Philippe de Rothschild forty-five years before, Prats' first thought when he came into his inheritance was to impress on the world that Cos was his wine rather than any merchant's, and to insist on compulsory bottling at the château. Rothschild had had to take the initiative, drag the other first growths with him, but Prats found that Borie and others were already moving in the same direction—as the enthusiasm for Barrow's services, which often resulted in the installation of bottling machines at individual châteaux, had already demonstrated.

The only hesitation came from proprietors like the Cruses at Pontet-Canet and Ronnie Barton at Langoa-Léoville, steeped in the idea that only their family businesses could properly bottle the wine. Indeed the argument still rages: experts in England, like Tony Berry at Berry Bros. and Rudd, acknowledged as the finest professional bottlers in the world, could legitimately claim that at most French châteaux "they do the bottling when they have a couple of hours to spare"—not necessarily at the right time or on the best equipment. At the worst the bottling can go on for months, occupying otherwise idle hours—but ensuring that the wine will be of very variable taste (it took nearly six months, for instance, to bottle Lafite's 1970 vintage). Other experts, like Harry Waugh, remember wine bottled in English establishments less reputable than Berry Bros. and capable of giving an undeserved reputation to the château concerned.

For in one sense compulsory château-bottling is a defensive move to protect a château's brand name. Pierre Ginestet at Château Margaux had allowed some of his wine to be bottled elsewhere until the late 1940s. The shock of finding some extremely dubious 'Margaux' circulating in Belgium finally changed his mind. But compulsory château-bottling, which did not arrive all of a sudden in 1969,* and was not confined to classified growths (Henri Martin, for instance, had been insisting on it for fifteen years or more), was a public declaration by the grower that his wine was not a commodity, but a brand. No matter that someone else was selling it, it was the grower himself, not the salesman, who was responsible for the quality of the product.

François Gardère, the broker son of Jean-Pierre, pin-points the practice as marking the end of the role of the 'négociant-éleveur' —the traditional Chartronnais who had bought the wine from the grower, either 'sur souches', before the grapes were even picked, or 'en primeur', immediately after fermentation, and had not merely bottled it, but had cherished it, topped it up, fined it, racked it, brought it up as a kind of adopted or foster-child. For the arguments between growers and Chartronnais resemble those between psychologists debating whether heredity (the vines, the grapes, the fermentation) matter more than environment (the years spent in the Chartronnais' cellars and the care lavished there on the wine). Inevitably the fact that the most influential class of vitiparents was determined to take care of its children from birth to maturity, until they were ready to be sent into the outside world on their own, was a major step forward.

It meant, above all, that the Chartronnais, deprived of their former glory as the foster-parents of Bordeaux's wine, had to find a new role. The growers had served notice that they were no longer needed in their former capacity, and they could, in any case, never hope to complete with the foreign groups as wine-buyers.

---

* Even after 1969 there were a few exceptions. The Cruses took a couple of years to come into line, and because the excise duties in Denmark and Switzerland differentiated between wines imported in bottle and those—paying less duty—imported in cask, sales to these markets were also excluded for several years.

19

Boom I: count-down

Prats, Borie, and their fellow-growers could not have chosen a better moment for their stand. For 1969 was the watershed, the year the American market flexed its mighty muscles. On the domestic scene the mergers of the 1960s culminated in the bid by Heublein—best-known for their Smirnoff Vodka—for United Vintners, the second biggest wine producers in the United States. Heublein's Managing Director, however, showed clearly that he knew the future direction for the combined group when, the same year, he summoned Michael Broadbent, the head of the wine department of Christie's Auction Rooms in London, to preside at the first of what were to be the most widely-publicized events of the American wine year—the annual Heublein auction of rare, fine and old wines. The sale made no profit for Heublein, but it symbolized the commitment of the American hard liquor business to the fine wine trade.

Broadbent, a decisive, competitive, ambitious wineman with a widely respected palate, was one of the many to have emerged from George McWatters' 'school' at Harvey's. Christie's had, intermittently, run wine sales for nearly two centuries, mostly of cellars from private houses, as a minor part of their regular auction business. They had not sold any wine since World War II, but by the mid-1960s were looking to get back into the business. Their opportunity arose in 1966 when Tom Taylor-Restell, head of a small auctioneers which ran wine sales in the City of London for the trade (and for a handful of journalists from the *Financial Times* whose offices were next to the auction rooms), suffered a severe stroke. His son Alan—almost certainly the fastest and most skilled wine auctioneer in the world—agreed to merge the family business with Christie's, and (largely thanks to Harry Waugh) Broadbent was hired to run the show.

The first season over £400,000 of wine was sold, and in the next few years Christie's business boomed, as the firm's socially ubiquitous scouts sniffed out a number of hitherto unsuspected cellars of fine old wines. The first, and most important, was that of the Earl of Rosebery, a sale which provided a major boost to Christie's business. It also provided a boost to the idea that there was money to be made out of old wines, which, previously, had been sold informally by merchants to especially favoured clients.* But, as early as 1967, a massive sale of 'Alexis Lichine wines' by Bass Charrington showed how useful the sale room could be as an outlet for surplus trade stocks—and as a means of publicizing a name previously little known in England.

The combination of Heublein and Broadbent was a symbol for for the next five years: the market for wine was shifting away from Bordeaux to London, while the final buyers of the best wines were increasingly being found in the United States rather than in their traditional home.

In 1969 even the political and economic auguries seemed bright: that implacable enemy of 'les Anglo-Saxons', President de Gaulle, had retired in the spring, and in the middle of August French wines suddenly became cheaper for Anglo-Saxon buyers when the franc was devalued. So the American market duly exploded: after a number of years in which Bordeaux's sales to the United States had risen 'only' at a steady 10 per cent annually, they rose in 1969 by nearly a half, a rate of increase faster than any seen in the later stages of the boom and, even more encouraging, prices rose at about the same 7 per cent rate seen in previous years.

The contrasts with Bordeaux's other export markets—apart from Canada, which followed the same pattern as the United States—could hardly have been more striking. Elsewhere 1969

---

* The French often accuse the British of an obsession with age as a quality in wines. Certainly the prices at the Rosebery sale led to the discovery of a number of other hoards. A classic writer like Maurice Healy went to town on a 1877 Vieux Château Certan: "At something like sixty years of age it was a very lovely and gracious thing. Its welcome had the dignity and charm of a dear old reverend mother at a very exclusive convent." Of another delicate bottle he wrote, "There enters leaning slightly on her stick a very old lady, but with a young heart, who speaks a few bright words to her guests and then departs." The last word on the subject was surely written by Allen Sichel in 1954, when, he claimed, he had been told "that the 1870 Château Lafite is nearly ready for drinking".

saw only a 5 per cent increase in sales. And, because the Americans turned increasingly that year to Bordeaux as the source of their imported fine wine requirements, the contrast with other French drinks exporters was also marked. It was the American demand for claret which gave Bordeaux a ninth of all French alcohol exports that year, a marked increase on the previous year.

Inevitably, the gap between the prices paid by the Americans and by other good customers like the Belgians and the British widened further—to nearly three times. Indeed the average prices paid by the British declined during the years between 1962 and 1969. But this change masked a most encouraging transformation of the British scene.

In the mid-1960s supermarkets were, for the first time, allowed to sell liquor; and the resulting intensified competition kept prices artificially stable. The widening of outlets also introduced French wine to a much less affluent public—one explanation why the British seemed to be buying cheaper wines from Bordeaux. But they were also clearly going to buy very much more wine given any sort of increase in general prosperity.

The 1969 vintage also helped things along: it had been a real cliff-hanger with appalling September rains, and fine weather at the beginning of October which had favoured those brave growers who had not started picking unripe grapes later the previous month. But it was very small—the smallest since 1961 and only two-thirds the average for the previous five years. Even more crucially, production of the basic Bordeaux rouge was down to only two-fifths of the 1968 vintage (when, naturally, a lot of wine theoretically entitled to better appellations had been declassed to a more basic level). And, as Peter Sichel explained:

"Bordeaux rouge is influenced by a different market to the more expensive wines. Probably 90 per cent of the crop is consumed in France and its price is closely affected by the prices of Beaujolais and Côtes du Rhône, these three appellations forming the basic diet of the increasing number of Frenchmen who are tending to drink less vin ordinaire and more wine that is entitled to an appellation. Nobody holds much stock, most of the crop is consumed within a year of having been produced. The quantity having been small in all three of these areas, there has been some almost panic-buying by home merchants, fearing that they would not be able to find enough wine to service their customers for the next twelve months."

For the next few years, indeed, these three wines chased each other up the scale, with basic Bordeaux Rouge usually the laggard, not only because there was so much more of it than of Côtes du Rhône or of Beaujolais (of the real stuff anyway), but also because there was a major upsurge of interest outside France in both the alternatives to Bordeaux Rouge. At the end of the 1960s the London *Sunday Times* revealed how much 'Beaujolais' came from other parts of the world, an exposure which greatly heightened English interest in the genuine article. The Americans saw in Beaujolais and Châteauneuf two 'generic' 'brand' names, easy to drink, to pronounce and thus to promote.

So, underpinning the apparently crazy price movements of the next few years, was a continuing demand from French customers for the most basic type of claret. But, of course, the publicity was concentrated on price movements at the other end of the market, by the continuing rivalry between the Rothschild 'cousins', based on a shortage of great clarets following the dreadful 1968s and the small 1969 vintage.

Baron Philippe was in full cry for promotion to premier cru. M. Nemès, acting for Baron Elie, was not prepared to relinquish the title 'Premier des Premiers' by letting Lafite's price drop behind Mouton's. The competition exploded at the beginning of 1970. In previous years Baron Philippe had been content to match the prices obtained by his 'cousins', at about 27,000 francs per tonneau (£3·35 a bottle in 1970 money) for vintages as superb as 1961 or 1966. But for the 1969s—less promising than either of the other two major vintages of the decade—Lafite demanded and obtained a record 70,000 francs a tonneau. Baron Philippe in revenge secured 75,000 for his. The other first growths trailed far behind with even the newly-restored Latour asking 'only' 48,000 francs, still double the 1966 price. For 1969, as the historians of the château noted, "marked a turning point in the quotations for the first growths". Opinions vary as to the effect of such stunning prices on the lesser wines.

A couple of years later Edmund Penning-Rowsell was to suggest, only half-jokingly, that: "When Bordeaux's central square, the Allées de Tourny, is restored after the excavations for an underground car park, all the 150 or so classified-growth proprietors should contribute out of their new prosperity to a sculpture group . . . the subject? Their two benefactors, Barons Philippe and Elie de Rothschild."

By contrast, Peter Sichel claimed that "It really doesn't matter at what prices first growths are sold. Say that between them they make 750 tonneaux, that's 75,000 cases or 900,000 bottles of wine. There are probably 180,000 restaurants, merchants, investors or godparents in the world who will be happy to buy a single bottle of each, and Presto! the crop is sold. The more expensive the better, it makes the gift more worthwhile and it makes the others wines on the list look that much cheaper. Probably only a few of the 900,000 will ever actually be consumed; they are for trading, not drinking."

Sichel sounds liverish, Rowsell rather starry-eyed. A more balanced appreciation might be that no boom is complete without a dramatic jump in the price of the first growths and that most are led by them. A rise as dramatic as that of early 1970 was bound to encourage lesser growers, although in 1969 the impetus came from below. For the Lafite–Mouton race had a solid enough base: it started only in May after the habit of selling their wine in two 'tranches'—lots—had already enabled some second growths, like Brane-Cantenac and Ducru-Beaucaillou, to ask 10,500 francs a tonneau for their second 'tranches' in April 1970, 50 per cent above the prices at which they had opened at the end of 1969. This pattern was followed also in Burgundy—where, however, the 1969s were recognized as unusually fine while in Beaujolais the 1969 vintage, according to Sichel "was by the spring of 1970 selling at a price nearly double the opening price, and shippers have often been reselling the wine well below replacement cost in order to retain their markets."

But it was the 1970 vintage which, rather belatedly, convinced the Bordeaux market that there had been a change as profound as that of 1955—or of the oidium years a hundred years before. For 1970 was the perfect vintage; "If I'd been God myself, I couldn't have done better," sighed one—anonymous—grower. But the vintage, as well as being obviously of the highest quality, was also enormous: for the first time since the war there were over 2 million hectolitres (nearly 45 million gallons) of red wine produced entitled to the AOC label. This was a third bigger than the 1967 vintage which had proved so indigestible for the market

8*

(less white wine was produced than in four years in the 1960s, largely because so many vines had been torn up by despondent growers in the succeeding years).

Inevitably the merchants, and especially the British-based buyers, tended to sit back, assuming that, whatever their early demands, the growers would be forced back to 'reasonable' prices by the sheer size of the vintage, as they had been so often before, as long ago as 1900, or as recently as 1967. More relevantly, they remembered how they had been panicked by the wicked press and the even wickeder Americans into paying so highly for that earlier "vintage of the century" in 1959.

In December even the shrewd Bamford was expecting only that prices would be broadly similar to the 1969s for the classified and top bourgeois growths. Interestingly, while he realized that "demand exceeds supply", yet he expected this only to peg, rather than increase prices. He even expected a fall in the price of the lesser wines, "as quantity is plentiful, and there is considerable pressure being exerted by the négociants to keep prices down."

The result of the conflicting pressures was a stand-off in the short-term, but one which, if correctly interpreted, was a major victory for the growers. Prices of the basic wines did not falter, and vast quantities were traded throughout the winter at prices roughly similar to those paid a year earlier for the 1969s. The trade was reasonably happy, not understanding the basic market rule that a rising volume of sales at firm price levels is a sure precursor of a boom, especially in a commodity where the next season's supply was exceedingly unlikely to be as large as 1970's exceptional crop.

The press and many outsiders, wine trade professionals closer to the final consumer than the Bordeaux wine market itself, saw demand escalating and realized the money to be made well before the Chartronnais—or the growers. The latter, aware that they were offering over twice as much wine as in 1969 and therefore were going to make a decent profit anyway, aware too of the merchants' pressure and of the lessons of 1966–67, started timidly enough.

They offered their first 'tranche' before Christmas at prices only a quarter above the initial price of the 1969s and significantly below the level they had since reached in the open market. But the trade had speeded up: no longer did the traditional English buyers dominate the scene, waiting eighteen months until the wine was ready for bottling before advising their customers on what to buy. The big new groups saw that they could place the wines in their own outlets, and there were hundreds of individual drinkers eager to lay hands on an outstanding vintage.

As in early 1970, so a year later, lesser wines did not have to wait for the example of the Rothschilds or anyone else before putting their prices up. Bill Bolter, who had bought two 'tranches' of Ducru-Beaucaillou from Jean-Eugène Borie, one in December and another in February, both for a mere 8,000 francs a tonneau, found himself paying 11,500 francs only a couple of months later. The same pattern applied elsewhere: the Taris had got only 6,800 francs for their December 'tranche': a month later they were asking 7,500 francs and by March 9,000 francs.

That month the irrepressible Baron Philippe stole the scene. He summoned the press to Mouton, declared that he was unhappy about the way prices were escalating, and announced that he proposed to sell a first 'tranche' of Mouton at a mere 36,000 francs, dramatically under half the price he had secured for the less magnificent wines the previous year—by 1971 he did not need to prove to anyone that Mouton was indeed worth its place as a first growth. And he insured himself by obliging buyers of the first 'tranche' to take an equivalent quantity of the second, whenever he chose to offer it.

The new owners of Latour were duly impressed by his magniloquent gesture in the fight against inflation and opened their wine at 'only' 40,000 francs. Haut-Brion followed suit with 44,000. Pierre Ginestet at Margaux then seized the opportunity to make up the ground he had lost during the 1960s and opened his wine at 45,000 (in the previous decade the two Rothschild wines had established themselves in a separate 'super-first' category, followed by Petrus, Haut-Brion and Latour, with Margaux, Cheval Blanc and Ausone trailing at a respectful distance).

But the 'cousins' at Lafite failed to respond: they asked for and got 59,000 francs—moreover buyers had to take an appropriate amount of the 'cousins' other estate, Duhart-Milon, as they had the previous year.

At that point Philippe de Rothschild, like the splendid old actor-manager he sometimes resembles, took his revenge.

Bowing, he claimed, to popular demand, he offered the eager populace another 'tranche' of his beloved wine at 65,000 francs, thus getting the best of both worlds—plaudits for his attempt to damp down 'speculation' and the satisfaction of again getting a price 10 per cent above that achieved by Lafite.

This was all good jokey stuff, especially when Lafite then offered a second 'tranche' at 75,000 francs, and even Margaux was asking 65,000. But even then there were a few voices worrying about the future. At a directors' meeting at Latour in June, Harry Waugh reported on the rapidly growing fear in the United States that the prices of the first growths, at least, had gone beyond all bounds and would meet consumer resistance. Translated into lay terms the figures being bandied about Bordeaux that summer did seem absurd.

The price of 75,000 francs per tonneau represented 'only' 65 francs (£5) a bottle. But this did not allow for all the costs incurred before the wine was bottled, let alone for at least a decade of interest before it was ready to drink, which would more than double the opening price. Nevertheless, the directors of Latour, probably the men in Bordeaux most in touch with external financial reality, concluded that summer that "after a long discussion the Board decided that it would be bad commercial policy unilaterally to reduce the price, especially as a reduction by Latour alone would not affect the market as a whole. Such a decision would only increase the buyers' profits and, in addition, there was the risk that the market would interpret any decline as an indication of lower quality." Inevitably Latour followed the others, and asked 65,000 for a second 'tranche' in a year when Latour's first wine provided its owners with sales revenue nine times that achieved from the 1955 vintage of blessed memory.

If the directors of Latour were worried in July, they would have been anguished in August. For that month President Nixon cut the link between the dollar and gold: for a few unnerving days the dollar seemed to lose all its value. Even after order was re-established financial life was transformed and a new element of uncertainty had been introduced into any internationally traded commodity: currency fluctuations could now upset even the best calculated of deals. But Bordeaux took no notice, the price levels established in the spring remained: if the second growths were

60 per cent above their opening price, why, even basic Bordeaux Rouge was nearly 50 per cent up, and there was not a single claret appellation less than a third above the price it had fetched the previous December. Despite President Nixon, growers enjoyed their holidays. The situation seemed perfect: exports virtually everywhere had risen steadily, so had the prices at which they were invoiced. Stocks of claret, which had been very low in mid-1970, were for the first time for decades at above the two million hectolitre level (over 42 million gallons). But nature had smiled on the Gironde: the weather during the 'flowering' in June had been miserable and it was already clear that the 1971 vintage would be a small one. So the momentum kept up: the volume of transactions was nothing like the record levels of the spring, but they were well above those of the previous autumn and, to use the increasingly appropriate language of the chartists of stock market prices, even the basic appellations "had broken through their previous highs on rising volume", the classic sign of another boost to a boom.

By the autumn the 1971 vintage could be measured and, to an extent, judged. Bordeaux's luck ensured that for the first time since the late 1940s the Gironde had enjoyed three vintages in a row of above-average quality and that the 1971 one was of a manageable size. Contrary to legend, it was not unduly small: a mere three-fifths of the record 1970 vintage, but it was only 10 per cent below the average for the last half of the 1960s.

By then, too, the growers had overcome their inhibitions: not for them the pussy-footing first offers of the 1970s. The proprietors of generally unconsidered wines were demanding, and readily getting, for their 1971 vintage as soon as it was made prices a fifth above the market prices for their 1970 vintage.

Yet, until late 1971, the prices in Bordeaux had done no more than allow the growers to catch up the ground they had lost in the 1960s, whether the figures were measured against inflation— or against comparable wines like Beaujolais. If Bordeaux's 1971 prices were a third up on those of 1960, even the cheaper Burgundies sold in cask had more than doubled during the same period, and the bottled variety, recognized as expensive even at the beginning of the decade, had gone up by a half. Nor was Bordeaux usurping an unfair slice of the export business: following the 1969 surge Bordeaux's market share relapsed, and in both

1970 and 1971 its share of French liquor exports fell below 10 per cent.

For even in the heady autumn of 1971 Bordeaux was still a relatively rational place. The proprietors of the better growths could sit back and survey the scene: seeing that lesser growers had asked for more than the market value of the 1970s, they too were confident that they could ask the same in the spring of 1972. But in the meantime it was in their interest to sell as large a part of their stocks of older vintages as possible. For the new year would see a radical change of the tax base of any grower with a turnover of more than 500,000 francs—and after the two previous years the class had grown to include virtually every proprietor of a classified or 'bourgeois' growth, and indeed anyone with forty acres of vines entitled to a 'respectable' appellation like St. Julien. No longer would he be taxed on a— usually low—'estimate', but on an up-to-date balance sheet basis. This would inevitably mean that owners with large stocks of older wines in the balance sheet at their original value, would be liable to stringent taxes on their newly-increased capital value. Inevitably owners sold a great deal of their stocks on to a willing market during the last quarter of 1971; and this shortage of the older and better wines was to be one of the forces which turned the next eighteen months into a vinous mad-house.

20

Boom II: blast-off

" 'Please send me six cases of Bordeaux Rouge,' a Bordeaux négociant
was asked by a private customer. 'Certainly, but I'm afraid I've had to
increase the price from Frs. 3 to Frs. 6.' 'Better send me twelves cases,'
was the immediate and typical reaction."

PETER SICHEL

"This crisis is perfectly rational. It was even foreseeable. The day I
saw in Time Magazine a photograph of a bank vault with a bottle of
Lafite in it I assembled my staff and told them 'The crisis has started.'
Indeed from the moment when you start to think of wine as an investment
and not as something to be drunk, that's the end."

ELIE DE ROTHSCHILD

In theory, the growers were better prepared for selling the
1971 vintage than they had been a year before. Led by the
ever-increasing prices of the more ordinary wines and by endlessly repeated stories of how they were nearly all sold even at
the higher prices, the owners of the better growths could wait,
could luxuriate, could confidently open their first 'tranches'
at well above the price their previous vintage was fetching in
the market, and not, as a year before, at below the going market
level.

So Henri Martin could ask 18,000 francs for his Château
Gloria, three times the price of his '70 vintage—and the same
as Léoville-Poyferré, a second growth, which itself had only
demanded 8,000 francs the two previous years. For classes and
relative prices were getting thoroughly confused: Bruno Prats,
for instance, was asking 19,000 for Cos d'Estournel 1971 in
January, the same month that his 1970 was fetching 21,500.
And by April that same wine was priced at 28,000—marginally
above the opening prices of the 1967 vintage of the top few first
growths.

Under the circumstances it was inevitable that these should start at fantastic prices: Margaux, Haut-Brion and Cheval Blanc in May at a 'mere' 75,000 francs, Lafite at 110,000 and in June the top three that year, Latour, Mouton and Petrus, at 120,000. Immediately the outsiders caught up, Haut-Brion asking 110,000 for a second 'tranche', and Lafite outdoing the execrated 'cousin' with a second 'tranche' at 135,00, exactly five times the prices asked five years before. (By that time Baron Philippe's Odyssey was nearing voyage's end. It seemed by then certain that he would be granted his precious title, in theory as the first part of an exercise designed to regrade all the classified growths, in fact, as everyone in Bordeaux knew, in a one-off rectification designed to satisfy 'le baron'.) So, just as two years before he had been at pains to assert his predominance, so, in 1972, it was Lafite which had to preserve its place as 'premier des premiers'.

Although the cousinly rivalry had been useful two years before, the booms in both 1971 and 1972 seemed entirely independent of any aid from the gods above. For that spring it appeared that a new reality was being born.

The CIVB was sure of it: a delegation had been told by one of their American colleagues "that if the per capita consumption in the United States doubled, not only will local production with its probable increase no longer suffice, but it would use up all available production of Europe, North Africa and South America put together."

This apparently hyperbolic remark was matched by the general feeling in the American market at the time, even by the most sober and widely-respected sources in the trade. The previous year the industry's "Wine Handbook" had predicted that "the consumption of wines in this country will grow at an unprecedented rate of 100% or more during the seventies." Moreover the market share of imported table wines was over a fifth for the first time in 1972. No wonder that year's catalogue of Sherry-Lehmann, the single most important wine store in the whole United States, reckoned that a 15 per cent growth rate in consumption was "modest". Optimists could say truthfully that Bordeaux's three best markets for good wine, Britain, the United States and Belgium, all came well down in the world league table of wine consumption, with the Americans drinking only ten bottles a head a year, a fraction of even the British figure—and consumption in Britain had doubled within a couple of years, simply because competition was keen, and duties had remained stable. "Some of you," concluded Sherry-Lehmann, "may have bought Château Lafite-Rothschild 1961 shortly after the harvest at about $100 the case and observe it currently being rationed at $750 the case. Will the same thing happen to the equally excellent '70? Barring a world depression even the most conservative economist would predict that the '70s will achieve equal heights in another decade."

No wonder the narrow Bordeaux market, swamped by visitors with open cheque books who had also read the catalogue— and *Fortune* magazine which was saying much the same thing— took off. Indeed, until May it had been possible for the statisticians at the CIVB to show that prices in the Gironde were merely catching up on those obtained by other French wines from Burgundy and the Côtes du Rhône, whose prices seemed to have jumped far more in the decade than had those of the Gironde's wines.* But in 1972 the spring was icy, reminding the wiseacres how few good vintages had followed a winter as warm as 1971–2. Moreover, after three above-average vintages, it seemed time for a disappointment. These gut feelings were seemingly confirmed by the weather up to the flowering. In 1972 it was in mid-July, later than any vintage since the 1932, considered by Daniel Lawton senior to have been the worst of the century.

The prospect of a poor vintage was a perfectly normal stimulus for a further surge in prices. Rationally it could also be argued that exports and export prices of competitive French wines had both risen faster than Bordeaux the previous year and it was about time for Bordeaux to catch up. It was not as though demand was coming only from the Americans. In Britain in the first quarter of 1972 Delor's sold three times as much

* These statistics were widely quoted, but were biased in Bordeaux's favour. The average price of the Gironde's exports was depressed by the cheap white wine not produced in the other two regions; and the base year, 1962, was one when prices had been artificially elevated in Gironde by the aftermath of the tiny 1961 vintage. Even so, the average price of Burgundies did rise at double the rate of Bordeaux from 1962–72, and this cannot be explained only by the continuing poor prices reached by the white wines of the Gironde.

château-bottled wine as the year before—so prices of wines bottled in Bordeaux and shipped to Britain rose faster than those being paid by the Americans. Even more significantly the Belgians, who still dominated the market in Pomerol, were prepared to pay up for their traditional beverage. By September basic Pomerol was up to 10,000 francs a tonneau—well above the prices originally asked by second-growth Médocs for their splendid 1970s. By then M. Thienpoint, the Belgian merchant who owned Pomerol's second-best estate, Vieux Château Certan, had demanded and obtained 48,000 francs for his wine, putting him fifty per cent above the market price for run-of-the-mill second-growth clarets.

The escalation of the prices of their wines, for the second year running, clearly hardened the hearts of the growers. In 1970 they had been cautious, had heeded the advice of the trade, and had been caught underpricing their wines. The following year they had pitched their prices above the market, and had still seen the merchants making an immediate killing. They would not be tricked a third time.

It was impossible then—and remains difficult even now—to persuade anyone in Bordeaux that the experiences of the wine trade in the Gironde in the two years before the October 1973 oil crisis were paralleled anywhere else. Yet other commodities, other wine-producing districts, enjoyed the same degree of overheating, the same massive swamping of supply by demand. In those crazy two years the Western world seemed short of everything except money. Finance was still cheap, but after the dollar crisis of August 1971 nobody any longer wanted dollars or, more especially, pounds. Investors, speculators, businesses were all desperately searching for solid objects, commodities, articles whose value could be relied on to keep pace with that new bogey-man, inflation.

Claret filled the bill perfectly and, most importantly, not only for individuals. The wine boom in the United States had led virtually every food and drinks producer in a trail to the Gironde, as to any other wine-growing area. Even today, there are chais in Bordeaux still piled high with crates of claret bearing the incongruous label 'shipped by Crosse & Blackwell', for the Swiss food giant, Nestlé, used its American subsidiary as a way into the wine business. The company bottling Pepsi-Cola in New York found itself the proud owner of Monsieur Henri wines, importers of the Spanish-made Yuri Sangria, at the time enjoying a fashionable boom.

But Pepsi and Nestlé were only peripheral: and so, despite the legends, were the private speculators and their favourite venue, the auction rooms. The examples set by Christie's and Heublein had speedily been copied: in the United States by the Sakowitz department store group with annual sales held in the company's home city of Houston—a far cry from the days only a few years previously when virtually no imported wine was sold between New Orleans and the Pacific Coast. In England, Sotheby's, which had traditionally been the pace-setter, was furious that Christie's had stolen a march, especially because the smaller house had sold the wine belonging to Lord Rose-bery, normally a client of theirs, and had set up their own wine department in 1970.

Because there were up to forty auctions a year in London, whereas Heublein and Sakowitz held their wine auctions only once a year, attention was concentrated on London. The American auctions were good talking points, useful opportunities for publicity-hungry owners of liquor stores to pay enormously for, say, a magnum of Mouton 1929, not unreasonably expecting to recoup the $9,000 outlay through increased sales of more ordinary wines. And in the longer-term the older French wines in the catalogue helped boost the many specially chosen Californian wines also at auction, wines which thus, by association, were elevated into the big league, a fact only understood by the French some years later.

But the London sales were different: by the end of 1971 they had proved beyond any doubt that earlier vintages of claret had proved a magnificent investment. The figures most often quoted were those of the first growths: more significant was the way that the 1961 vintage of second growths such as Ducru-Beaucaillou and Cos d'Estournel had more than trebled in price since they had opened a decade before. Palmer was even more special: its opening price in 1961 had been between £16 and £20 a case. The 1971 auction figures varied between £68 and £80. These prices, it could be shown to potential investors, were not freaks but relatively run-of-the-mill events at reputable, regular sales.

The auctions, backed by Michael Broadbent's relentless style of salesmanship, have borne a great deal of the blame for the explosion in prices of 1972–3. This is unfair, part of a more general attempt by the Bordelais to shift the blame from themselves to external forces. In fact Christie's, like any other saleroom, is only as powerful as its customers. In Broadbent's words, it was "the barometer, not the storm", as the contrast between the market in claret and that in vintage port shows clearly. In Christie's very first sale in 1966 it was the price of a celebrated port (Quinta do Noval '31) which provided the greatest sensation. "There were," wrote Edmund Penning-Rowsell, "distinct reverberations in port cellars throughout the country. As a result this rather rare wine came on to the market with surprising frequency, though with diminishing return to the sellers." For, as it turned out, there was simply not enough demand for vintage port from anyone outside England for it to be a satisfactory investment (despite attempts made by some American advisers to shift their clients into port at the end of 1972).

Nor were Burgundy or German wines good investments. Apart from a few millionaires prepared to pay almost anything for the precious 'Trockenbeerenauslese' wines made in tiny quantities, the Germans themselves refused to pay excessive prices for their own wines (at one Christie's sale in Düsseldorf there was much more enthusiastic bidding for French than for German wines). Foreigners are put off by the complications of the labelling and the relatively limited life of even the best hocks. Burgundy, too, provided an unfruitful soil for investors: the quantities were too small, and the names (apart from Romanée-Conti and Echézeaux) too unreliable an indication. Characteristically, the best-publicized event in Burgundy was the annual auction at the Hospices de Beaune of new wines which then disappeared into private cellars—and obscurity.

But claret was a different matter: quantities were large, names simple and well known, the track record good, and the 1855 Classification—duly amended—an apparently reliable guide. "A jeroboam," enthused the *Investors Review* late in 1972, "is an investor's best friend." Not all the investment was by new-comers or amateurs. Justerini and Brooks ran a scheme as early as 1970; another early venture was organized by Southard's, a long-established wine merchant which had originally been based in Bordeaux, and had once numbered a Gilbey among its partners. Moreover the wine side of Southard's business— itself part of a much larger drinks group—was managed by Lionel Frumkin, who as a young man had written a guide to Bordeaux's wines. Southard's was one of a number of companies which had previously run similar schemes for investing in single malt whisky, which resembled claret in that supplies were limited, and which benefited from several years in cask (it should have been a warning that the whisky market had been severely upset in the late 1960s because of overcrowding and over-investment in the much more easily distilled grain whiskies).

In his sales document Frumkin could point to some fabulous profits for earlier investors: for by March 1972 the prices of the 1964, 1966 and 1967 vintages (in Bordeaux rather than at Christie's) were three or four times the levels at which they had opened not so many years before. He also thoughtfully arranged for investors to be able to insure their investments. So euphoric was the atmosphere surrounding wine that summer that a major British insurance company would, for only a one per cent premium, insure the lucky investor against possible losses over a two-year period.

Other schemes were less solidly backed. By the autumn any expert was almost permanently buttonholed by eager promoters, or simply milked for free advice. Bill Bolter remembers a lunch where "a tall intellectual looking stockbroker sat quietly saying only 'how interesting'." Harry Waugh, Michael Broadbent, any independent expert was asked to participate in schemes of all sorts. The most reputable involved some of the best 'new names' in the business. The wines—to be held in an Investment Trust—were to be chosen by a panel which included Alexis Lichine and actually bought by Bernard Ginestet. (Other schemes were less formally presented. One involved John Train, Nicholas Barrow and an investment counsellor working out of Mexico City and proposing to set up an operation based in Luxembourg. This was pushed to one expert by an intermediary at a 21st birthday party in London, an opening which led the harassed expert to reply that "perhaps 3 a.m. in the morning after all that drink is not the best time to discuss investment in wine".)

These schemes were much discussed—and not always at 3 a.m. after a lot of drink—but they accounted for much more publicity than actual wine buying. More characteristic was the advice given through a variety of outlets by such professional advisers on investing outside the Stock Market as Richard Rush, an American professor. His arguments for buying claret always seemed to stem from a particularly lucky purchase he had made in 1969 in the English cathedral city of Canterbury where he had stumbled upon an expert wine merchant of the old school.

Rush could point to the opportunities offered, not only by the previous rise in prices, but also by the relative anarchy in the American price situation: as late as October 1971 he was buying Lafite 1962 in a Washington store for $12 a bottle, under half the then normal price in New York. At another Washington store he could buy Duhart-Milon 1966 for just over $2·50 a bottle, a mere quarter of the price reached by the inferior 1962 from the same estate the previous May at the Heublein auction.

Although French wine was gradually becoming a more important part of the business for liquor dealers, yet these market imperfections ensured that London remained the centre of the market in wine, as it is for so many other commodities (and financial instruments like Euro-dollar notes and bonds) where the number of British holders of the underlying assets is relatively unimportant. The major London wine merchants still held relatively large quantities of earlier vintages. These helped to stabilize a market which was less hysterical than Bordeaux and was boosted by the principal asset of British dealers, their reputation for honest dealing and their willingness to deal on narrow margins, provided the quantities were sufficiently sizeable. In July 1972 Edmund Penning-Rowsell noted that "while prices of château-bottled clarets appear extravagantly high to English consumers, to others the apparently boundless auction-room supply of classed growths of the vintages of the '50s and '60s, at prices moderate by Continental and American standards, is very attractive." For by the end of 1972 even leading Paris restaurants, not a class likely to flinch from having to charge exorbitant sums for their wines, were complaining that they could offer their customers the best champagne (itself a drink whose price had risen relatively rapidly) cheaper than even a run-of-the-mill claret.

It was easy for the British onlooker to gasp at, say, the £270 a dozen paid at Christie's for a dozen of Latour 1961. This was roughly treble the opening price of the new 1971 vintage. But ullage, fining, bottling and storage charges would add at least 25 per cent, and a decade of interest charges would double the resulting sum. If the 1961 wine was going to cost £40 on a restaurant's wine list, then that euphoric autumn no one seemed unduly worried. And even the sums being done about the 1971, proving that they would cost £100 or more a bottle when they were ready for drinking, were no deterrent.

That year's Heublein auction showed the mood well enough. The star turn was a jeroboam of Mouton 1929, eventually purchased by one Joseph Zemel for a record $9,200 (nearly £4,200). Zemel's interest "began with the wine we used to have with our Passover meal", from which blessed beginning "my tastes slowly matured to drier French wines. Now I prefer Pomerols", a taste he had the freedom to exercise because his father-in-law owned a large liquor store.

For all the slightly mocking tone of the reports there was sound sense behind such extravagances. When the owner of a liquor store in the Bronx district of New York advertised "Gold $58 an ounce—Wine $47 an ounce" because he had just bought an extremely expensive bottle of hock, he was, in fact, merely tempting readers into buying wines that cost a hundredth of that figure (which he had exaggerated slightly anyway). But the equation of gold and wine was natural. That autumn both were hot investments.

Wine became an even hotter property with the 1972 vintage, the latest to start in forty years. Despite good weather for the harvest, the miserable cold earlier in the year had ensured that the vintage was likely to be acid and hard, as indeed it has since proved to be. But, for the first time in Bordeaux's history, the sale at excessive prices of a vintage which everyone knew would not be of the top quality was guaranteed before a grape had been picked. Corporate finance combined with modern marketing forecasts seemed sufficiently impressive for the basic rules to be broken. Even at the height of the pre-mildew boom the buyers who swept the Médoc in October 1868 were sure they were buying a superb wine. There had been other widely-acclaimed and eagerly bought vintages, from 1868 to 1959, which had turned, financially at least, sour, but the idea that the world was waiting eagerly for an overpriced glass of hard red wine was new.

It was encouraged by the world-wide interest in the vintage: "If anyone was burnt after a cool dull summer," wrote Edmund Penning-Rowsell disgustedly, "it was not from the sun but from exposure to the battery lights of the TV film teams who pervaded some of the better-known châteaux so extensively that at times it was hard to see the grapes for the cameras."

Nevertheless the warning signs were already there: sales to those normally loyal customers the Belgians and the Germans stopped rising in the last four months of the year and they were by no means buoyant in other 'rational' markets such as Norway and Sweden. Moreover everyone knew that sales to Britain were already being inflated in anticipation of the arrival of Value Added Tax the following April, which would, it was feared, add an additional impost on to wine.

Nevertheless the scene for a further boost in prices was being set elsewhere in France: at the 1972 Hospices de Beaune sale prices were up by a fifth. Foreign—especially American—demand for Châteauneuf du Pape had sent prices of Rhône wines soaring; and by the end of the year, according to a leading merchant, "between 80 and 90 per cent" of the 1972 Burgundy vintage "had already been sold to the shippers . . . where thirty years ago it was quite common to see wines maturing in the cellars of the grower for three years."

No wonder the opening price of Bordeaux Rouge was 3,500 francs, 15 per cent above the level reached by then by the 1971s—which themselves had been only 2,100 in January—and nearly three times the opening price of the splendid 1970s. Nevertheless the market seemed insatiable: shippers were more concerned to fulfil the sales for which they had contracted in a year when wine exports were to rise by nearly three-fifths than to think about the wine's price or quality. If the growers of ordinary wines needed spot cash for the first time in a century proprietors of better growths could afford to wait. And given the way

that the trade had, in their eyes, made such fortunes out of the
'70 and '71 vintages, they saw no reason not to. After all, it was
not so long since owners of even the 'crus bourgeois' had been
glad to get the same price, 3,000, as was now being paid for
Bordeaux Rouge. And these owners had been shown no mercy
by the shippers at that time—when the owners were not getting
the 4,000 francs or so they needed to maintain their estate and its
wine-making equipment in a proper state. It was their turn
now.

So they were intransigent; and it was, fundamentally, their
opposition which killed a number of initiatives that winter to
try and restore order to the market. The first attempt was made
by Peter Sichel, as Chairman of the Merchants' Federation,
who in November proposed a 'three-year contract' between
shippers and growers, which would ensure that prices did not
rise by more than 15 per cent in any year. The owners wanted
something more and they got it, thanks to the combined initiative
of Henri Martin at the CIVB and Daniel Doustin, the 'Super-
prefect' appointed from Paris with considerable powers (as
usual, Chaban-Delmas was pursuing a policy of masterly
inactivity so far as wine was concerned).

The Martin scheme provided for a massive increase in production. At least another 75,000 acres would be replanted, to
bring the area under vines in the department back to its pre-
war level. At the same time the CIVB would have powers to
establish a band of prices within which wine had to be sold,
and funds would be made available for a stock of wine to be
built up in bad times to stabilize the market in the longer term.
But it meant that the shippers would have to surrender their
basic freedom and accept a controlled market. And they were
certainly in no mood, or financial position, to be defeatist, to
surrender to the growers or the CIVB—not yet anyway.

Meanwhile, the customers were still wandering around
Bordeaux with open cheque-books (it did not take many of
them for such a gossipy community to get the impression that
there were uncounted hordes of such 'speculators' abroad),
and the trade and the growers' attitudes were still light years
apart.

Ever since then the growers have been accused of 'greed'.
At one extreme Harry Waugh declared that they had "got

away with their 1969s, a vintage of no extraordinary quality at a price well above their value", which seems a bit hard. But the English wine trade magazine, *Harpers*, summed up the result of generations of ill-will: "It is also ironic that in some circles among the Bordeaux négociants, there is a movement afoot to form committees in conjunction with these same proprietors, the idea being to produce a 'shock absorber' effect on prices. All of which sounds very public-spirited and liberal, until it is realized that such committees are merely to whistle against the very hot wind blowing today called 'world demand'. In any case, it might well be asked where such committees were some ten to fifteen years ago when many a small proprietor lived a life of penury because of the poor prices his wines realized in Bordeaux."

But for the moment the growers could wait. In Peter Sichel's words: "Up to 1971 in an average year a grower of Bordeaux Rouge even if he sold his entire crop probably had to borrow money to finance the production for the following year. Today he can finance 1973 by selling only half his crop. In St. Emilion or the Médoc he only needs to sell 25 per cent of his crop. Perhaps a first growth could cover its costs by asking shippers to pay for their samples."

All the shippers could do was to diversify, to try and find other sources of acceptable wine, and to tie up as many 'abonnements' as possible. The search for alternatives was frantic, especially in France, where the sales of Bordeaux were closely linked to their price. In early 1973 for instance a major chain started to sell wine from the Midi in claret-shaped bottles, at 2 francs against 7·50 for St. Emilion—sales of which dropped to less than half the previous year's figures (they also alleged that only five out of the forty 'Bordeaux' wines sold by their rivals came from the Gironde).

Similarly, Nicolas heavily promoted its 'vins de terroir', entitled only to the 'VDQS'* label, below AOC, a class of products made all over France. These had been heavily promoted in 1971 by the French government in the United States under the umbrella of 'country wines of France'. In early 1973 Hugues Lawton, who was working for Barton and Guestier, shocked the traditionalists by arranging a tasting in Bordeaux itself,

* Vins Délimités de Qualité Supérieur.

but not of claret—his company was buying properties in the Rhône and in Beaujolais (similarly Pepsi-Cola bought a major estate in the Rhine at the height of the boom). In the Gironde, by contrast, the prices of actual estates had escalated even faster than those of the wines they produced, so that, despite a lot of publicity, virtually none changed hands.

Even more shockingly, Jean Calvet announced that for the first time in his family firm's century-and-a-half history he would be selling VDQS wines produced not in Burgundy or in Bordeaux—he was also selling, as 'Vieux Calvet', a non-appellation wine with at least one year in bottle (in the event Calvet was both clever and lucky: a severe fire had destroyed the family cellars five years before, and the insurance had proved inadequate to enable the family to rebuild their stocks—though not their warehouses. So he did not have the funds with which to speculate: he also relied heavily on a long-serving employee, M. Guimberteau, who remembered past follies and exercised an effective brake).

Calvet's had never owned châteaux and, though members of Group A, were not heavily involved with owners. But other shippers felt obliged to return to that basic Bordeaux practice, the long-term 'abonnement', making a long-term gentleman's agreement with a grower to take his wine. This was different from the defensive impetus behind Group A; for the groups involved were, generally, bigger and they had a more direct access to the final consumer than the members of Group A—which still had a few exclusivities left, notably Beychevelle.

But there were, seemingly, sound reasons why a large modern group should imitate the habits of long-dead Johnstons and Bartons. For one, salesmen, agents in foreign markets and their customers, especially restaurant-owners, wanted assurance of continuity; they did not wish to have to disturb their range of wines too frequently or too drastically (only monopoly state buyers in Sweden or Norway could afford the luxury of absolute choice among myriads of small estates). Besides, the men at the top of the new groups were used to modern methods of marketing, in which the promotion of a brand name was an expensive, long-term business. And to justify the expenditure they had to have assurance of continuity of supply. Michael Longhurst, a keen young salesman who had worked as

Bamford's assistant at Loudenne since 1970, put it succinctly: "It seemed extraordinary that a luxury product was being offered by thirty or forty different people. Their natural reaction was that 'I can't set up a business with that sort of capital merely to speculate'." And 1972 would be the test of the genuineness of the many new arrangements made in the previous year: "We'd set up ongoing exclusivities . . . if we hadn't bought the 1972s then we would have been stuck forever."

Gilbeys was one of the three or four groups which, between them, had arrangements with fifteen or twenty châteaux each (and these excluded the groups of estates actually owned by merchants, like Cordier, Cruse, Moueix and Eschenauer). The others were Lichine and Ginestet, the only one without major external sources of finance. But every case was different: Bamford and Longhurst were buying, not only for IDV's own outlets, but also for Ab Simon at Austin Nichols, who, secure in the profits he had shown on his massive purchases of earlier vintages, was probably the biggest single buyer of all. But, to complicate matters, he was also buying large quantities of wine from Gilbeys and through Nathaniel Johnston: significantly 'Natty', the oldest-established merchant of them all, had grasped the fact that a Chartronnais could no longer afford to make investments mostly on his own account, but would have to act principally as an intermediary, a sort of super-broker, responsible for buying, storing and shipping the wines but not for the financing of stocks.

Ginestet, no longer able to rely on a spread of wines from the family estates, had reacted in the opposite direction to 'Natty' and arranged 'abonnements' on a large scale. But not as heavily as Lichine. The firm of that name was no longer in the hands of Lichine himself, but of Jacques Théo, a dapper, charming little man who, as the local manager of Lloyds Bank, had helped Bass Charrington with their take-overs in Bordeaux and had then been invited to run their operations in the Gironde. He, too, could claim that he was buying not on his own account, but because of actual or forecast demand from other companies within the group, or Bass's American agents, Dreyfus Ashby.

In England, too, Bass Charrington were bullish. Once the combined group had run down its stocks it had returned to the Bordeaux market in a big way with the '69s and, unlike some of their hesitant American equivalents, had also bought a lot of the '71s. By the end of 1972 they were pressing all their Bordeaux suppliers, especially Philippe Cottin at La Bergerie, who had not raised the price of his Mouton Cadet, which consequently was selling so well in England that he could supply only half of BCV's requirements. (In the United States Cottin's situation was less happy. La Bergerie's former agents, National Distillers, had fallen into the hands of men more interested in hard liquors and who were selling only 33,000 cases a year; an actual reduction on the 1960s figures. So in December 1972 in an inevitably well publicized and dramatic move Baron Philippe removed the agency from National Distillers and formed a joint company with the Buckingham Corporation, which he felt had performed miracles for Cutty Sark Scotch. He was soon sued for breach of contract by National Distillers.)

The build-up of exclusivities reduced the choice of wines for other major buyers, like Delor, which did not have many contracts, or Barton & Guestier, which would have liked to have more than it did. And the new 'abonnements' and the way they narrowed the market together with the growers' new-found security, provided the basis for the hysteria which erupted in the first half of 1973.

But the underlying factors were much confused by the general hysteria over 'speculators' at the auction rooms, and, in particular, by the impression, rife that winter, that Japan was poised to replace the United States as the newest and most exciting market for claret.

This was always nonsense, for the Japanese never looked like becoming major wine buyers. As always their commercial policy was very clear: they had effectively prevented imports of wine until their own industry was strong enough to cope (the same tactic they had employed with Scotch, imports of which were liberalized only when Sun Tory had established a stranglehold for its own—by no means unsatisfactory—brands). Indeed import restrictions on wine were lifted only in 1970 and even when imports started to boom a couple of years later wine still took a bad fourth place to beer, saké and whisky among Japanese drinkers. Not that Japanese wine was or is any good. Reporters inspecting the tiny vineyards worked out that "on your production that means you are getting approximately three bottles of wine from each grape. By the way, why are those barrels marked 'return to Bulgarian State Railways'?"— for the simple reason, as the reporter knew perfectly well, that Bulgaria was the source of much 'Japanese' wine.*

The appetite for wine, previously non-existent, had been encouraged by the increasing numbers of Japanese travelling abroad, by the growing appetite for meat (for their former, fish-based diet was no encouragement for claret salesmen), and by the influence of the thousands of foreigners who had visited the Olympic Games in Tokyo in 1964 and the Osaka World Exhibition six years later.

Claret, like whisky and many other foreign imports, was strictly a luxury business, designed to provide impressive offerings for the twice-yearly Japanese business gifts habitual in Japan. And it was the prices paid by the Japanese, rather than the quantities involved, which so excited the Bordelais imagination. In reality, even in 1973, the peak year for Japanese imports, they bought less claret than, say, the Canadians, though the average price they paid for the wines they imported in bottle— 20 francs—was higher even than that paid by the British, and a quarter above that paid by the Americans. Jean Calvet pioneered the market, because his company's wines were imported by Sun Tory, but in 1973 Barton & Guestier started to swamp the market.

The result of the Japanese eagerness was that today wine lists of leading hotels contain some sensational and startlingly-priced wines. Sun Tory's *cave de vin* lists a range of Latours from 1919 to 1970, with prices up to 70,000 yen (£140) for a bottle of the 1937 and the 1945.

But the reality—a sharp increase in a hitherto virtually non-existent market—was much less interesting than the legend, which consisted of hordes of yellow men spreading through the Gironde, carrying either notebooks (to learn how to imitate claret and Sauternes) or open cheque-books (to buy up French vineyards). The classic story concerns the alleged attempt by a group of executives from Canon Cameras to buy Château

* The basic joke about the Japanese and wine concerns the alleged advertisement for "Genuine Scotch Whisky made from real Scotch Grapes".

Canon in St. Emilion from its formidable owner, Mme Fournier. In the event the Japanese bid openly for only one estate, the unremarkable Château Caillavet, south of Bordeaux. Sun Tory offered the remarkably elevated price of 11·5 million francs (over £1 million) for a hundred acres of vines in March 1973; and the timing and size of the bid both fed the flames of hysteria very nicely.

By then two streams were reaching their flood tide. In the first quarter of the year Christie's conducted an unusually large number of sales, through which early speculators managed to re-sell a great deal of wine in advance of April 1st—when Value Added Tax would increase the price paid for most lots bought at auctions. The trade was surprised that prices did not fall as a result, and the ability to absorb apparently endless quantities of wine created a general feeling of resignation: that prices were, indeed, crazy, but that there was really nothing much that anyone could do about it.

This feeling of helplessness was not confined to foreign buyers. Late the previous year, Raymond le Sauvage, the President of the brokers' union, had expressed a feeling widespread in Bordeaux that they were "all helpless spectators, buffeted by external events". So the owners of the major growths took their time, luxuriating in their new-found ability to sit back, serene in the assurance that they would infallibly be wooed by innumerable potential buyers. They knew their wine was not great: but they also knew the price their neighbours were getting. And it was this 'keeping up with the Jones' factor which, added to the historical suspicion of the trade, prevented any sanity in the marketing of 1972's wines.

Harry Waugh put it succinctly: "I arrived in Bordeaux at the end of March 1973 and was able for the first time to taste, but not enthuse over the young wine. Upon remonstration, grower after grower admitted the price was very high, but explained if he did not stick to it, his neighbour would succeed and he would lose face. The fact of the matter is the growers had become greedy and I do not think I overdid it when I compared their attitude with the parable of the Gadarene swine in the Bible, for over the precipice they have gone and with a vengeance. Incidentally that was not at all easy to put into French."

For warning signs there were aplenty. In the previous December Waugh, as buyer for a major wine-buying cooperative society, had enthused over the 1970 crus bourgeois one of which 'was rated higher than any of the classified growths' at a blind tasting. At one important auction Penning-Rowsell noted that "American buyers were less prominent than usual"; yet the American market was at least still expanding, though slowly. By the first quarter of 1973, however, the cannier Canadians and Belgians were buying noticeably less wine than the previous year: and sales to the Norwegians and Swedes had slumped by more than a half. But there was a far more ominous sign. Sales of the basic 'appellations' to the French public had steadily diminished as it grew more expensive than its competitors, Beaujolais and Côtes du Rhône. And in the second quarter of 1973, for the first time in a generation, both these out-sold Bordeaux in the French market.

Nevertheless, the traditional relationships between growers and shippers, and between different growers, prevented any response. For even in 1973, in the immortal phrase of Colin Anderson, one of the leading British wine buyers, prices in Bordeaux "were still set by five growers lying to each other. Prices are paid practically on pure hearsay. It would be laughable if so much money weren't involved." Attempts to reason them down inevitably broke on the same rocks: an inherited refusal to believe the merchants, pride in their wine as expressed in its price, and, in 1973, the fear that the price that year would be taken into account in any future re-classification. For Baron Philippe had, early in the year, finally been elevated to the first rank and, in theory, the re-classification was due to be applied to other 'classified' growths. So, in a typical incident, Natty Johnston believed he had convinced the owner of Léoville-Poyferré to open at a 'reasonable' 18,000 francs—the same as for his 1971s—and even confirmed the deal at the weekend on the golf-course. But on Monday came the news of an inferior château selling at 24,000 to Bernard Ginestet: and Léoville-Poyferré duly opened at 32,000.

Henri Martin's account of what happened to him is probably typical. Early in the year he received a telegram from Aymar Achille-Fould, the minister who was chief proprietor of the family-owned Beychevelle, one of the few châteaux still sold

through Group A—mainly because of Achille-Fould's friendship
with Roland Duvivier, the abrasive managing director of de
Luze. A group of growers, including Borie, talked at length
over 'un sirop écossais'* and the next morning Martin told
Fould that he thought 18,000 was a reasonable opening price
for his wine. He then left for a cruise and when he returned
six weeks later found Daniel Lawton on his doorstep with the
news that a lesser neighbour had asked for, and got, 24,000. So
Martin in his turn demanded 32,000.

Similar tales were being told the length and breadth of the
Gironde—Longhurst remembers day-long haggles at dozens
of châteaux, with intervals in the office devoted to dealing with
an uninterrupted stream of telephone calls from frantic buyers.
By April wine was, apparently, so short that British buyers
were 'faced with a virtual ultimatum', were being told bluntly
to buy their requirement now or their normal allocations would
be sold elsewhere. But by then the peak had been reached—
with a record price of 42,000 francs being paid for Léoville-
Lascases, probably the last major estate to offer its wines for
sale.

Indeed, by the time the first growths opened in June, their
prices looked almost reasonable, a mere 90,000 francs for
Mouton or Haut-Brion, 100,000 for Lafite (though with minimum resale prices fixed at between 116,000 for Sweden to 132,000
for the USA). These prices, nearly four times the last 'normal'
year of 1967, were under three times the average prices of the
second crus. And for all the sound and fury of the intervening
years, the basic price of Bordeaux Rouge had still not risen as
fast as had the better wines. Indeed the major difference, a very
welcome one, was that, as had happened in the earlier boom
of the 1860s, the price of the 'crus bourgeois' had risen sufficiently—though not much more than other wines—to make it
worthwhile for growers to take some pride and care in their
wine-making.

But an eerie calm descended over the scene in the second
quarter: prices of Bordeaux Rouge drifted downwards, but
not very much, and not many deals were struck. In that other
market, Christie's wine auctions, prices again drifted, but not

* Literally "A Scottish liqueur". It seems likely that the fate of
claret prices was decided over glasses of Drambuie.

9

dangerously so: in July, Penning-Rowsell commented on the "standstill quality mixed with record prices for special items that has marked the wine saleroom scene since the pre-VAT torrents were disposed of earlier in the year".

Cynics, believing that large companies together with their management consultants, marketing experts and whiz-kids all move together at the same time and precisely in the wrong direction, could point to the opening of major and expensive new warehouses for Barton & Guestier at Blanquefort (by Chaban-Delmas) as one portent of evil times to come, to the announcement by Delor of their plans for equally expensive new premises as another, and to the take-over bid launched in April by the British Bowater-Ralli company for de Luze as a sure sign that the boom was at an end. For Bowater was run by the whizziest of financial kids, and the manager of its French operation was a former management consultant at McKinseys.

Less biased observers would have absorbed the implicit warning to Bordeaux contained in a comment of *Beverage Media*, the American trade magazine. "Remember," an editorial advised that June, "American interest is not just limited to drinking one wine. The American consumer is probably tasting more wine than any European who confines his preference to one local wine with no curiosity or interest to try any other type." In that sort of market Bordeaux had no hope of selling its over-priced '72s. Its future lay in the path being mapped by Baron Philippe's new partners, who were preparing to spend $300,000 a year—or 75c a bottle based on existing sales—on promoting Mouton Cadet. Yet this lay in the future; the present lay with Henri Martin's euphoria, which reached its peak that June.

A few sporadic attempts were made to rationalize the relationship between growers and shippers: Bernard Ginestet gathered together the owners of the estates he had under contract, with no very clear result; although one grower, young Pierre Tari, son of Nicholas at Giscours, showed the way with a far-reaching new type of 'abonnement'. He agreed with Martin Bamford to relate the buying price of any given vintage to the market position at the time, allowing the grower to mature at least some of each vintage in his own cellars, thus enabling him to share in any sudden surges in price.

But by then the 1973 flowering had come, and it clearly

indicated that a very large vintage was in prospect. "Horror of horrors," said Longhurst, remembering the 50,000 cases of château-bottled wine he had in Gilbeys' cellars sold to Ab Simon to cover his requirements over the next few years, "the size of the 1973 vintage could be seen."

He may have been worried about his levels of stocks: but many other shippers were still obsessed by the wine they had committed to deliver which they could not buy—not if they wanted to stay in business, that is.

21

Winegate Act I: the raids

The 'greed' of the growers, combined with the sheer physical shortage of wine bearing the precious AOC label, had reduced many shippers to desperation. For a year they had happily been selling, at inflated prices, wine they did not possess, confident of being able to buy the necessary quantities in time to meet the delivery dates. Nevertheless, by the spring of 1973 they were seemingly faced with only two, equally unappetizing, alternatives: failing to deliver the wine or buying it at prices so far above the level at which they had previously sold it that their fragile finances could not stand the strain.

Relief for half a dozen of the less scrupulous was sudden, if unexpected. It came in the person of old Louis Bert's notoriously disreputable grandson, Pierre, accompanied by an apparently unlimited supply of 'acquits verts'. Pierre Bert had learnt all the tricks of the trade from his grandfather. He had learnt to love wine but to despise the rules which surrounded its sale—an attitude highly convenient for anyone whose livelihood depended on turning the law's restrictions to his own ends. For Pierre Bert possessed all the attributes required in someone destined to expose the essential hypocrisy of French wine laws—and the tricks of those who had to comply with them. He was and remains a compulsive exhibitionist, a trait which has invariably led him to expose many of his schemes to discovery by the police, the Ministry of Agriculture's Fraud Squad, or the tax authorities (he displayed this compulsion early in life: he was clever enough to be considered for the 'prix d'honneur' at the Jesuit school he attended, but ruined his chances by being caught singing the 'Internationale' in the street just before the prize-giving).

For he is the brightest and most engaging of souls, small and perky, witty and literate,* able to clothe his cynicism and his misdeeds in a style entirely suitable for an age which cherishes anti-heroes of the requisite quality and panache.

His career, however, had already been rhythmically punctuated by brushes with the law. Like Jean Cordier he had inherited his business from his grandfather; his father had died after a short spell of imprisonment on charges of collaborating with the Germans. So when Louis Bert died at the age of ninety—after an heroic attempt to ward off the effects of a severe winter by sliding bare-foot on the ice—he bequeathed a business in very poor financial shape. Pierre found that he owed 15 million old francs to the authorities to compensate for the excess profits made during the war, a fine he could meet only by selling Château Rolland, the lovely house in Barsac his father had given him as a wedding present. So he cheated in the simplest possible way: he started to fill in his record books indistinctly, hoping to ensure that the authorities could not follow the pattern of his trading practices. But, true to form, he felt impelled to boast of his misdeeds: an informer told the Fraud Squad: another fine was imposed, this time 300 million old francs—the equivalent of four months' sales. So he had to sell a 75 per cent controlling interest to a well known but equally well-detested local character, M. Grenouilleau, who, in theory, took over the responsibility of paying the fine. But, through an unforeseen legal oversight, this had been levied on Bert in person, not in his capacity as managing director of Louis Bert & Cie. Grenouilleau promptly refused to pay and an interminable law-suit ensued.

So Bert became a broker, welcomed by the many shippers who disliked Grenouilleau—and especially by the wholesale merchants on the Quai des Paludates. In 1969 he finally won his case against Grenouilleau and was able to set up again as a merchant after a dramatic reconciliation with his cousin Bertrand de Pinos who had originally helped Grenouilleau oust Bert from the family firm. By this time Bert was an expert on every type of wine fraud: and he was soon 'cooking' wine on a large scale,

---

* *In Vino Veritas*, his account of his life and his part in 'Winegate', is a delight, beautifully written, witty and—as far as I can judge— largely accurate. Although Florence Mothe, of the local paper, *Sud-Ouest*, helped to ghost the book, much of its quality is due to its nominal author.

melting sugar in a jam-making cauldron to produce a syrup which in its turn would boost the alcoholic content of a 'Barsac' or a 'Sauternes' and thus increase the price. Unfortunately his partner bought all his sugar, ninety tons of it, from a single grocer and this alone was quite enough to arouse suspicions. After a slapstick episode when Bert, fleeing from the Fraud Squad, hid a crucial 'acquit vert' under the cloth covering the high altar of a village church before handing it over to his customer, his ingenuity was again rewarded only with a massive fine.

Nothing daunted he soldiered on, only to be caught, like so many of his colleagues, short of suitably accredited wine. Then in the offices of an old friend and good customer, a self-made shipper called Lucien Castaing,* he noticed a secretary using a small machine to frank 'acquits verts' with an official stamp. For, in an effort to simplify the administration of the wine laws, the authorities had allowed suitably approved shippers to stamp their own 'acquits verts' to avoid a visit to the local tax office every time they wanted to move a load of wine. The controls were still stiff enough: the master certificate, green for AOC wines, white or straw-coloured for the cheaper 'vins de consommation courante', table wines, travelled with the wine itself; when it reached its destination a detachable coupon was torn off and returned to the tax office nearest to the seller's place of business, which also received the seller's copy of the certificate.

Bert noted that the detachable coupon did not indicate the colour of the wine involved, or, indeed, its 'appellation'. So the tax office had no means of telling if the colour of the wine received by the purchaser was the same as that sold by the vendor. Only a comparison of the certificate itself (held by a completely different office) with the copy sent to the vendor's own tax office would reveal any discrepancy.

The difference of colour which could thus be concealed was absolutely crucial: for although *red* Bordeaux with the precious AOC label was worth over three times as much as a run-of-the-mill red wine, the difference was only 10 per cent in the case of white wine. So if Bert could buy ordinary red wine and AOC

* In his book Bert mispells the name as 'Castaingt', curiously the same as one of the most distinguished of Mauriac's 'fils'.

white, and then switch the certificates so that he was selling ordinary white but AOC red, he would lose only 10 per cent by demoting the white wine while gaining 300 per cent by promoting the red. The possession of a franking machine would enable him to do just that: the original 'acquit' would travel with the red wine, the detachable coupon would then be returned to his own tax office which would already have received an 'acquit' relating to a similar quanity of *white* wine. Bert had only to remove the carbon paper separating the original from the copy before filling in the different colours on each one. Moreover, if he sold only to other merchants, the size and price of any transaction would not have to be officially reported to the CIVB—as were all sales to a retail or foreign customer.

For Bert, facing losses of 300,000 francs (£25,000) he could not hope to cover, the idea was a life-saver. But to carry it out he needed a supplier of good red wine which could pass as claret, he needed cellars and, above all, he needed a front man without a criminal record, for not even the most gullible tax office would entrust a franking machine to him personally. The supplier was easy to arrange: even in early 1973 there was plenty of wine available in the Midi at a reasonable price and of the right quality —for 1972 claret was hard and unattractive, qualities not much in demand without the precious 'acquit'. And after a frantic search lasting several weeks he also found a broken-down warehouse forty miles from Bordeaux at St. Germain-en-Graves, a hamlet so small that it did not even have a café, and leased the place (which would, however, hold only 18,500 gallons) from its accommodating owner, M. Ballarin. For his front man Bert selected his driver, a simple soul called Serge Balan, who, crucially, had no convictions against his name. Balan entered into the spirit of his new role so thoroughly that he even suggested painting a sign on the warehouse proclaiming its importance as the headquarters of 'Serge Balan et Cie'. Finally, his friend Castaing recommended one Barnabé as a driver who knew how to keep his mouth shut.

It remained only to convince the local tax office at Langon that S. Balan et Cie was a solid enough enterprise to allow the issue of a franking machine, and then to deposit the necessary 10,000 francs as evidence of financial solidity (since the theoretical alternative, a banker's reference, was clearly not a practicable proposition). The tax-man at Langon proved amenable. According to Bert he even complimented young Balan on his choice of instructor in the technicalities of wine-trading. This seems unlikely: but Balan fulfilled the necessary conditions, a clean record and the necessary deposit. For once, French official machinery worked speedily and the franking machine was issued on 20 February, only a month after permission had been granted.

So S. Balan et Cie was in business—and on a grand scale: although it was only four months before the law caught up with the conspirators, the profits in that time amounted to 4.7 million francs, an annual rate of over £1 million. For the quantities were, relatively, enormous. Eventually, the judge concluded, S. Balan et Cie sold 29,712·67 hectolitres of wine—enough to fill four million bottles. Of this staggering amount 90 per cent was sold accompanied by the faked acquits, the other 10 per cent was merely not of the quality appropriate to the appellation under which it was being marketed.

The fraud itself looks larger when compared with other irregularities discovered by the Fraud Squad and the tax authorities. In 1972 they had carried out 6,000 inspections throughout France, had uncovered 177 offences serious enough to warrant prosecution: but, in all, these had involved only 25,000 hectolitres of wine.

In Bert's book he compares the four of them—Balan the ex-chauffeur, Ballarin the helpful owner of the warehouse, Barnabé the driver and himself to the four Musketeers, but with one crucial difference, that the latter-day d'Artagnan and his companions were destined actually to be caught by the lackeys of the Cardinal Richelieu—in the improbable disguise of the inspectors from the Tax and Fraud Squads. Yet, despite the squalor of the setting, the leaky warehouse in the muddy hamlet, he makes the whole affair sound grand, innocent fun—the comings and goings of innumerable impatient tanker-drivers, placated by the urbane Bertrand de Pinos, the discovery that Ballarin enjoyed acting as housekeeper (though Bert himself saw to the supply of wines), the wonderment of the locals, their attempts to sell him wine and to pump Mme Ballarin, the local school-teacher, for information.

Bert's heart, so he says, was innocence itself: his attitude that of a smuggler using a false passport to transport goods on which duty had in fact been paid. For, he claims, he was selling only wines of decent quality, thus shielding the public from less scrupulous suppliers.

Whatever the attitudes, his discovery of a magic source of AOC claret made him welcome to half a dozen merchants; and, through them, some of France's biggest retail outlets became indirectly involved. But none of the names of Bert's own customers were well known and certainly none could remotely be described as Chartronnais.

In the third week of April, however, there was a dramatic development. Bert chanced his arm and invited himself to the august—if dilapidated—offices of Cruse et Fils Frères. Bert (who may merely have been hoping for a good story rather than a sale) found in the event that the Cruses, like many of their lesser brethren, were desperately short of AOC claret: indeed they had American customers who had rejected perfectly good wine unaccompanied by the requisite 'acquit vert'. But Emmanuel Cruse had retired in 1964 at the age of eighty and since then the business had largely been in the hands of his 'cousin' Yvan, who did the purchasing, and of Emmanuel's son Lionel—who had the misfortune to be born a hunchback in a family noted for the swagger and physical distinction of its style. Emmanuel was a difficult act to follow. To make it worse, the family had in the past managed to balance commercial ruthlessness with gentlemanly charm. Emmanuel had (amply) provided the toughness, while his brother Christian had brought complementary qualities: he was a great gentleman, much loved by the English merchants whom he visited for nearly half a century, and a sure guide to the intricacies of Bordeaux—Edmund Penning-Rowsell, for example, freely acknowledges that his classic work on the Wines of Bordeaux could not have been compiled without Christian Cruse's store of knowledge, and his freely-shared wine cellar. With their retirement the balance had gone, and only a cynical, arrogant toughness remained.

Lionel, Yvan and their uncle Hermann, who together effectively ran the business (there were five other directors, none, to outsiders, of any real importance), knew of course of Bert's reputation; they had been at daggers drawn with the Bert family for generations. So they hesitated before buying from him: five times in one week Bert visited their offices, thoroughly enjoying

9*

his transformation from a mere supplicant broker into a supplier of a status sufficient to allow him to see Lionel, Yvan or their manager, M. Jaubert. Even when the Cruses agreed to buy from him they insisted that the 'AOC' wine they purchased would be exchanged for a similar quantity of 'consommation courante' wine. Moreover they would not buy from so transparently artificial a company as S. Balan et Cie. Old habits die hard: the Cruses, normally accustomed to satisfying their requirements through only one broker, their 'cousin' Lawton, would unbend enough to admit as suppliers only Bertrand de Pinos and Pierre Servant, another of Bert's inner ring.

It seems absurd that the Cruses should have expected to delude anyone with these transparent precautions. The alleged need to dispose of cc* red wine contrasted with the fact that they were buying large quantities at the same time as they were, supposedly, offloading their unwanted surplus on Bert's associates (and, what is more, at a price well above the going market rate). And the refusal to deal with S. Balan et Cie—except as a buyer of cc wine—looked equally hollow, for all the 'AOC' wine came direct from Balan's warehouse and all the dealings were done with Bert himself, ignoring not only Balan, but the nominal suppliers, Servant and de Pinos, as well.

The margins were so good that there was money in it for everyone: the Cruses were 'buying' AOC red wine—mostly, in theory, basic Bordeaux, but also some of 'superior' appellations like St. Emilion and Margaux—at about 15 per cent below the market price (when everyone else in Bordeaux was clamouring for the same wine at any price) and selling cc wine at above the market value: de Pinos and Servant were getting a 2 per cent brokerage fee and also a turn on the 'wines' they were 'buying' from Balan and 'selling' to Cruse.

However, once the system had got going in late May, no wine needed to change hands (or tanker lorries for that matter). Even before they had started to buy wine from Bert, a number of tankers had arrived at the Cruses' warehouses carrying wine from the Midi bearing an 'acquit blanc', had immediately been equipped with an 'acquit vert' and directed to another Cruse warehouse at Ambares. The Bert-Cruse system took this idea to its logical conclusion: Barnabé would drive to their warehouse, hand in

* Consommation courante.

his 'acquit vert', wait a little while and then depart with the 'acquit blanc'. In the first fortnight of June the Cruses—not counting Bert's other customers—received over 87,000 gallons of wine, although Balan's cellars would hold only a fifth of that amount and themselves received only token amounts from outside. Indeed, once the paper really started flying, the only wine which changed hands were the little bottles of samples, scrupulously supplied to cover each transaction.

Eighteen months later the judge's summing up spelt out how Barnabé spent a typical day, in this case 7 June. Work started at 7 a.m. when he left the Balan warehouse driving a tanker containing 3,400 gallons of red wine bearing an 'acquit vert'. By 8.30 he was parked in the street in front of the entrance to the Cruses' cellars. He took the 'acquit' to the reception, where they told him to wait. This he duly did (except for ten minutes during which he left his vehicle to buy breakfast, but the period was, the court eventually concluded, too short for even a part of the wine to have been unloaded). He was then given an 'acquit blanc', which he checked to see that the quantities corresponded with the 'acquit vert' he had handed in. Then he drove back to St. Germain-en-Graves arriving there at 11.20, and parked his lorry in front of the warehouse (which was full of white wine). At 12.30 he drove off again with another 'acquit vert', arriving at the Cruses about 2 p.m. After an hour's wait (this time he didn't even go off for a snack) he returned to St. Germain, unloaded and was off-duty by 4 p.m.

In the mythology which soon came to surround the whole operation the alarm was originally sounded by the locals at St. Germain. They, so the story went, suspected that something unusual was happening at the warehouse because there were so many comings and goings—like Barnabé's on 7th June— between mid-day and 2 p.m. when all self-respecting inhabitants of the Gironde stop work. In reality the operation was so blatant, involved so many people who as time went on drank a little too much and found local girl friends, that discovery was inevitably only a matter of time. The prosaic fact is that the Bert-Cruse prosecution resulted from a tip-off, probably by someone on the fringes of the business, since the authorities did not immediately grasp the nature of the fraud.

For it was only three weeks after Bert/Balan/de Pinos/Servant

started to deliver to the Cruses that two squads from the Tax
Office descended on Bert's office in Bordeaux and on the warehouse. At the office they rummaged through all the papers and
address books.

At the warehouse there was a typical piece of Bert slapstick:
the inspectors naturally asked his secretary for the register
containing the details of wine transported to and from the
cellars. But, immediately they had arrived, Bert had kicked it
under a cupboard, in the kitchen, and it was only finally unearthed
that afternoon. The inspectors then departed bearing with them
documents and samples of all the wine they found (according to
Bert's account they were only jolted by de Pinos, who breezed
in and thoroughly disconcerted them with his aristocratic disdain
for their activities).

Bert did not warn the Cruses—a piece of forgetfulness which
suggests that in the back of his mind had always been the idea
either of revenging himself by dragging them down with him,
or of sheltering behind the protective screen which everyone
assumed surrounded a house so important, so close to Chaban.

Five days later, on the 27th, the Cruses finally unbent enough
to agree to buy—a little—St. Emilion directly from S. Balan et
Cie, without going through Servant or de Pinos. But the next
morning, sharp at 9 a.m., ten inspectors from the Tax Squad
turned up at 124 Quai des Chartrons, demanding an immediate
inspection. They were received by M. Jaubert, the maître de
chai, who kept them waiting half an hour while the Cruses
pondered what to do (he also telephoned Bert, who rushed over,
saw the inspectors outside the door and promptly strolled past
on the improbable pretence that he was merely a passer-by).

Finally the Cruses graciously received the inspectors in audience
and agreed to co-operate in what, they later claimed, they understood was to be merely a routine inspection—though they
naturally objected that this moment, just before the holidays,
was their busiest season, that they were two months behind with
deliveries anyway, and that it would need their whole staff to
explain to the inspectors what was going on.

But they then started to mobilize their forces: they telephoned
their lawyer, M. Rozier. More crucially, they telephoned Peter
Sichel, that year's President of the Merchants' Federation. They
told Sichel of the inspectors' arrival, and of their unprecedented

demand for an immediate inspection. But they gave him the impression, then as later, that the proposed inspection was purely a routine affair, and thus covered by the gentlemen's agreement of 1913—which emphatically would not have provided a cover for an inspection in a criminal case. The failure to tell the whole truth was unfortunate, for Sichel, who had settled in Bordeaux only in 1961, was more English than Chartronnais, a man of the highest moral qualities (which was why he had been elected to the job relatively so soon after his arrival). His first instinct was to believe what his fellow merchants told him, and to back them to the hilt. But he was not the sort of man to continue such support if he found that the Cruses were deceiving him.

For the exceptional nature of the inspectors' visit had become clear on the afternoon of the 28th. At about 4 p.m. Lionel Cruse, emboldened by the results of his telephone calls, began to argue that the inspection was too unprecedented, involved too much upheaval, to continue. An annoyed Inspector Desrau snapped back that they were really interested in 94,000 gallons of wine bought from Bert. Cruse immediately offered to let the inspectors look at the wine involved (although he knew perfectly well that it had never existed). But the inspector pointed out that an inspection of one type of wine was useless, it had to be all or nothing. At that point Lionel, notoriously an impatient man, blew up. He refused to let the inspection continue further—an act which technically constituted obstruction of justice.

But for the moment the heat was off the Cruses while the inspectors, comparing the different copies of the 'acquits' franked on the Balan machine, worked out the mechanism of the fraud. In a careful letter written to the director of the tax organization on 9 July, Lionel Cruse amplified the defence he had first adopted on the afternoon of 28 June: while denying he had refused entry to his cellars, at that period of the year any surprise inspection was bound to reveal considerable confusion, and to disrupt the running of the business for weeks.

In a narrower, more legalistic form, this was also the attitude Lionel, Yvan and Hermann, accompanied by their lawyer, maintained at a special meeting of the Merchants' Federation called a fortnight later. At that stage, and whatever the rumours they had heard, their fellow-merchants had no positive reason not to believe the Cruses. So they protested formally against "the intolerable suspicions and the methods of the agents of the tax authorities", which, allegedly, involved "untimely" and "unreasonably niggly" inspections. They naturally hoped that a compromise would be reached, that the Cruses would admit to a technical breach of the regulations, that honour would be satisfied all round with a suitable fine in the absence of prosecution. Such a sequence of events had happened before, though not involving a shipper as important as the Cruses.

The meeting was discussed sufficiently to reach the ears of Jack-Henry Prévot, the well-informed wine reporter of the local paper, *Sud-Ouest*. On 31 July he reported that "despite the holiday atmosphere, something has happened in the Gironde regarding inspections of cellars", but he could find nothing definite.

In reality, the tax authorities had pieced together the fraud, but it had been so ingenious that "we had certainties but no proof", as one inspector put it. Proof required a full-scale inspection of the Cruse cellars, never a job to be undertaken lightly, and even less so after the formal protest made on the 13th. Inevitably the decision had to be made in Paris.

There again the Cruses were unlucky: the Minister of Finance who had to give the ultimate go-ahead for a further raid was Valéry Giscard d'Estaing. He and everyone else in French politics knew that President Pompidou was a dying man, and he was one of the two candidates most talked of as a successor. The other was the Cruses' friend, Chaban-Delmas.

Even before the holiday period Giscard was storing up large-scale fraud cases on which he wanted to be seen to act decisively and openly, thus giving the impression that he was not the sort of minister who followed French tradition in hiding cases involving major public figures by prosecuting only the smaller fry involved—indeed after the holidays he did proceed with two other less well-publicized cases, each involving as much money as the Bert–Cruse affair.

But the Chaban–Giscard tension was in the forefront of the Parisian mind that summer, exacerbated and kept there by Chaban's other woes—which included a divorce and the revelation that he had found ways of avoiding the payment of any income tax for a couple of years. This interesting tit-bit had been leaked the previous year to the leading French satirical-political weekly, *Le Canard Enchaîné*, almost certainly by disgruntled junior tax officials, fed up with the dodges employed by the more powerful members of French society, but not available to less influential tax-payers.

It was probably the same officials who leaked the news of the investigation into the Bordeaux trade to *Le Canard* in August 1973. It was naturally assumed by the French that the leak had been organized from the top, from Giscard's own office, and that without the political tensions between Chaban and Giscard the investigation would have been taken no further. This is unlikely: for all their friendship with Chaban, for all their long and proud history, for all their local importance, the Cruses were simply not important enough to benefit from a cover-up of a fraud as sizeable as theirs. Even after a century and a half in France, they were still "strangers in a strange land", helpless if the state turned against them.

Le Canard's first article on the raids appeared on 15 August. The article did not name the Cruses, but referred merely to a "fraud big enough to make a wine-grower blush" adding up to 800 million old francs and involving "one of the best-known shippers in Bordeaux".

The news broke on the public holiday celebrating the Assumption of the Blessed Virgin Mary, in lay terms, the height of the French holiday season. Nevertheless—or perhaps because there was no other major story around—the first revelation ensured that for the next ten days the French papers seemed to be full of Winegate. *

Many of the stories concentrated on the rivalry between Chaban-Delmas and Giscard d'Estaing—one newsletter owned by an enemy of Chaban's even claimed that Winegate was only one out of five financial scandals being stored up by the Finance Minister to implicate the Mayor of Bordeaux. And most of the others, including *Le Monde*, assumed that the nub of the affair was what *Canard Enchainé* described as "dyers who transferred white wine into red"—processes which threw suspicions on the quality of the wine, and thus of any wine from Bordeaux.

The problem was that the fraud was so ingenious that very

* The first use of this magnificent word I have come across is in an article of Jack-Henry Prévot's on 24 August. But it was, probably, its use as a headline in *Newsweek* on 10 September which spread the fame of the expression world-wide.

few of the stories then or later spelt out that the inherent quality of the wine was not in question; the trouble lay in the names it was called and the documents which accompanied it.

Even the INAO "as guardian of the national heritage formed by AOC wines" got into the act, threatening to sue anyone who had acted in a way prejudicial to the good name of French wine. This threat was followed by other interested parties, all of whom turned up at the trial fifteen months later to demand their— usually nominal and symbolic—damages from the Cruses.

But the Cruses made matters much worse. Their official statement denied that "they are implicated in any misuse of Appellation Contrôlée. They will proceed against any persons or body making any allegations of such misuse and making any statements prejudicing the reputation of Cruse or the good name of Bordeaux wines". Prévot was quick to point out that the Cruses had gone beyond the bounds of a legitimate defence by assuming that any attack on them was, by definition, an attack on all Bordeaux's wines (in the event, they started only one action, against the weekly magazine *L'Express*, which had, probably, been the first to name them).

Even worse, Lionel Cruse, irritated by the constant attention of press photographers, compared himself with Richard Nixon, who, he said, was also the victim of unjustified press smears; and, to top off an object lesson in what not to say, issued another statement that "the personal and friendly relationship that the house of Cruse enjoys with M. Chaban-Delmas does not enter this controversy."

The resemblance between the Cruses and Nixon was real enough. Both 'Wine' and 'Water' Gates involved the 'irresponsible press' hurling 'unthinkable allegations' at institutions whose repute had been of the highest, attacks which subsequently proved to be more than amply justified.

But there is a more specific resemblance. Nixon did not destroy the tapes which finally incriminated him. And, in the two months which followed the raid on 28 June, the Cruses did nothing to regularize the paperwork in their cellars. Yet, once the news had broken, a further inspection was inevitable (even if the Cruses' unyielding attitude had not previously removed the possibility of any compromise). For, although the inspectors by then understood the mechanism of Bert's fraud, they had, as yet, no direct evidence that the Cruses had worked with him—only indications, through the (tapped) telephone call made by the agitated maître de chai on 28 June, and the refusal later that day to admit the inspectors. For when, on 26 August, he was interrogated for the first time, Barnabé the driver had told the inspectors nothing about his round trips to the Cruses' cellars.

That same day the inspectors' superiors met—and sealed the Cruses' fate. Although their conference was held in Bordeaux, it had already been decided that "investigative resources on a national scale " would be needed to get "to the bottom of the affair". The officials knew, as one of them put it, that "we are faced by people who have put a great deal of thought into their operations and have benefited from a number of gaps in the official controls. This case has nothing in common with the usual run of small-scale frauds."

At the conference were officials from the Ministry of Agriculture itself, from its special fraud squad and from the tax service: all day they went through the case, laying out in full the mechanisms by which the frauds had been committed. Only when they had satisfied themselves that they already had a case did they move into 124 Quai des Chartrons again. But once the decision was made action was immediate.

On Monday the 27th, the first working day after the conference, the Ministry of Finance vainly tried to cool the situation by saying the opposite to what had been secretly agreed the previous Friday. The Ministry wanted the public to believe that this was a fraud like any other. But while the statement was being issued, a squad far more senior than that of late June had descended on the Cruses' offices.

The first day the two chief inspectors involved, Le Derff and Ruffié, concentrated on trying to familiarize themselves with the methods used by the Cruses to keep track of their wines. But they also got a damaging admission from Alain Cruse, who told them that 'an excellent wine from the Midi' was used to top up the vats allegedly containing 'AOC' wine. This, of course, ensured that none of the contents of any of these vats could then be sold as 'AOC' wine, since even the smallest proportion of non-AOC wine was sufficient to declass them. (The elder Cruses' explanations that Alain was not a technical expert did not help much, especially as it subsequently

emerged that the Cruses used only four types of red wine in all
to top up their many vats.)

The next day the inspectors started examining the books in
detail. In particular they looked through three school exercise
books which the Cruses called the 'chemical notebooks', and
a register which the Cruses called their dictionary. Le Derff
immediately "noticed some extraordinary entries. In the dictionary containing the analyses, there were notes like 'red wine,
Côtes-du-Rhône type' or 'Burgundy type'. Every time I asked
for the corresponding stock sheet, the employee would disappear
for half an hour and then return to say that it couldn't be found."

Overnight the Cruses panicked, and when the inspectors
returned the next day it was to find that the register giving the
daily analyses of wine in stock, as well as the three 'chemical'
notebooks, had disappeared from the table in the office where
they had been working, and that the 'dictionaries' they had
looked at the previous day had been tampered with. Entries
which had naturally drawn their interest had been scratched out,
obliterated or written over.

The stock sheets themselves had been numbered up to about
37,000 and, to avoid confusion, claimed Lionel Cruse, had been
restarted from 40,000 up. To avoid further error in what was
seemingly a not very numerate establishment, the earlier stock
sheets relating to the renumbered wines had been destroyed.

At that point the inspectors felt in a strong enough position
to request permission to start a prosecution, thus allowing them
later that day to remove the famous 'dictionary' to prevent any
further alterations. A few days later the three 'chemical' notebooks
turned up again, and Lionel Cruse delivered them to the police,
protesting the while that his firm had never been guilty of
non-collaboration with the authorities.

The day after the inspection Bert, who until then had been
the mysterious 'Mr. X' in the affair, spoke up on the radio
station Europe Number 1, and in *Sud-Ouest* Jack-Henry Prévot
published a photograph and details of the 'modest, indeed seedy'
warehouse at St. Germain-en-Graves. He also showed clearly
how the fraud was carried out—although the explanation was
so belated that the rest of the world was still left with the impression that the basic fraud had involved tampering with wine,
rather than paperwork.

A fortnight after the first inspection a much more senior official, Commissioner Mohsen, turned up at the Quai des Chatrons armed with a formal warrant to search the premises. At first he would not show Hermann Cruse the document, explaining that it provided too many details of the way the officials were to act. The search started, but still Mohsen would show Cruse only the first page of the warrant. At that point he told them to leave. This was far more serious a step than Lionel's refusal to help on 28 June; and Mohsen duly returned the next day reinforced by the whole weight of the French law—including bailiffs and the senior examining magistrate in Bordeaux.

In the meantime the inspectors had had the opportunity to examine a notebook which led them to suspect that the Cruses had been using unauthorized chemicals to treat the wine. This notebook, coloured orange-yellow, had disappeared, but the evidence, including fifteen pounds of lime, remained and were found on the 15th. Throughout this time the Cruses were protesting, first that the various documents were merely rough drafts and had no official standing and, further, that the authorities were entitled only to examine documents relating to the wine laws.

The dramatic events of 13–14 September formed the climax to Winegate Act 1. The case should have been sent to the prosecuting attorneys on the 17th of the month: but, because of the complexities, it was only a fortnight later that it was officially handed over. (The authorities were so worried that in the meantime the French customs had been ordered to take samples of any wine exported, in cask or bottle, from Bordeaux.) By then the Cruses had, in the public's eyes, already been judged and found guilty. The 55-page document from the Fraud Squad setting out the heads of the case against them had been leaked to *Canard Enchaîné*, which quoted a particularly damaging summary:

"The different examples quoted below—which may not be the only ones—demonstrate that the firm of Cruse respected neither the idea of 'appellation' (because cc wines were given the names of 'AOC' wines or that a lot of one appellation is divided into shipments bearing the names of different appellations, or that they mixed AOC with cc wines) nor did they respect the idea of a 'cru' because the same wine could bear different châteaux names, nor the idea of a particular vintage, because dates were allocated to wines which lacked them when they arrived in the cellars."

All these alleged offences were a far cry from Bert's original scheme, which seemingly got lost under the weight of the other horrors discovered at the Cruse cellars. No wonder that Chaban-Delmas (who had publicly refused to interfere in the course of justice) was heard later that month to hurl imprecations at the head of Lionel's mother, the formidable Margaret de Luze, whom he had so publicly thanked 'for what you did for me when I first arrived in Bordeaux' when he had presented her with the Légion d'Honneur a few years previously.

In late October the official legal mechanism got going, when Bert and the Cruses were officially charged with 'criminal practice' and 'tax avoidance'. On 28 October the 'examining magistrate' —who in French law acts as a sort of one-man Grand Jury deciding if and how the case should be brought to trial—started work on a case so complex that it was only a year later, after Valéry Giscard d'Estaing had duly defeated Chaban-Delmas, that the trial started.

22

Bordeaux in a trance

"Gold, oil and claret have all trebled in value during the last three years. . . . Claret was the first to increase so dramatically and the picture of the Gnomes of Zurich and the Sheiks of Arabia taking their cue from Bordeaux peasants is pretty to say the least. . . . Bordeaux is now determined that its product should no longer be an article of speculation and is also becoming dramatically aware that it is not a sheikdom that holds a strong hand over its customers. It can be hoped that out of the crisis will come good."

PETER SICHEL

In private, the Bordelais thoroughly enjoyed the discomfiture of the Cruses, a family which had behaved in too supercilious and arrogant a manner for too long to too many people to expect much sympathy. But in public the decencies were preserved: as the judicial machine ground into action at the end of October, Philippe de Rothschild bravely delivered a memorial address to Roger Cruse to the Academy of Bordeaux. Roger Cruse was not the only survivor of the older generation of the family (Emmanuel still had over a year to live): but the oration sounded very much like the epitaph to an era, and to the family perhaps most associated with it.

The address was the more poignant because Roger Cruse would far rather have written works of social philosophy and morality than work in the family firm. But in his generation the discipline, social, economic and religious, was still too strict to allow him to escape—as it had been for another member of the family, Frédérick, who had wanted to take Holy orders. In Roger's case, apart from his attempt shortly after World War I to formulate a social family policy for the Médoc (and thus he hoped, for France), his views were not known to a wide public. The eulogist himself had been luckier: the accident of birth and of temperament had enabled him to combine more than one role.

But this gesture was a shining exception in a dreary scene. The scandal surrounding the dead man's younger relatives had tarnished the good name of Bordeaux—almost every report on the 'Affair' still referred wrongly to wines which had been 'adulterated'. It was all very well for the Rothschilds of Lafite to launch the most elaborate 'ban des Vendanges' ever seen in Bordeaux, complete with an ultra-fashionable night-club imported from Paris. Everyone knew that the vintage being celebrated would be virtually unsaleable, whatever its quality—and relations between the 'cousins' were further strained when *Sud-Ouest* published photos of the festivities with captions proclaiming that they were taking place at Mouton rather than Lafite.

For the 1973 vintage was precisely what the Gironde did not need: it was enormous in size and very variable in quality. The total of red wine entitled to one of the innumerable 'AOC' certificates was a fifth above the record 1970 vintage, an increase largely concentrated in the lesser 'appellations', where production was up by a quarter. Although total production was still not up to pre-war levels, it was nearly four times the average for the five years which followed the 1956 frosts and double the estimated pre-1970 world annual consumption. Coming so soon after the 1970 vintage it served notice that the new generation of growers—cultivating their land with greater discipline, using only the best grafts for their vines, able to afford new types of pesticides and increasing quantities of fertilizers—were likely to establish new crop records in any year when the weather was favourable. Moreover these record figures applied to AOC wines, thus creating a different kind of problem from that being felt in other French wine-growing areas, where the surplus consisted virtually entirely of the most basic wines.

Moreover the quality was, inevitably, mixed. The weather had been perfect until the middle of September, when it had rained heavily. So the grapes were swollen with water they had not had time to absorb when they were harvested. Growers took full advantage of the laws which permitted them to make up to 64 gallons per acre. Some, it was said, made even more.

So their wines tended to be very light, if not actually watery. Some conscientious owners could afford to balance nature's deficiencies, either, like Henri Martin, by a ruthless selection of wines or, like the estates owned by Jean-Pierre Moueix, by allowing the wine to ferment for longer than usual and thus boost its strength.

But the vintage—and the warning note it sounded—had two immediate effects: it ensured that any slump in prices would be prolonged, and, more immediately, it spurred the French Government into reforming the regulations which had allowed so much wine to be awarded an AOC certificate.

But these were only being formulated during the terrible winter of 1973-4, when, whatever the size and quality of the 1973 vintage, Bordeaux would have suffered. The outbreak of the Middle Eastern War, the sharp fall in the price of the dollar, the quadrupling of the price of oil, recalled the slump in world trade which had begun exactly a hundred years earlier and had started Bordeaux off on a long decline from which it had only just recovered. The only major difference between the two cases was that Winegate provided an excellent excuse for inaction in customers who would certainly not have bought any wine anyway.

The situation was equally bad at both ends of the market: in France the consumption of basic Bordeaux Rouge had stopped declining, to be sure, but at a level a third below the 1972 figure. It was only a half of the five bottles consumed by every household in France in 1970 (the decline was even worse in Bordeaux's best domestic markets, in the north of France and in Paris).

Abroad the position was even worse, because the supply pipelines were so much longer and because they were all so full of wines ordered on the assumption that drinkers' thirsts were inexhaustible. Moreover the pattern of ordering during the previous three years ensured that the blockage would not be cleared away: for the better wines were being bought and paid for in the year following fermentation, and remained in Bordeaux for up to two further years awaiting bottling and shipment. To make matters worse many of the new entrants to the American wine scene shared the Bordelais' own assumption that the American market would continue to drink claret, at whatever price. "What confused us," says Bill Bolter, "was that we were still receiving orders from America; we did not realize just how aggressive our salesmen were being."

The momentum of the previous couple of years could not quickly be slowed down: so the shipments continued, even to markets like the United States, Canada and Great Britain, where it was clear they would no longer be needed, for the decline was not confined to the classiest wines. It was hastened by the tax increases necessitated by the economic crisis—in England duty was raised repeatedly from March 1974 onwards —further depressing a market already hit by price increases; when Bass Charrington increased the price of Mouton Cadet by over 70 per cent to £1·80 a bottle sales slumped by two-thirds. But in other cases the shock was further delayed.

Bowater, for instance, still went ahead with its purchase of de Luze at the end of October, once the French Government had become convinced that no French buyer could be found, although it could have backed out of an increasingly unpromising deal in the meantime.

But even in the autumn of 1973 the Bordeaux market was virtually paralysed: in principle the price of the most basic Bordeaux Rouge reverted only to 2,200 francs, the same as was being paid in the happy days of May 1972. The only difference was that no one bought the wine at that price, and the growers were not prepared to come down—for the moment anyway. And among the better wines the only activity was that Jacques Théo persuaded the eighteen estates 'abonnés' to Bass Charrington to reduce their prices by 20 per cent compared with 1972—in hindsight a pathetically inadequate gesture.

It was paralleled by events at Christie's that month, where "a re-adjustment of prices that had gone almost too high for investors and certainly for consumers" resulted in prices of first growths dropping by a quarter or more and lesser wines by a tenth, "a healthy sign," proclaimed the *Financial Times*, "in a previously over-heated market". Even so the results of the early stages of the boom were, apparently, here to stay, "consumers must realize that fine, reasonably-mature, château-bottled claret must cost them about £60 a case". As in Bordeaux, so in London, the consequences of the end of the boom had not been fully digested, a fact which lends an air of unreality to most of the events of the following year.

That winter it was not clear if Bordeaux would use the new misfortunes to re-organize itself, or whether it would revert into old habits—a tendency exemplified when, early in the New Year, the association representing the 'crus' classified in 1855 went to law to claim that the 1973 ruling which had given Baron Philippe his heart's desire was null and void because the Chamber of Commerce did not have the right to initiate proceedings. The suit came to nothing and, significantly, the Baron was supported by a number of other growers, some of whom (like Jean-Eugène Borie of Ducru and Frank Lahary of Pichon-Longueville) had nothing either to gain or lose from a new classification.

The other face of Bordeaux was shown by the continuing efforts to try and establish some form of buffer stock to absorb the flood. In January a small group of the more enlightened shippers, led by Peter Sichel, launched what they called a 'cry of alarm'. They took up the plans launched the year before to stabilize the market through some form of regulatory mechanism, but it was not until April that Daniel Doustin managed to get both sides to agree and then to get the ideas presented to the central government. These were an elaboration of schemes first publicly aired a year previously and included giving the CIVB the power to regulate prices, and cheap credits to help finance maturing stocks of red wine. But the chances of acceptance were reduced when, in the absence of any official from the Ministry of Finance (which would have to pay for any such idea), it was examined only by the Minister of Agriculture. And even he was not interested in the more radical ideas being put forward by Louis Marinier, representing the growers of Bordeaux and Bordeaux Supérieur, who demanded immediate action on a buffer stock of 6 million gallons or at a price of 2,000 francs the tonneau.

Marinier pointed out that there were three different markets for the Gironde's wines: the 'grands crus' virtually all sold abroad, the wines entitled to the 'better' appellations, either 'Médoc' or single villages, and the third class which he represented. Significantly he described his members as 'the third estate'—the 'lower house' which had set off the revolution in

1789, an upheaval which itself had been sparked off by a short period of economic unhappiness.

For by the spring all three classes were unhappy. A mere two years after they had started to lift into the stratosphere, prices of basic Bordeaux slumped by two-thirds. The official price remained at about 1,800 francs—below the 2,000 francs Marinier had tried to get for his members, and itself a price which only just carried production costs. By the summer most transactions were going through at 1,500 francs or less, with some as low as 1,000 francs, the pre-1968 level. Yet buyers still held off, either because they themselves were overstocked, or because they were waiting for even lower prices, which seemed inevitable as the market continued to stagnate.

The producers of white wine were less unhappy: not that their prices were any better, but at least their export outlets had increased—or rather their major market, Germany, was back in business. Encouraged by the strength of the D-Mark the Germans bought a record 6,250,000 gallons in 1973-4, three-quarters more than the previous year and, in quantity anyway, three-tenths of all Bordeaux's exports. But this was a minor consolation: so was the return of the Swedes to the market in a big way—their purchases, largely of cheaper wines in cask, jumped nearly four-fold. Without these two markets Bordeaux's exports would have dropped by over a fifth.

The malaise was just as bad further up the market. Early in the year a few of the 'crus classés' had crept on to the market. Far from the 20 per cent reduction negotiated by Théo, these were offered at 35 per cent below the 1972 prices. Much later the Rothschild cousins not only cut their prices drastically to just over 50,000 francs, but also offered a couple of barriques of their 1972 wine for every tonneau (four barriques) of the 1973 bought off them.

An early victim of the crack-up was the one major remaining contract held by Group A, Beychevelle. The members took one 'tranche', only to find that Aymar Achille-Fould was negotiating through the good offices of an American brother-in-law with Dreyfus Ashby, one of the biggest of American importers, to sell the rest of his wine at a price substantially below the price he had been given by Group A.

The result was a legal action over the price paid for the 1972 vintage, the final demise of Group A, and "the end of a beautiful friendship between Achille-Fould and Roland du Vivier of de Luze" (such is the absurdity of Bordeaux that Achille-Fould remained on friendly terms with Bernard Ginestet, although the latter stood against him in the 1974 elections which also saw the triumph of Valéry Giscard d'Estaing).

But these were local problems: the backwash of the unwillingness of the Americans and British to buy over-priced French wines was only starting to be felt. The figures were frightening: although wine imports as a whole to the United States fell only by 7 per cent in 1974, sales of French wines slumped by 42 per cent, and France dropped from first to fourth place as a foreign supplier of wine to the Americans, who were quite prepared to try any reasonably-priced alternative. Julius Wile, one of New York's most respected importers said bluntly that "with many of the famous French wines retailing at the cost of a bottle of whisky, consumers have changed to the less expensive wines of other countries and found some of these to be more than adequate for their needs." He himself was concentrating on French wines from areas other than Bordeaux and Burgundy. For the average cost of a gallon of wine from France was $8·42, from Germany $6·40 (despite the strength of the D-Mark), from Italy $3·68 and from Spain only $2·46. Americans ranged even further afield. The biggest growth in 1974 was in wines from Argentina: "the New York wine establishment," wrote Gerald Asher, an English wine expert, "is becoming as familiar with the uplands of Mendoza as it is with the Médoc and the Napa Valley."

But the real threat to Bordeaux's better wines came not from rival imports (which, even in 1972–3, accounted for only a seventh of all wine drunk in the United States), but from the rapidly-improving products from California. Asher quoted in evidence the wine list of The Four Seasons, then, arguably, the most fashionable restaurant in New York. California wines, he noted, "for years a mere coda to the wines of Europe, now dominate the list. Indeed, traditional headings like 'Bordeaux' and 'Burgundy' have been dropped, and to find a Volnay, for example, you must look among the Pinot Noir wines"— a salutary lesson for Médocains, apt to brood about ever additional percentage of Merlot mixed with the Cabernet Sauvignon in their Lafite.

At the same time as the Californians were increasing their reputation for quality, the Girondins were losing theirs. The trade was full of graphic descriptions of what happened to wines left for a couple of weeks in twenty degrees of frost on the quay-side in New York, then exposed to sub-tropical temperatures in a warehouse in the South lacking air-conditioning. In a market as fussy as the American, even the deposits usually found in older clarets were deemed unacceptable. These problems were curable (a high-powered technical mission concluded that a combination of filtration, using only the best corks, and a decent amount of air between them and the wine would do the trick, but by then the damage was done).

The only exception to a miserable year was Baron Philippe. He had settled out of court with his previous distributors for $100,000 ("it was like a divorce," says Cottin); and the new importers were spending up to 50c a bottle in promoting Mouton Cadet. By that time Rothschild and Cottin were offering it in both red and white versions. Originally the white was made sweet, following an obviously rather primitive market survey which had shown that the consumption of sweet white wines was greater than of dry. But the lesson was soon learnt, and the wine formulated to give a drier taste, using mostly the rather characterless Semillon grapes (Cottin's own taste was for the fruitier Sauvignon, but, as a good marketing man, in the end he offered the public what they, rather than he, preferred).

In the dismal year of 1974 Mouton nearly doubled its sales to over 100,000 cases, a significant achievement even though far short of the figures achieved by other foreign brand names, like Blue Nun Liebfraumilch or the Sangrias and Rosés which formed the spearhead of most importers' ranges.

Baron Philippe needed to be lucky, for the tables had been turned since 1970, and instead of Mouton-Rothschild financing the promotion of Mouton Cadet, the parent needed financing for several years, especially for major expenditure on new 'chais' blasted out of the rocky soil of the Médoc.

But he was even more exceptional than usual, and by summer

1974 desperation was the general rule in the Gironde. Stocks of claret had jumped by over a third to over 60 million gallons or even possibly more by the end of the year. Many of the growers were still stuck with much of the 1972 vintage, of which they had only sold a first 'tranche' before the market seized up. Most refused to sell any of their precious 1970s and 1971s; and all were suffering from the jump in interest rates which had accompanied the general economic crisis of 1973-4. So their financial charges had often quadrupled (both stocks and rates having doubled). And the French Government, fed up with the growers' trickery, had abandoned an earlier scheme under which wine destined for export had enjoyed the advantage of lower interest rates—too many growers had obtained these favourable terms on wine that was either non-existent or destined for the home market.

In the summer the first signs of cracking appeared. In London the domestic side of Bass Charrington was called in to stop the rot in Bordeaux. In an imaginative gesture they decided to cut the Gordian knot by putting some of their surplus stocks up for auction at Christie's. Some rather tense negotiations followed, since most of the wines they wanted to put on offer were relatively undistinguished minor clarets, though finally Michael Broadbent contrived to include rather better clarets and a great deal of burgundy and hock.

The sale, in the middle of July, was a widely-publicized sensation. Although the wines from outside the Gironde went for reasonable prices, the presence of hundreds of enthusiastic amateur buyers often in syndicates from offices, clubs or colleges ('clearly unaccustomed to the ways of the auction rooms', noted one expert reprovingly) ensured that the first day's sale, on which the majority of the claret was disposed of, would be a roaring success. If Christie's had been the butt of attacks accusing the auction house of over-boosting the price of wine, no one could reasonably complain of its new role as a cushion absorbing the shock of re-entry by enabling over-stocked shippers to get rid of astonishing quantities of wine at one fell swoop. In the two days Christie's disposed of 36,000 cases of wine for nearly £1 million. In some cases the quantities were mind-blowing: "If," as Edmund Penning-Rowsell noted, "the Mouton-Rothschild '70 and Latour '70 fell from the record 1973 price of £160 and £125 a dozen to £54 and £50 this was for 100 and 50 case lots that few could run to."

The Bass Charrington sale set a pattern: for the next couple of years it would seem cheaper to buy wines at auction than through merchants (who sometimes advertised wines 'at auction prices') whereas before the break in prices the opposite had been true. This trend helped those shippers and growers sizeable and enterprising enough to take advantage of the new outlets, since they could relieve their cash problems at one fell swoop, though it provided too powerful an alternative for English merchants' comfort.

But the sale was the only glimmer that summer—and, even then, it was clearly an act of desperation. More typical of the London scene was the bankruptcy a couple of months later of the London Wine Company, one of the leading promoters of wine as an investment in the previous few years. Growth had simply been too fast—with turnover multiplying ten times in three years. Ironically, as Nigel Baring, the managing director, pointed out, he "was in talks with a public company a little more than a year ago but turned down any possible take-over on the grounds that he considered the company at that time was trading so profitably."

But Baring's collapse introduced an agonizing element of uncertainty into the situation: for his cellars contained wines allocated to dozens of different owners, and at first the principal creditors, the giant National Westminster Bank, seized the lot. It was only after many months of argument that the bank allowed the wine's owners to claim their property (and even then the bank could, legally, have been infinitely tougher). But for a time it seemed that not only were people's wines dropping in value, they were not necessarily safe in anyone's custody.

But the position in Bordeaux was even worse. In August the growers, boiling with resentment at the merchants' refusal to help and at the total lack of action by the Government on their reform scheme, walked out of the CIVB, followed by the substantial figure of the Gironde's leading lawyer, Pierre Siré, a director of Latour and an expert on wine laws.

More tragically, that same month, Hermann Cruse, unable

to face the forthcoming trial of his family, threw himself off a bridge into the Gironde.

No wonder 1974 is one of the few years in Bordeaux's history when the vintage seems relatively unimportant.

23

Winegate Act II: the trial

"Stand by for a rash of 'after the Bordeaux trial' wine jokes. One of the first concerns some Japanese wine which is now on the market in bottles marked 'Beware of French imitations'."—Financial Times

Hermann Cruse committed suicide the same month President Nixon, that other victim of 'press calumnies', resigned office. The two events formed an unhappy prologue to the second act of Winegate, a tragedy which was to fulfil one primitive function of the dramatic form—to purge a community through the ritual sacrifice of one of its members. For the other Cruses had been twice judged and found guilty even before the trial opened at the end of October.

Earlier that month the merchants' association had met in solemn conclave to decide whether to join other injured parties, like the INAO and the growers' associations, in claiming damages from the Cruses. The occasion was especially unpleasant for that year's President, Hugues Lawton, called upon to sit in judgment over his 'cousins'. By all accounts the Cruses mounted a dignified defence, admitting that they had allowed Midi wines disguised as Bordeaux into their cellars, but protesting their good faith throughout. Their listeners knew that they, too, had almost all been guilty of the 'mistakes' which the Cruses were admitting. But group self-interest prevailed. And by a vote of 18 to 10, with one abstention, the association decided to be represented at the trial.

In itself this was only a symbolic act (most of the parties in a similar position were claiming only a single franc in damages): but it finally undermined the Cruses' original defence—that any attack on them was an assault on the reputation of Bordeaux's wines as a whole; and the decision could also be used as evidence that their fellow-merchants did not believe the Cruses' innocence.

Nor did the press: for the French publicly discuss the defendants in a forthcoming trial on the assumption that they are guilty. A fortnight before the trial, Le Monde, France's most important newspaper, cheerfully based its discussion of the case on the 55-page report submitted the previous November by the Inspectors of the Fraud Squad to the prosecutors (in the event, because the authorities did not proceed with one of the charges in the report, Le Monde went too far even for French law and had to apologize, but the damage had been done).

The earlier publicity merely whetted the world's appetite for seeing how such distinguished burghers had slipped on such interesting banana skins. The court-room was packed with friends of the accused, with local notabilities and with the world's press—few of them wine correspondents, mostly representing the drinking classes anxious for their revenge on the supposed 'experts' who had aired their superiority so publicly for so long.

The trial began on 28 October. It was originally scheduled to last only three days, but the timetable was never a practicable one. There were eighteen defendants—Bert, Balan, the Cruses, two of their employees, de Pinos, and a number of their more-or-less innocent customers. Moreover they were accused of a wide variety of alleged offences, ranging from outright fraud, through obstruction of justice to the alteration and falsification of legal documents (the judges' summaries allocating responsibility cover over a hundred pages). And during the trial each defendant was naturally represented by one or more legal counsel, all of whom deemed it their right to have a lengthy say whenever their client's interests were possibly involved. Moreover the number of institutions clamouring for damages to their supposedly injured reputations had grown alarmingly, to include such seemingly irrelevant institutions as the Gironde's 'Union of Family Associations'.

The French judicial system allows every accused person to have his or her say and be interrogated by the presiding judge before witnesses are called, so the three days originally scheduled for the whole trial were all occupied in hearing the accused. The trial itself lasted two weeks, sessions enlivened by the inability of the presiding Judge Lief to keep order, or to understand much of the wine-talk with which he was bombarded—a reference to a 'Saint Médoc' wine provoked particular hilarity. Chaos was compounded by the bad acoustics in the courtroom and by fierce competition among the dozens of lawyers present to get at the only microphone.

The first day's hearing was the most sensational, for it exposed to the world the full range of Pierre Bert's talents. Following some legal wrangles—including an attempt to get the Cruses' elderly and respected oenologist, M. Baillot d'Estivaux, tried separately—he took the stand. His attitude was simple: he clearly saw himself as the instrument of revenge against the hypocrisy of French wine laws, and of the shippers who lived so well by abusing them.

"I am guilty," he proclaimed, "but it was not I who invented fraud. There are thousands as guilty as I . . . I didn't do anything very original. Out of 1·5 million hectolitres entitled to be labelled Bordeaux, there are 700,000 to 800,000 that are magnificent. The rest are little Bordeauxs, modest wines, that cannot be offered to a foreign clientèle . . . there are two markets for Bordeaux. For the second market there must be a mixture. The mixers are the vineyard owners and the sellers. And they sometimes make a good mixture."

Following this opening outburst, the naivety of the presiding judge made him the perfect feed-man for the star witness—and an ideal representative of the consuming public, intrigued above all by the mysteries of the wine business. Lief, for example, remarked on how audacious it was of Bert to mix his wines. On cue, Bert replied that "no, it's a common practice. It's called 'baptism'. The role of certain dealers is to collect bad Bordeaux and improve them. There is perhaps a risk, but I didn't invent anything." The president then filled in by asking whether the differences could not be exposed in the tasting. Bert left that to the experts, but proclaimed proudly that, in thirty years in the business, no one had ever complained about the quality of his wines. (If that was the case, he must have been unique: Bordeaux merchants were notorious for not keeping their quality stable, especially when additional shipments were made of a previously well-received wine.)

Living up to his role, the judge then asked whether he had really mixed white wine with red. On reflection Bert was glad the judge had asked him that. "Yes, that happened," he replied. "A little white doesn't harm the quality when there is too much tannin in the red." "Yes, but it's not legal," said the judge, "No, but it's good," replied Bert.

Having set the scene, Bert went on to launch another bombshell, declaring that Barton & Guestier were also guilty, because they had received a consignment of his—or rather Balan's—wine from Lucien Castaing. Bert had already tangled with Hugues Lawton a couple of months previously, when the latter had gone into his firm's new warehouse at Blanquefort only to find that one of the security staff had a familiar look. Sure enough it was Bert, out on bail, earning an honest living in a manner characteristically guaranteed to maximize the embarrassment of the wine-shipping fraternity.

At the trial, however, the Barton & Guestier revelation proved rather a damp squib. The firm promptly denied the allegations, and stated that it had refused to buy any of the wines it had been offered by Bert, because the quality was not good enough. Nevertheless his wider accusations were nearer the mark. It was hypocritical, he proclaimed, for the merchants' association to join the injured parties, since so many of them were guilty of so many of the offences with which the Cruses were charged. The CIVB understood the point: they had laid on elaborate facilities for the journalists, with proper briefings, and tastings, not for once confined to the most internationally famous of châteaux, but including generic wines with which the journalists were not familiar.

Nevertheless Bert had succeeded in one major aim: he had ensured that the trial would not confine itself to the narrow events surrounding the Cruses' cellars the previous summer, but would also discuss the wider questions of the guilt or innocence of the whole wine trade—and, more especially, the hypocrisy of the regulations surrounding its operations. He distinguished sharply between legal requirements and the inherent qualities of the wine: mixing red and white wines, for instance, may not have been legal, "but in reality, it was an operation which had no regrettable consequences, rather the converse." Similarly, he quoted Jean Cordier's godfather, the Abbé Dubaquié, that a wine whose contents were *too* correct was suspicious. Provided the chemical analysis conformed to legal requirements, the "rest was a matter of personal appreciation."

Most of the rest of a long day in court—nine hours in all—

the two Cruses were interrogated on precisely this point: the fallibility of the human palate, especially when dealing with young wines. It was crucial to the Cruses' defence to present themselves as the most upright of shippers, accustomed to the highest standards in their suppliers (which was why they were not prepared to take wines directly from Balan, Bert's front-man), but genuinely deceived by the wines offered.

To insiders, Lionel Cruse's protestation that he had no reason to suspect Bert was the sheerest hypocrisy, given his previous notoriety and his track record. Nevertheless at the end of the day their position seemed relatively intact. Lionel Cruse had early established the basic point: "It would not be denigratory of Bordeaux's wines," he said, "to say that there are excellent table wines in France. I don't want to be Bordeaux's grave-digger, but, yes, I must say that confusion is possible, if the wines involved are young, mixtures and are transported in tanker-loads."

The prosecutor, M. Dontenville, pressed Yvan Cruse on the point. But the stand remained: that, since the particular qualities of Bordeaux's wines developed only with ageing, confusion was possible with younger wines. Nevertheless, insisted Dontenville, "there's a vine somewhere in the business. How can you be secure in your purchasing policy, how do you make sure of the quality of your goods?" Yvan Cruse's reply was dignity itself, "You must remember that what we buy we will be obliged to sell one day. And the firm of Cruse is known by all the brokers who have dealings with it to be very strict in its purchasing policy."

The tone was reinforced by the impersonal tone employed by both Cruses: their family firm was to them more than merely the people who happened to work for it at any one time, it was an institution in itself. Indeed they presented their rôle in relation to the family business in the same way de Gaulle talked of himself, not just as a person who happened to be president, but as the representative of a far loftier unity—in his case the French nation.

The first day, seemingly, had produced more smoke than fire: Bert was duly surrounded by journalists, to whom he gave further lurid stories of the activities of his fellow-merchants; and one journalist summed up the day's activities by asking where he could get the name of the supplier in the Midi who, for a mere 3 francs, could supply wine which was indistinguishable from Bordeaux, even to experts like the Cruses.

This note of cynical disbelief was sustained on the second day, which started with the appearance of six of the Cruses' foreign distributors to testify on their behalf. The first was David Rutherford, whose family firm had dealt with the Cruses for generations. He was loyal and, as an Englishman, naturally argued that no one should be presumed guilty before a trial. He admitted that from time to time his firm bought wines which turned out to be corked, but these, it transpired, came from a number of sources, not only from the Cruses.

The other witnesses served mainly to confuse the issue of whether the inherent qualities of a wine were readily distinguishable early in its life. The Dane, Mr. Torben, was particularly prodded by the prosecution. Yes, he could tell the difference between a run-of-the-mill table wine and a Bordeaux of a better class. No, it would be difficult for him to tell the difference between, say, a St. Emilion, and a wine from Languedoc, if only because his firm did not import any wine from the Midi. But, yes, he could tell the difference between a St. Emilion and a 'vin de table'.

The Dutch witness, Mr. Verbank, who was also his government's official taster, agreed with the point, which directly contradicted Lionel Cruse's statement the previous day that confusion was almost inevitable.

But it was André Donzé, a major Swiss importer, who went to the heart of the matter. He relied, he said, on chemical analysis, but also on the French 'acquits', based on the world's strictest wine legislation, and on the firm selling the bottle. "Now, can we have any confidence in anyone or anything?" he cried. "If you want my opinion, at present you are conducting a trial of the wine itself. And that's bad for French wine" an opinion echoed in the blunt words of the Dutch witness that "given the publicity surrounding this affair, it is going to be very difficult from now on for us to promote and to popularize the wines of Bordeaux, indeed, French wine in general."

But the trial sheered away from more general considerations and the rest of the day was spent in a detailed examination of the Cruses on the state of the wines—and the paperwork—in their cellars the previous year, and how they had behaved when confronted by the inspectors' demands. Many of the arguments were technical, concerning the illegal substances allegedly found in the cellars, and the audience began to get bored. Nevertheless, there were more dramatic moments, when the argument started on the apparently haphazard way the Cruses had labelled their vats. The Cruses were by no means convincing when they tried to explain away the use of the words 'base' on a number of vats, and how wines could serve alternatively as Meursault or Puligny-Montrachet, and why the contents of one particular vat would 'serve as Beaujolais for the American market'. Nevertheless, the battle was tough: the Cruses' lawyer protested that his questions were too often interrupted by the judge, who snapped back that he was leading the questioning. "But it is I", retorted Maître Rozier, "who's leading the defence."

The Cruses, however, stuck to their positions, reinforced by such tell-tale mistakes as the mislabelling of one vat as Graves when it had previously been called Médoc: the renaming, far from increasing the Cruses' profits, would have cost them money, since at the time, a year earlier, a tonneau of Graves was selling 1,500 francs below the value of a Médoc.

Only once was Yvan Cruse provoked, when the prosecutor talked of 'a Bordeaux shipper of the reputation you used to have'. The past tense was too much: Yvan's reply, "Yes, I'm untidy, I erase things, scratch out entries, but I'm telling the truth", echoed through France.

The situation was no clearer after Wednesday's hearing, which was largely confined to preliminary examinations of the many other shippers who had bought wine from Balan (who was formally questioned before each of 'his' customers, only to confess his ignorance). If anything the day's hearing helped the Cruses, and not only because other witnesses confirmed how 'ungiving' and indistinguishable the wines appeared to experts. ("The trial has certainly removed much of the mystique from wine-tasting," said Hugues Lawton.) The parade of lesser shippers gave a glimpse into the underside of the wine trade, the innumerable middle-men, percentage merchants gaining their living without cellars, tankers or assets of any kind save only a telephone. In that company the dignity and expertise of the Cruses shone out brightly (the only major relief, as usual, was Bert, behaving on that day as a Greek chorus lamenting how his former customers had disowned him).

But one point stood out: the desperate needs which had driven Bert's other customers to deal with him. Inevitably the source of the trouble was located anywhere but the Gironde: "In 1972," said Lucien Castaing, "we witnessed incredible follies. Because a number of Anglo-Saxon countries had monetary problems they became obsessed with claret, which suddenly resembled gold bars; I even had rubber companies and cigarette manufacturers asking me to take their money." (This was not as absurd as it sounds. The single biggest buyer of all, Austin Nichols, was owned by a cigarette manufacturer; and at the time the London Rubber Company, best-known for its rubber contraceptives, also owned a chain of off-licences).

But Thursday was the turning point, although the Cruses' defence counsel, Maître Rozier, himself a wine-grower, made theoretically the most telling point of the whole trial: that there was, as the judge had already remarked, 'no corpse' in the case; the wine in question had never actually been brought into court, never submitted, as M. Rozier suggested, to a blind tasting.

Had Bert and he succeeded, then they could have exposed the fundamental flaw in the whole legal apparatus: that the inherent qualities of the wine sold by Bert to the Cruses were not in question. Had the wine been called as a witness then the irrelevant nature of the French wine laws, their purely formal and theoretical quality, their failure to guarantee any special qualities to the wines they labelled would have been exposed for all to see. As it was, the debate was confined to the technicalities of the law. "Written proofs are enough for us," declared Inspector Gardia of the Fraud Squad. And on that Thursday he and his colleagues from the Tax Squad mounted the most detailed and damning description of how they stumbled across 'the affair' (sources included 'an informant' and the divisional office at Langon, which had requested additional help to deal with the unprecedented amount of paper-work being churned out by Bert and Balan's franking machine). They went on to give details of their descents into the Cruses' cellars, and what they had found there, the chaos, the obstruction, the missing paper-work. Their mastery of detail was impressive: so was their awareness of how unprecedented the affair was ("it was

the first time in twenty-two years' service," said one of them,
"that I had ever had to resort to a formal warrant"); and so was
their understanding of Pierre Bert's character. "It wasn't his
first attempt," said the formidable Inspector Eugène Gardia,
"but relations with him, our exchanges, were courteous, which
is why he comes over as so likeable. It is regrettable that the
need to cheat is second nature to him, and a second nature,
moreover, which the Bordeaux wine trade was fully aware of"
—a statement aimed directly at the Cruses, with their claims that
they knew nothing against him.

The court then adjourned for a well-deserved long weekend
break to celebrate All Saints Day, and when it resumed on the
Monday morning it heard evidence which finally convinced
everyone that the Cruses were guilty. The day started with
some more of Inspector Gardia's pithy characterizations: of
Lucien Castaing, "a man who is discreet, wary, circumspect and
who keeps everything in his head . . . you wouldn't find com-
promising account books in *his* cellars"; and of another defendant,
François George, that he was "highly intelligent, had an answer
to everything, and was certainly not a dupe of Bert's."

But these were mere hors d'œuvres: the first main dish was
solid evidence of the Cruses' guilt on the charge of topping up
AOC wines with others not entitled to any appellation. This
was technical stuff, designed to lull the court before the excitement
of the afternoon session. Then the chauffeur, Barnabé, gave the
game away. He described his activities in minute detail, leaving
no one in any doubt that the Cruses knew exactly what they
were up to, had indeed conspired with Bert, had simply been
buying the precious green pieces of paper from him without
any wines to accompany them. The inspectors could merely pin
them down on technicalities: Barnabé could turn them to
conspirators.

The rest of the day—and indeed the trial—was anti-climactic.
The audience was naturally interested to hear poor Hugues
Lawton, in his role as defendant of the good name of the wines
sold by the Gironde's other wine merchants; it was intrigued
to hear from Raymond le Sauvage, the widely-respected president
of the Brokers' Association, of an embarrassing wine tasting at
St. Estèphe the previous spring when a distinguished gathering
had accepted as worthy of the commune label a sample from the

Lot-et-Garonne, up-river from Bordeaux in the 'Haut Pays'.
Daniel-Georges Lawton, Hugues' brother, made a moving plea
on behalf of his 'cousins'. But, after the chauffeur's evidence,
it only remained for the defence lawyers to try and salvage some
mitigating circumstances from the wreckage of their case.

Before the final submissions came a day of arguments from
lawyers representing the aggrieved parties claiming damages.
Most were obvious, ranging from the 4 million francs (£370,000)
claimed by the INAO from the Cruses and Bert to the mere
80,000 francs (£7,400) demanded by the Gironde's Ligue des
Viticulteurs, the pioneering growers' association founded nearly
seventy years earlier. The lawyer representing the growers of
Bordeaux and Bordeaux Supérieur, in dignified contrast, asked
for only the traditional one franc: "the immense prejudice"
caused to his members' reputation "was beyond price". And
there was one moment of pathos from the lawyer representing
the growers of the Midi who had supplied the wines which
were so easy to pass off as products of the Gironde: never forget,
he remarked, that half the wine produced in the Midi is sold to
shippers in Bordeaux and Burgundy to emerge in bottles bearing
their valuable labels, to the detriment of the growers and the
extortionate profit of the merchants. Finally, the lawyer representing the tax authorities rose to demand a total of 82 million francs
(£7.5 million), a sum ridiculed by the more knowledgeable
spectators as merely a hollow gesture in view of the certainty
that some form of accommodation would be reached.

Indeed, the next day the prosecution's summing-up made it
clear that the Cruses would not be going to prison. Dontenwille
started in bucolic-philosophical vein, reflecting out loud on
"those, growers and merchants alike, for whom wine is their
whole life, and not only a source of profit. For I am fully aware
the pain they have suffered through this trial which afflicts them
so unjustly"—a theme more fully spelled out by that day's
Sud-Ouest which reflected bitterly on how the 'fraud perpetrated
on Bordeaux wine' of summer '73 had gradually become 'the
affair' to end as 'the trial of Bordeaux's wine'. It remained only,
said the paper, to describe the affair as the trial of wine in general.

But Dontenwille went on to be more specific, to ask for
penalties which ranged from a year in prison for Bert to simple
fines for the outer ring of his customers. As for the Cruses,

10*

Dontenwille agreed he was attacking a firm with a long tradition. But this, he argued, although it conferred rights, also created obligations, "especially that of being absolutely exact in its commercial transactions, of deserving the credit the house possesses". Nevertheless, the case "covered events of relatively limited duration, and Lionel and Yvan Cruse were involved only in a transitory fashion in the world of fraud", so he asked only for a suspended sentence. In contrast, the less well-connected Castaing, described as the very mirror-image of Bert, should go to prison (a cleaner at a shipper's warehouse had just been sentenced to two years' imprisonment for stealing a few cases of château-bottled wine from her employers).

Then the defence lawyers had their day—or rather their two days and a half. Their arguments were varied and ingenious. Bert's lawyer concentrated on the religious vocation felt so strongly by his client during the 1960s. The Cruses' lawyers deployed a battery of explanations. The most convincing was the plea that no one had ever complained about the quality of the wine involved and the least plausible the complaints about the allegedly bad behaviour of the inspectors and the allegation that the mere possession of the name of Cruse was being treated as an aggravating circumstance. The press came in for a beating, but the biggest sensation was reserved for the statement by the lawyer defending François George that the whole affair was political, that it resulted from an agreement between the then Minister of Agriculture, M. Chirac, and the former Minister of Finance, Valéry Giscard d'Estaing, who had just appointed him Prime Minister (the whole accompanied by heavy hints that they had been assisted by 'a former champagne merchant installed in the Place Vendôme'—a reference, clear enough to a French audience, if not to outsiders, to Pierre Taittinger who had recently become Minister of Justice and operated from the Place Vendôme). He compared the world-wide notoriety attaching to 'Winegate' with the oblivion into which a similar case involving merchants in Burgundy had fallen. But the defence naturally did not spell out the difference in scale: if Barnabé had kept up his 'deliveries' for a year at the 7 June rate he alone would have 'baptized' three times as much wine as Pomerol had produced in 1974.

Exhausted, the court adjourned, and the three judges went

away, with an estimated 10,000 pages of evidence, to consider their verdicts to be delivered just before Christmas, on 18 December.

There were few surprises: only eight out of the eighteen defendants were found guilty and only Bert was given a prison sentence. The Cruses, still protesting that the whole affair was a politically-inspired put-up job, were given suspended sentences, as were Balan, Bert's cousin Bertrand de Pinos and four of his major customers.

But more damaging were the fiscal penalties: the guilty men's businesses were to be kept under strict legal surveillance for three years. Moreover the Cruses and Bert would have to find 38 million francs (£3.5 million) to satisfy the taxmen's demands, far higher a figure than anyone had suspected.

The last word was inevitably left to Pierre Bert. He spent most of the day of his conviction conducting a series of impromptu press conferences, asserting that, like a hero in a Western, he 'had merely done what he had to do', announcing that he was going to write his memoirs, and providing a foretaste by claiming that the market in wine was influenced by four factors, the growers, the merchants, the brokers 'and women'. He then completed a star performance by turning to one of his accusers and saying, simply, "You've won, let me offer you a glass of champagne."

24

The dark days

Despite the relative leniency of the sentences, all the convicted men appealed, though when they were heard in May 1975 there was only a handful of journalists—all of them French—present to record the scene. This was a pity: for it was only at this late stage that François George's lawyer touched an exceedingly raw nerve: the implicit guilt of the French authorities in allowing one of their precious franking machines—supposedly confined to the most reputable of wholesalers—into the hands of Serge Balan and his puppet-master, the notorious Bert. How, argued M. Dumas, could Bert have become an untouchable for reputable shippers so soon after he had been trusted with a machine? And Dumas rubbed salt in the administration's wound by unearthing a previous accusation of fraud on Balan's own part.

Following these revelations it was not surprising that the 'affair' was allowed virtually to lapse and in July, as a result of the appeal, the sentences were greatly reduced. All the guilty parties were to benefit from the pardon automatically granted by a new President—which, for instance, relieved the Cruses from the three-year judicial supervision of their business decided by the court the previous December. Pierre Bert himself received a remission which, effectively, set him free.

Although he appeared much subdued at the appeal (no longer the 'sorcerer' of the original trial), Bert had bounced back sufficiently to have written his sensational book, *In Vino Veritas*, during the first quarter of the year. It was more than his amplification of his testimony at the trial to the idiocy of the law and the consequent endemic cheating among the wine growers and shippers. Its first chapters provided an idyllic picture of the life lived among the growers of Barsac before the war.

It was, naturally, a huge success: the first edition, timed to appear just as the appeal was being heard, was quickly sold out, and Bert himself signed copies at Feret's, the bookshop named after the original publisher of Bordeaux's bible. Indeed writing books seemed to be the only way to make money out of wine in 1975. Another merchant in deep financial trouble, Bernard Ginestet, published his compilation *Bouillie Bordelaise*; the distinguished American wine writer, Robert Daley, published a long and lurid thriller, *Red Wine Deep as Blood*, featuring a wicked (and sexually exceedingly kinky) merchant. And France's greatest comic-strip hero, 'Asterix the Gaul', stout defender of French freedom against the wicked Romans, got into the act with a volume clearly based on the great wine boom.

('Obelix and Company' was firmly based on the French assumption that the whole crisis resulted entirely from the wickedness of foreign speculators, taking advantage of simple but innocent Gauls.)

For in 1975 there was no profit in wine itself. In fact the year saw a sell-off of wines good and bad at an unequalled rate, and a sorting-out among the shippers, who by then were suffering appallingly from the financial strain. But in the end, the process, although it was painful and involved a number of casualties, had beneficial results. It opened new sales channels and forced every single shipper to sit down and reappraise the future of his business.

The pressure was not helped by the 1974 vintage, which was roughly the size of 1970, giving three vintages out of five nearly a third above what had previously been considered 'normal'. It was not that the wines were bad, simply unwanted: "1974 is, at this early stage," wrote Peter Sichel in April 1975, "reminiscent of the 1967 vintage. Under different circumstances, thoroughly useful wines and no doubt one day they will be wanted. Today they are the unwanted orphans of a shattered market place."

Yet, even when Sichel was writing these words, the first signs of light were appearing—in France itself.

Immediately after the trial, a French market research firm had examined its effect on the future habits of French wine-buyers. The results provided a useful indicator to future patterns. Over a third of the customers surveyed thought that Bordeaux's wines in general had been on trial, and nearly four-fifths thought (correctly) that only shippers and brokers had been in the dock —only a fifth believed that the scandal also involved growers.

More crucially, the customer showed an enhanced interest in the name on the bottle: brand names and shippers' reputations had suddenly become of enormous importance. And, finally, 95 out of every 100 said they would continue to buy wine from Bordeaux.

In fact they did more than that: the last quarter of 1974 marked the turn of the tide for Bordeaux's products on the home market. Encouraged by the slump in prices, consumption started to increase and within a year, the Gironde's red wines had recaptured their historic position ahead of Burgundy and Côtes du Rhône. And in the early 1970s claret-drinking had spread more evenly throughout France: although consumption in Bordeaux's two former strongholds, the industrial north-east and the Paris region, was slow to recover to pre-boom levels, any shortfall was more than made good by increased consumption even during the height of the boom in the rest of France.

This tendency was encouraged by the ability of some of Bordeaux's merchants to use the rapidly-spreading hyper-markets to sell even château-bottled wines: the theory being that wives shopped during the week seeking only the cheapest possible beverage, but that husbands were increasingly helping with the major shopping trip of the week on Saturdays, and were easily tempted into buying fine wines to accompany Sunday lunch. So the average price paid by French buyers for claret continued to rise and, for the first time in history, the domestic market became an important factor even for sellers of classified growths.

Historically the French wine trade was just not organized to cope with the change in purchasing patterns. In 1971 there were 7,000 wholesalers dealing in wine servicing over 350,000 retail outlets, with only a few large distributors. Within Bordeaux the majority of the shippers tended to be either uninterested in the home market, concentrated on direct distribution to private clients, tied up (like the Moueixes) with a handful of powerful, regional, outlets, or (like the Calvets) in the hands of the 'agents multi-cartes', the powerful travelling salesmen each representing a wide range of alcoholic drinks, and virtually unsupervised by head office. (Typically, Calvet employed only five inspectors to supervise 98 'agents multi-cartes.')

The increasing importance of the home market inevitably led to greater professionalism in the marketing within France of good clarets and Sauternes. Wholesale wine merchants like Jean Castel moved into Bordeaux in a big way (in 1976 Chantovent, the biggest of them all, bought Château Chasse-Spleen to provide a major brand for the top of its range of wines); and a few Bordeaux houses, especially Cordier, increased their domestic operations (Lichine was less successful, being forced to cut back its efforts very sharply within a couple of years).

Nevertheless the vast majority of the Gironde's wines sold through normal French retail channels remained cheap: not surprisingly the rush of bargain-hunting French buyers (through direct buying as well as through normal retail channels) was felt first at the bottom end of the trade. By April 1975 Prévot was noting in his weekly column in *Sud-Ouest* that the market in lower-priced wines was firm, although not many deals were being done—despite a late frost which provided a theoretical boost for the market. By June the position was even more polarized. At the upper end of the market virtually none of the 1974 wines had been offered at all, and 29 appellations of 1973s were simply not quoted. Yet by the end of the month the growers had, overall, disposed of a third more wine—red and white—as they had the year before. No wonder that by the end of August even the co-ops were getting 1,300 francs without question for Bordeaux Rouge, with suggestions that the price was actually rising.

The topsy-turvy nature of the market was reinforced by what was happening abroad. In the three markets which had taken the bulk of the better clarets during the boom—Japan, the United States and Britain—sales were still depressed. But in the rest of the world the buyers imitated the French, and sales during 1974-5 rose by 30 per cent in volume and a fifth in value over the previous year.

But the three 'difficult' markets were completely swamped by the tactics of the firms which had been such major buyers during the boom: having destabilized the market on the way up because of their size, they prevented a peaceful landing by equally panicky dumping tactics on the way down—an influence increased by their enormous stocks. Two alone were alleged to have 5 million bottles of château-bottled wines in stock in

Bordeaux. Their influence was felt first by Bass Charrington's sale at Christie's in July 1974.

During the two-and-a-half subsequent years, however, Christie's proved its usefulness to growers and shippers anxious to increase their liquidity without ruining the market. The precedent was set in June 1975 when Baron Philippe and M. Nemès of Lafite combined to sell a vast range of Lafites and Moutons. Their success stabilized the market and relieved the universal fear that the market had no bottom. Subsequently Delor and Calvet were able to follow Bass Charrington's example and Jean Cordier followed the Rothschilds by selling an incomparable range of the classed growths he owned.

But in 1975 itself any sales method had to be tried. Gilbey's, faced with what Michael Longhurst calls 'a buyer's market of the worst description', went out for new customers, through direct sales in France and, most spectacularly, through the biggest advertisement ever seen for wine in Britain, a whole page in *The Times* in February 1975.

Nevertheless the combination of tax increases, a continuing decline in the standard of living among Britain's traditional wine-drinking classes and the application in Britain of the French 'Appellation Contrôlée' system consequent upon Britain's entry into the European Common Market completely destroyed the British market. For several years, indeed, the British were interested almost exclusively in Bordeaux's cheapest wines. No wonder the three British groups which had been so active in Bordeaux lost considerable sums: Allied Breweries—owners of Delor—and Grand Metropolitan Hotels—which owns Gilbeys —both had to write £2 million off their stocks while Bass Charrington admitted to losses of over £6 million.

While the British were grubbing for bargains among the cheaper wines, the Americans were making hay at the upper end. Much of the wine sold through Christie's and Sotheby's went to them, and the liquor stores, especially in New York, were awash with bargains. The 1972 vintage of Henri Martin's precious Château Gloria was offered at a mere $3 (£1.35), and 1970 Beychevelle was going at $5 (£2.20)—a price which dragged down the level at which the 1974 vintage was being offered. Most of the second growths were available at around the same price, with the firsts at between $12 and $15 (£5.20 to £6.60), a mere fraction of the prices at which they had opened a couple of years before.

Most of these bargains were useful publicity for French wine, but one of the most spectacular offers rather rebounded. Sherry Lehmann advertised their 1968 Lafite at $4.99 (£2.20), a cut in price of $10 (£4.30) a bottle, and took an advertisement in the *New York Times* to announce the fact. But the wine was not distinguished and many buyers were disappointed.*

Despite the immense stocks, and although the only shipper to increase his sales in the USA was Baron Philippe (who at one point was reckoned to account for one bottle in five of Bordeaux wine entering the US), in fact French wines did not suffer too badly in the American market. During the year the Americans turned against the Sangrias and Rosés which had accounted for much of the boom in imported wines, and although sales of Bordeaux wine were a fifth down in the 1974-5 campaign year (which starts on 1 September) sales picked up later.

Much worse was the position in Japan, which was 'drowning in a lake of wine'. Imports had shot up more than ten-fold in the previous three years: and the improbable newcomers to the import business had included the trading arm of the Toyota Motor Company, anxious to find some imported product to offset against the soaring foreign sales of its vehicles. These massive purchases and a (relative) slump in sales meant that by the beginning of 1975 the Japanese had enough wine in stock to last for at least a year. Moreover the warehousing costs were enormous and the effects of Tokyo's steamy summer climate disastrous. So, as elsewhere, the dumping was ferocious. Mitsukoshi, Tokyo's most distinguished department store, was offering the best 1971 and 1972 clarets at under a third of the original price. And the effect of such cuts was far more

---

* A generation earlier, Charles Walter Berry had reacted violently to the sight of a Latour of the dreadful 1930 vintage being offered cheaply at the Hotel d'Orsay in Bordeaux for propaganda purposes: "What mentality," he exploded: "if ever there was a bad vintage here you have it . . . run through your mind the two together—Latour 1930 and then imagine what the public will think. 'This must be good we will try it' . . . and then comes the fall, the great disappointment. 'If this is a specimen of the finest red Bordeaux (they probably know nothing about the vintage) then may I be spared from drinking it again.'"

severe in Japan than elsewhere. In other markets buyers are proud of bargains, and appreciate them the more the greater the prestige of the original item. By contrast the growth in the Japanese market for claret had depended very largely on the habit of giving gifts of obviously considerable value twice a year, to employees, relations and friends. And if the value of the possible gift was being publicly demeaned, then it was automatically devalued in Japanese eyes.

No wonder sales to Japan slumped by nearly three-quarters in 1974–5 compared to the previous year. Then, the sheer length of the pipeline had ensured that exports remained virtually static, even though it became increasingly clear during the year that there were no customers for the wine at the other end.

Although the Japanese scene was the most spectacularly awful, the carnage elsewhere ensured that 1975 was a ghastly year for all those involved in growing and making and selling the better wines.

The shippers suffered worst: indeed the surprising thing is that virtually all survived, more or less intact. Even Ab Simon survived: Austin Nichols packed up its wine business, but he simply moved over to sell similar wines for Seagrams. The saddest casualty was Bill Bolter. He was struck by the bankruptcy of two of his major American regional distributors in Seattle and Rhode Island and the desire of his partner to get out of the business, so the firm went into voluntary liquidation—characteristically Bolter remained in Bordeaux, still living on the 'Pavé', and acting as a sort of 'super-broker', as intermediary between foreign buyers and major estates, a role previously adopted to a great extent by Nathaniel Johnston. And only one shipper sold out: Grenouilleau, the man who had bought up Pierre Bert's family firm, sold a half-share in his business to a Los Angeles-based firm, Mifuku Inc., best known as the American distributors of such luxury products as Dior perfumes.

Only by acting as brokers could shippers avoid the financing costs which, in the absence of any help from the French government, were crippling their business—up to an eighth of their sales revenue was being swallowed up by financing charges, and short-term loans amounted to nearly half the (much reduced) value of their stocks. The announcement in September that the government would help to finance stocks of over twenty million gallons only helped growers, not shippers.

Some of the biggest losers (like the English) had their parent groups to fall back on; others, like Dourthe and Cordier, had considerable reserves. But even these were rapidly eaten into. Unlike most of his fellow-shippers (who between them reduced their work-force by over a thousand), Jean-Pierre Moueix refused to sack any of his employees, so they simply sat around, among stock valued at up to £4 million for six solid months during which the firm sold not a drop of wine.

But even the Cruses survived (amazingly, in the year after their conviction they still exported more wine than de Luze, Eschenauer—or Bollinger champagne for that matter). Like many other Chartronnais before them, they found a solution to their financial problems in selling one of their estates. The Cruses were still financially stable enough to be forced to sell only one of their properties, albeit the biggest, Pontet-Canet. Even then the purchaser was Lionel's brother-in-law, Guy Tesseron, who controlled a large cognac business. (They also had to rearrange the legal position of their business, bringing in a number of respected outsiders, effectively as trustees.)

More serious was the position of the Ginestet family. Bernard's brother had died, leaving the expected inheritance duty problem. It was the only firm with major obligations to growers which did not have substantial backing from a foreign parent company: it was also exceptional in trying to hang on to them, and in being absolutely scrupulous in honouring what were in most cases unwritten contracts. (Termination involved the most dreadful arguments. "It's surprising how ungentlemanly people can get when unscrambling gentleman's agreements," says Michael Longhurst.)

For Ginestet the figures were frightening: the firm's debts— reckoned to be over 50 million francs (£5.5 million)—were a third greater than its annual turnover; and the interest alone was unlikely to be covered by profits for years to come. So the Ginestets had to sell their only real asset: Château Margaux, which it had taken Bernard's grandfather and father a quarter of a century to buy in its entirety.

They spent much of 1975 arguing with the Rémy Martin cognac firm which clearly scented a bargain but could not find the cash. So it teamed up with a major insurance company, Union des Assurances de Paris, to bid for the château and the family business, both at bargain prices: but the Ginestets would not agree, because the purchasers would not guarantee the jobs of the people employed by the estate and the business, nor the continuance of the 'abonnements' with the growers.

In 1976 Bernard thought he had found a buyer, National Distillers, an American liquor business whose major previous venture into the wine business had been the purchase in 1967 of the Almaden vineyards in California. Agreement was speedily reached: National Distillers would buy Margaux alone for 82 million francs (£10 million). Moreover they would guarantee the jobs of everyone on the estate.

The Ministry of Finance immediately blocked the sale, claiming that the Ginestets must find a French buyer. This reaction is normal with any foreign take-over bid for any French asset (let alone one as precious as Margaux)—we saw earlier what high-level politicking it took before control of Latour could pass into English hands.

But during 1976 there is no doubt that the French government did lean most unpleasantly on the Ginestets. Outsiders automatically believed that the cause of the trouble was Aymar Achille-Fould, Minister, owner of Beychevelle and Bernard's successful opponent in the 1974 elections.

The Ginestets deny this, saying that they are still friendly with him, that the trouble came from much higher, that they were subject continuously to pressure from a Presidential level to accept any French bid. For eventually, after six months of rumours, the Crédit Agricole, France's semi-public agricultural bank, offered a mere 60 million francs (£7.2 million), barely enough to pay off the family debts together with their accrued interest. Without any apparent encouragement from their fellow-growers or merchants, who could well have found themselves under similar pressure, the Ginestets refused the bid. In mid-November Bernard announced that in the absence of a decent offer the family would put the château up to auction at the end of the year, a desperate device which precluded any guarantees about the buyer's attitude towards the château or the wine.

But a month later the most improbable of Father Christmases

suddenly appeared on the scene, a French company prepared to pay, if not the full asking price, only 10 per cent below it— 75 million francs (£9 million). It was Félix Potin, the most solidly French of grocery chains, still, in an age of supermarkets, wedded to the continuing profitability of the corner grocer's shop. Sighs of relief all round. The joke was that Potin itself had been rescued from a slow death twenty years before by a lively entrepreneur, André Mentzelotoulos, who, as his name suggests, is Greek-born and bred, still a Greek citizen, in character "Greek to the ends of his fingertips" in the words of a close friend, and majority shareholder in Potin.

In other words, the 'French solution' demanded by the government turned out to be effectively foreign after all. At this early stage it seems to be turning out a happy compromise: the new purchaser is allowing Pierre Ginestet and his wife to live out their days in their old home, and the first news out of Margaux is that the buyer (and his French wife) are hiring France's leading interior decorator to refurbish the Médoc's noblest pile. Since this was built and owned for half a century by Spaniards, its rescue by another foreigner is entirely appropriate.

25

From the ashes

"To return this autumn to Bordeaux, battered by nearly three years of crisis, is rather like re-visiting a friend's family that has been sadly afflicted by an accident, to a degree unknown to the visitor. Who, one asks cautiously, have died, how many are alive and well, and how are the convalescents? In Bordeaux one quickly discovers, not only that the family is very large, but that their circumstances differ widely and that there are some serious family disagreements."—EDMUND PENNING-ROWSELL, *November 1976.*

1976 was the year that the framework, personal and institutional, of the new Bordeaux scene became clear. And very different it was from the image or the reality of Bordeaux before the boom.

The breakage of past links which formed such an important part of the change was unhappily symbolized early in the year. In January the seventy-year-old Max de Pontac, the direct descendant of the Parlementaire who had originally pioneered the making of fine wines on a grand scale in the Gironde and their sale in England, sent in the bulldozers to plough up the vines at Château Myrat. Under the older version of its name, Mirat, the vineyard had been classed in 1855 at the top of the second growths of Barsac and Sauternes—the white wine equivalent of the position held in the Médoc by Mouton-Rothschild.

Cynical observers might allege that the Count "spent more time in the pink-painted library of his Louis XV château than among his vines", but the fact remained that he, like virtually every other conscientious maker of Barsac or Sauternes, had been losing money for a decade or more. They themselves attributed their losses to the flood of unworthy wines produced for so many years under the names of Barsac and Sauternes; charitable people in the trade put the blame simply to a change in drinking fashions.

Other changes were less dramatic but more far-reaching. For

the crucial event of the year, the reorganization of the CIVB and the introduction of a special 'Bordeaux contract' armed with all the powers necessary for its enforcement, marked the final triumph of the growers, nearly seventy years after they had first founded the Ligue des Viticulteurs to defend themselves against the wicked shippers.

But the new generation was not merely defensive. It had explored a refreshing range of selling methods. The Co-operatives in St. Emilion had virtually taken over the town after an internal coup d'état the previous year. And they were working with Paul Jauffret at Dourthe and even with a similar co-operative in California. One group of twenty-five growers had banded together to promote wines grown without any of the chemical aids permitted under French law. The collapse of 1973-4 had induced many others to sell directly—one, Château Timberlay, even took on salesmen who had left Bass Charrington's Lichine business. At the other extreme Bruno Prats had set up his own distribution business: he had even developed his own brand (Maître d'Estournel) cashing in on his proudest possession. And in the United States he had formed a joint distribution company with Julius Wile, later becoming confident enough to take over the whole business.

But the most startling example of growers' initiative came from Paul Glotin who, together with Jean-Paul Jauffret and Prefect Doustin, was to be the key figure in reorganizing the Bordeaux system. Glotin is not physically impressive. Short, square, balding, his remaining hair plastered carefully over his pate, he resembles a cartoon figure depicting the unremarkable politicians who dominated France between the two world wars. The physical contrast with the typically Anglo-Saxon Chartronnais—lean, sporty, Savile Row-suited—is equally marked in business terms, but in this case totally to Glotin's advantage.

For a long time Glotin has worked for Marie Brizard and was responsible for the firm's success in the Spanish market. But he also inherited a property in the Graves de Vayres, Château Goudichaut. The house itself is a splendid eighteenth-century affair and the estate a fine one, once the country retreat of the Archbishops of Bordeaux. But its surroundings, five miles west of Libourne, are less remarkable. For the parish is in one of the smallest and most downtrodden of the Gironde's wine-growing districts, under 3,000 acres in all, producing in most years under 300,000 gallons of unremarkable white wine.

Nevertheless, quite quietly, Glotin persuaded his fellow-proprietors to spend money on their properties and to sell their wine collectively. He organized a proper marketing study and this led the growers to a single distributor in Germany prepared to take the whole vintage, year after year. He persuaded his fellow-growers to spend money on advertising, and delegations of growers would go to Germany to talk directly to the shoppers in German supermarkets who were buying their wines.

Subsequently, while still working for Marie Brizard, he was elected head of the growers' organization and formed a perfect foil to Jauffret. They were not alone. In fact it was Glotin who, together with Prefect Doustin, largely worked out the recommendations of the commission, which in early 1976 rewrote the constitution of the CIVB. This in itself was possible only because of earlier initiatives which had culminated in a law passed in July 1975 granting a reformed CIVB the necessary powers. But it took nearly another year before the new body was formed, and it was only in October 1976 that the changes affecting the Bordeaux market itself were announced. (By that time Doustin had left Bordeaux. His talents had been recognized by promotion to be Chef de Cabinet to the French Prime Minister, Raymond Barre.)

The committee deliberated under happier circumstances than might have been thought conceivable even a year before. The 1975 vintage was exactly what Bordeaux had been longing for since 1970: it was of potentially very high quality and was by no means enormous in size—an eighth bigger than 1971, a quarter smaller than 1970, partly because of some unseasonal September hailstorms. Markets at home and abroad continued to respond to price-cutting—by the third quarter of 1976 Bordeaux was selling almost as much red wine in the home market as its two chief rivals, Beaujolais and Côtes du Rhône, together. Abroad, although the German market suffered a temporary collapse because of a change in the regulations surrounding the Common Agricultural Policy of the European Common Market, still their total value went up by a fifth. For prices recovered to the 'sensible' levels of the early stages of the boom, those at which the 1971 vintage had opened.

The 'new' CIVB was set up in February and in June Jauffret became President (the growers would have preferred Glotin: but Marie Brizard would not allow him the necessary time off). He took on the job saying—and meaning—that it was to be for one year only, and on the understanding that he would be allowed to carry through the changes agreed by the refounding committee. Everyone was astounded when he fulfilled both conditions.

The new organization he announced in October was sweeping enough. For a start, although Bordeaux's 47 'appellations' were not abolished, they had all been allocated into five groups. Three were for claret—the basic appellations, the superior ones in the Médoc, the 'Libournais' group covering St. Emilion and Pomerol—and two for white wines, sweet and dry. A price was fixed for every appellation, and all transactions were to be conducted within ten per cent of that figure. Moreover the CIVB was to have the power to ensure the registration of each transaction. A compensation fund was to be set up to enable the CIVB to buy and store wine surplus to market requirements at the proper market price. Longer-term contracts, the concentration of sales at the beginning of the 'campaign' year soon after the vintage, and the hope of public financing of growers were other items on the future agenda.

In theory and to an extent in practice this new regime, called 'The Bordeaux Contract', was a revolution. It inhibited speculation, it brought the growers near the reality of the market place, it prevented shippers from playing growers off against each other. It is a mark of Bordeaux's backwardness that roughly the same form of agreement had been in operation for years in other wine-growing districts of France—yet its chances of survival in the chronically speculative Gironde were by no means guaranteed.

The backers of the new contract were also lucky in that the merchants were divided. Many of the older generation were hostile or sceptical. But where not so long ago it was the shippers who had been a small united group, holding the whip hand over a disorganized and mutually suspicious army of growers, now the boot was on the other foot. The idea of the Bordeaux contract trampled over the whole basis of the Chartronnais' world—their power to set prices by dividing and ruling over the growers. But they had been destroyed by their own greed, and by the intrusion of far more financially powerful forces from outside.

The names of the new CIVB gave the game away. They included a Lawton—but he was working for an American-owned company; a Schÿler was president of the Merchants' Association—but half the capital of his family firm had been bought by A. Moueix (the non-Jean-Pierre branch of the family); more typical were Jauffret, with his partnership with the St. Emilionnais, Yves Pardes from the English-owned Delor, Glotin, and Pierre Coste from Langon, an earnest, bearded, much-respected merchant, dedicated to the proposition that good claret could be drunk young, and working with a number of growers to make their wine so that it was indeed very drinkable after a couple of years.

Peter Sichel—who himself had reservations about the contract but loyally went along with the decision—summed up the end of the Chartronnais powers quite simply: "What's out for the future are family companies holding a stock of wine and selling to a free international wholesale clientèle that doesn't need them any more"—a perfect description of the Chartronnais. Earlier that year Martin Bamford had pointed out that the "1975 vintage has sold well in European markets, but for the most part Bordeaux négociants have acted merely as brokers, making only minimum profit. This leads us to question the traditional distribution system . . . only long-term concentration on a few prestigious labels backed by exclusivity and continual investment will produce a return". And this was a game only a few independents could play: Cordier (who was setting up wholly-owned distribution companies abroad) certainly, Calvet and the two halves of the Moueix family possibly, Peter Sichel—but only because of the profits made from Blue Nun Liebfraumilch by the other branch of the family company.

Nevertheless the Chartronnais had a few last tricks up their sleeve. The winter of 1976-7 was exceptionally mild: Nathaniel Johnston, sure that this foretold some form of disaster, speculated heavily on the '75s and '76s. And at the end of March 1977, after the vines had come early into bud, a severe frost wiped out up to a third of the earlier Merlot variety, ensuring that, in St. Emilion and Pomerol at least, the 1977 vintage would be only half the normal size. This provided an early test of the new contract, which proved flexible enough to absorb the strain. Although the 'contract' price should have lasted a full 'campaign' year, in April, only half-way through, prices were raised by 10 per cent (and of course the 'crus classés' which Johnston had bought went up even more).

But old habits died hard: at a marketing seminar (the first in Bordeaux's history) held in June, a Belgian distributor complained that the St. Emilionnais, not content with the 'contract' price, were hoarding their—still considerable—stocks, claiming that they had no wine to sell. Jauffret was chairman and therefore unable to sell directly to the thirsty customer. But after the session it was noticeable that a number of shippers clustered round the dissatisfied distributor and he did not leave Bordeaux unsupplied.

But it was this same seminar, itself a revolutionary innovation, and bringing together all the new men of Bordeaux, which also clearly demonstrated that Bordeaux's ambivalence between orderly marketing and the desire for an unconsidered bargain remained. The clue was provided by the chief buyer for the Swedish state liquor monopoly: on the first day he emphasized how Bordeaux must concentrate its efforts on a few brands and discourage the proliferation of names; by the second day his tune had changed, and he was hoping that the upheavals in the Bordeaux scene would not mean the end of the many little châteaux which had provided drinkers in Sweden, as in the rest of the civilized world, with so much good wine at such reasonable prices for so many years. Mr. Petersen was reflecting the inevitably contradictory feelings of buyers the world over—which is why the Bordeaux market-place remains so much the most interesting in the world of wine and, because of the quality of the commodity, one of the most fascinating in the world.

Acknowledgments

The prime sources for this book were the large number of busy people, in London and in and around Bordeaux, who were kind enough to talk so frankly to me. My special thanks are due to Hubert Mussotte and Jean-Louis Viaut at the Conseil Interprofessionel des Vins de Bordeaux, who supplied me with so many statistics, and to Michael Broadbent for his patience. Peter Sichel kindly gave me permission to quote from the newsletters written by his father and himself. The librarians and staff of the Bodleian Library, the London Library, the Bibliothèque Municipale in Bordeaux, the Guildhall Library, and the *Financial Times*, *Le Monde*, and *Sud-Ouest*, were unfailingly helpful. Jenny Phillips provided the material on Japan and Laurie Zimmerman did a great deal of work for me in New York. Rita Towler somehow translated my type-scrawl into legibility.

Sources

This book is not the result of any original or scholarly research. It is, rather, an attempt to look at often well-known material in a new light. Indeed, a few key words provided the framework for the historical sections of the book:

PENNING-ROWSELL, Edmund, *The Wines of Bordeaux* (Penguin Handbooks, 1976), by far the most comprehensive study of the subject— and the only work to devote several chapters to the Bordeaux shippers themselves.

Histoire de Bordeaux, edited by Professor Charles Higounet. Bordeaux.

Vol. V—Bordeaux au XVIIIe siècle. ed. F-G Pariset, 1968.
Vol. VI—Bordeaux au XIXe siècle. ed. Louis Desgraves, 1969.
Vol. VII—Bordeaux au XXe siècle. ed. Joseph Lajugie, 1972.

La Seigneurie et le Vignoble de Châteaux Latour, edited by Professor Higounet, 1974.

DION, Roger, *Histoire de la vigne et du vin en France*, Paris 1959.

Gilbey Diaries: these invaluable documents are lodged at Château Loudenne, where Martin Bamford, Priscilla Bonham Carter and Michael Longhurst gave me every opportunity to consult the transcripts.

The number of books on Bordeaux and its wines is mind-bogglingly large. Among those I found useful:

CAMPBELL, Ian Maxwell, *Wayward Tendrils of the Vine*, London 1947.

CHASSAGNAC, Pierre, *La Vente des Vins de Bordeaux* (Unpublished thesis in Bibliothèque Municipale, Bordeaux).

COCKS, Charles et FERET, Edmond, *Bordeaux et ses Vins*, 12th edition revised by Claude Feret, Feret et Fils, 1969.

COCKS, Charles, *Bordeaux: its Wines and the Claret Country*, 1846. (In French: *Bordeaux, ses Environs et ses Vins*).

COWLES, Virginia, *The Rothschilds, a Family of Fortune*. London, 1973.

FERET, Edmund, *Biographie des Notabilités Girondins*, Statistique Générale du Gironde, 1889.

FRANCIS, A. D., *The Wine Trade*, London 1972.

GUÉRIN, Jean et Bernard, *Des Hommes et des Activités Autour d'un Demi-siècle*.

GUYON, J-R, *Au Service du Vin de Bordeaux*, 1956.

LEROUX, Alfred, *La Colonie Germanique de Bordeaux 1462–1870*, Bordeaux 1918.

MALVEZIN, F., *Bordeaux: Histoire de la Vigne et du Vin en Aquitaine*, Bordeaux 1919.

REDDING, Cyrus, *A History and Description of Modern Wines* ("Redding on Wines"), 3rd edition London 1851.

ROUDIÉ, Philippe, *Le Vignoble Bordelais*.

SALAVERT, Jean, *La Commerce des Vins de Bordeaux*, Bordeaux 1912.

SHAW, T. G., *Wine, the Vine and the Cellar*, London 1864.

Tovey, Charles, *Wines and the Wine Countries*, London 1877.

Vizetelly, Henry, *Glances Back Through Seventy Years*, London 1893.

CHAPTER 3

Passim   H. Enjalbert's "Comment Naissaient les Grands Crus", in *Annales*, 1953.

Page 24   *The Life and Letters of John Locke*, Lord King, 1871.

Page 26   René Pijassou: "Le Marché de Londres et la Naissance des Grands Crus Médocains", in *Revue Historique de Bordeaux* (henceforward RHB) 1974.

Page 27   "Sir Robert Walpole's Wine", by J. H. Plumb in *Men and Places*, 1963.

Page 27   The merchant, Charles Walter Berry, quotes the story in *A Miscellany of Wine*, 1932.

CHAPTER 4

Passim   Robert Forster: "The Noble Wine Producers of the Bordelais in the 18th century"—*Economic History Review*, 1961.

Pages 37–9   *The Papers of Thomas Jefferson*, Ed. J. P. Boyd.

CHAPTER 5

Page 42   Henry Cockburn, *Memorials of his Time*, London 1860.

Page 45   Stendhal, *Travels in the South of France*, translated by Elisabeth Abbot, London 1971.

Page 46   On 'French Tom' Barton: Cyril Ray, *Fide et Fortitudine, The Story of a Vineyard*, privately published.

Page 47   Paul Chevreau, *La Formation Topographique du Quartier des Chartrons*, RHB 1928–9.

Page 47   The "unsympathetic observer" was Alexis Lichine qv.

CHAPTER 6

Page 50ff   M. Guy Schÿler kindly allowed me to use his unpublished work on his ancestor Daniel Guestier. On the Bartons, see Ray, op cit.

CHAPTER 7

Page 67 Edmund Penning-Rowsell has written a number of useful articles on the history of Christie's wine auctions in Christie's Reviews of the Year 1972–7.

Page 68 Nathaniel Johnston's letter books quoted in H. Warner Allen, *A History of Wine*, London 1964.

Page 69 The "contemporary English visitor" was Angus B. Reach, *Claret and Olives*, 1852.

Page 69 Bernard Ginestet, *La Bouillie Bordelaise*, Paris 1975.

Pages 69–70 Mr. John Bossey kindly led me through the theology of the "spiritual guide" and drew my attention to the *Institutiones Theologae Morales*, by J. Buccerone, Rome 1900.

CHAPTER 8

Passim A. Charles, *La Commerce des Vins de Bordeaux sous la Deuxième Empire*. In RHB 1962.

Page 78ff On the Gilbeys, see H. Warner Allen, *Number 3 St. James's Street*.

Page 85 Cyril Ray, *Lafite, The Story of Château Lafite-Rothschild*, London, 1968. *Mouton-Rothschild*, Christie Wine Publications 1975.

CHAPTER 9

Page 90ff The standard work on phylloxera is George Ordish's painstaking *The Great Wine Blight*, London 1972.

Page 93 Beatty Kingston wrote *Claret, Its Production and Treatment*, 1895.

Pages 99–100 M. Jean Calvet kindly loaned me the material on his family's history.

CHAPTER 10

Pages 105–6 The "recent visitor" to the Cruse mansion was Lyn Macdonald, quotation from her *Bordeaux and Aquitaine*, London 1976.

Page 106 Quotation from Bohne from Anthony Rhodes's *Princes of the Grape*, London 1975.

Page 107   Charles Walter Berry, *In Search of Wine*, London 1935. See also chap 12.

Page 109   Pierre Bert, *In Vino Veritas*, Paris 1975. See also Chaps 21 and 23.

Page 110   Stephen Coulter, *The Château*, London 1974.

Page 115   Poussou was writing in the *Histoire de Bordeaux*, Vol. VI.

CHAPTER 11

Page 115   On the Bordeaux agreement, see Bernard Ginestet, op cit.

Page 127   André Simon, *The Blood of the Grape*.

CHAPTER 12

Page 138   Maurice Healy, *Claret and the White Wines of Bordeaux*, 1934.

CHAPTER 13

Passim   J. Masson, *La Crise Viticole en Gironde*, Bordeaux 1938.

Page 145   Waugh was writing in Christie's *Wine Review*.

Page 150ff P. Barailhé, *Eléments de Legislation Viti-vinicole*, Bordeaux.

Page 153   Charles K. Warner, *The Wine-growers of France and the Government since 1875*.

CHAPTER 14

Page 158ff For the origins of the CIVB: Paul Barailhé, *L'Entente Interprofessionelle du Vin de Bordeaux*, in RHB 1953.

Pages 158–9 M. Pierre Campana of Cadillac was kind enough to give me issues of *L'Union Girondine* chronicling the origins of the CIVB.

Pages 159–60 *Jacques Chaban-Delmas, Ou l'Art d'etre Heureux en Politique*, by J-C. Guillebaud and P. Veilletet.

CHAPTER 15

Page 166ff On Alexis Lichine see Joseph Wechsberg in the *New Yorker*, 17 and 24 May, 1958.

Page 171ff For Henri Martin see Robert Daley in the *New York Times Sunday Magazine*, November 1976.

Page 175ff On St. Emilion see Pierre-Marie Doutrelant, *Les Bons Vins et les Autres*, Paris 1976, a witty book which is especially perceptive on the wine boom.

CHAPTERS 16 to 25

Apart from the works by Ginestet, Doutrelant and Bert, I have relied principally on interviews with many of the participants and on reports in a few key newspapers: *Le Monde*, *Sud-Ouest*, *Le Figaro*, the *Financial Times*, *Wine and Spirits*, *Harpers Wine & Spirit Gazette*, *Impact*, and the *Revue Internationale Viticole*.

The Author and publishers would like to thank the following for permission to quote copyright material: Edmund Penning-Rowsell for quotation from *The Wines of Bordeaux*, Cyril Ray for quotation from *Mouton-Rothschild* and *Fide et Fortitudine*, Lyn Macdonald and Batsford Ltd. for quotation from *Bordeaux and Aquitaine* and Constable & Co. Ltd. for quotation from *Claret and the White Wines of Bordeaux* by Maurice Healy.

For permission to use photographs of material in their possession the publishers are grateful to Gérard Rancinan for 1a, to Frank Spooner for 1b, to Photographie Industrielle du Sud-Ouest for 2 and 3, to John Hillelson Agency for 4a, to Photo Luc Joubert for 4b, to Société Civile du Château Beychevelle for 5b, to Société Civile du Château Lafite-Rothschild for 6a, to Baron Philippe de Rothschild for 6b and to Chris Smith for 8.

The maps were drawn by Patrick Leeson.

Index

Major entries are indicated by bold figures